The Environmental Justice

The Environmental Justice

William O. Douglas
and American Conservation

Adam M. Sowards

Oregon State University Press
Corvallis

The paper in this book meets the guidelines for permanence and
durability of the Committee on Production Guidelines for Book
Longevity of the Council on Library Resources and the minimum
requirements of the American National Standard for Permanence of
Paper for Printed Library Materials Z39.48-1984.

Library of Congress Cataloging-in-Publication Data
Sowards, Adam M.
 The environmental justice : William O. Douglas and American
conservation / Adam M. Sowards.
    p. cm.
 Includes bibliographical references and index.
 ISBN 978-0-87071-567-9 (alk. paper)
 1. Douglas, William O. (William Orville), 1898-1980. 2. United
States. Supreme Court--Biography. 3. Judges--United States--
Biography. 4. Environmental justice--United States--History. 5.
Wildlife conservation--Law and legislation--United States--History.
6. Environmental law--United States--History. I. Title.
 KF8745.D6S69 2009
 347.73'2634--dc22
 [B]
                                        2008042773

First published in 2009 by Oregon State University Press
Printed in the United States of America

 Oregon State University Press
121 The Valley Library
Corvallis OR 97331-4501
541-737-3166 • fax 541-737-3170
http://oregonstate.edu/dept/press

for Elizabeth

Contents

Acknowledgments

This book has been a decade in the making. In the course of writing and rewriting it, I have accumulated a long list of debts. I am happy to finally be able to acknowledge the tremendous help I have received along the way (and ask forgiveness from anyone I have inadvertently forgotten).

Like all historians, I remain indebted to my teachers. *The Environmental Justice* began as a dissertation, and I received incomparable assistance from my co-advisors, Peter Iverson and Steve Pyne. For years, both of them have supported me unyieldingly in what I wanted to do professionally. Peter is a model of humaneness in the academy, a quality I hope I can emulate to at least a modest degree in my own career. Steve has shown me the value of staying true to the research interests I feel most strongly about. Both Peter and Steve helped shape me into the historian I am, and I feel fortunate to have been their student. Even before graduate school, I received uncommon mentorship. When I was a junior in college, Drew Isenberg inspired me to become an environmental historian, and I cannot imagine what my professional life would be like without that inspiration. I continue to rely on him for advice and friendship. I am grateful to you all.

As a researcher, I owe great thanks to librarians and archivists. I spent many hours in the archives at the Library of Congress, the Denver Public Library, and the University of Washington. Others have helped from a distance, including the staff at the Bancroft Library at the University of California at Berkeley and the Sundquist Research Library at the Yakima Valley Museum. The Yakima Valley Museum graciously gave permission to reprint the photographs in this book. The individuals who staff these archives make a historian's task an easy one; I appreciate the work you do. Thanks, too, to Eva Strand for the maps.

This book has taken several previous forms. I learned from the comments of panelists and audience members at professional conferences, including the annual meetings of the Western History Association and American Society for Environmental History. Pieces from this book also appeared earlier in *The Human Tradition in the American West*, the *Western Historical Quarterly*, and the *Journal of the West*. I appreciated the opportunity to test evolving ideas in print and am grateful for permission to draw on those materials.

I remain convinced that environmental historians are the most collegial group of scholars working today. Over the years I have benefited from dozens of conversations with historians, many of whom have read and commented generously on various pieces of this book. These helpful scholars include Kathy Aiken, Lisa Brady, Karl Brooks, Elizabeth Carney, Bill Cronon, Sara Dant, Tom Giesen, Drew Isenberg, Derek Larson, David Rich Lewis, Kevin Marsh, Michael Nelson, Sean Quinlan, Jeff Sanders, Aaron Schab, Paul Sutter, and Jay Turner. Anonymous reviewers of the book and article manuscripts pushed my thinking and saved me from errors. There are many others whose work profoundly influenced my view of history and this book but are too numerous to name. Shortcomings that remain are my own fault.

One more colleague deserves special mention. There were times when I felt that everything I ever learned about wilderness history I learned from Mark Harvey. Mark read this book when it was still a dissertation—and many times since—and gave the best advice I ever received: "Take it apart and see how many different ways you can put it back together." I hope that he recognizes his influence in this book; it is present on nearly every page.

When I arrived on the Palouse in the inland northwest, I was adopted into a group of environmental historians by its leader, Paul Hirt. The "Palouse School," as we affectionately refer to it, has sustained me in friendship and supported me in scholarship in ways I cannot adequately articulate or repay. Although he quickly left the Palouse, Paul has shown me a path to mentorship and remains a valued colleague and friend. Jeff Crane demonstrates a zest for academic life and recognition of the more important things in life I greatly respect. Andrew Duffin and I have shared many trials and tribulations, and I admire his talents and persistence more than he knows. Michael Egan has been my good friend the longest, and he remains my model of professionalism and continues to offer avenues of support I value. Kevin Marsh has mentored me in wilderness and northwest history and has been a friend through all seasons; I cannot imagine having written this book without his help. I thank you all for adopting me.

I am so pleased to publish this book with Oregon State University Press. The entire staff has been as professional and friendly as a writer could hope. Jo Alexander, Tom Booth, and Micki Reaman have made the process a joy, and they have improved the writing and the book's appearance immeasurably. Mary Braun deserves my special gratitude.

I have known Mary for nearly as long as I have been working on this project. Her sustained interest and encouragement have succored me on numerous occasions, and her friendship remains steadfast. I doubt this book would be what it is without her.

The process of writing a book begins at home. Without the sacrifices, unconditional support, and love my parents and brothers shared with me throughout my entire life, I would never have been in the position to achieve any of my academic success. I do not tell them enough how important they have been to my journey. My daughter, Ella Mae, shares her smiles and love with me every day, and that brightens my world more than she can possibly realize. My wife, Elizabeth, has supported me and sacrificed for me in innumerable ways for more than a decade; I am so grateful for that companionship. She has read this book dozens of times and listened to me natter on about Douglas for years; surely, she is the only person happier than I am to have this book finished. I cannot fully express my gratitude, admiration, and love for her daily inspiration, care, and love; I hope the book's dedication is a start.

A Public Intellectual for Conservation

We should leave behind a land where those yet unborn will
have an opportunity to hear the calls of loons and come to
know that they are more glorious than any whir of motors.
William O. Douglas, "America's Vanishing Wilderness," (1964)[1]

In the middle of summer 1964, thousands of Americans opened up the most recent copy of *Ladies' Home Journal* to find "America's Vanishing Wilderness." Sandwiched between articles on choosing paint for home decoration and the continuing importance of homemakers, "America's Vanishing Wilderness" tackled an issue of increasing public significance— preserving the country's natural heritage. Written by a sitting U.S. Supreme Court Justice, the article hardly seemed typical reading for the popular domestic magazine.[2]

In his feature, Justice William O. Douglas described dire threats to America's natural world. Tragically, Douglas explained, the environment through which Lewis and Clark had traveled no longer existed. No longer could Americans enjoy free-flowing, clean rivers, because dams blocked them and sewage poured untreated into streams. Grasslands, once six feet high, now had been trampled underneath thousands of hooves, never to recover. Diverse eastern hardwood forests lay reduced by loggers and bulldozers. We have lost wild nature, Douglas explained, and with that loss an uncertain future beckoned. "A boy or girl should have the opportunity to grow up in the Daniel Boone, Thoreau or Muir tradition—learning about survival in the woods, ridding the mind of fear, filling the heart with affection for all the mysteries of the forests, acquiring reverence, wonder and awe for all the handiwork of the Creator," Douglas implored. Wilderness built character, after all. With so much wilderness already gone and so much more currently threatened, Douglas wanted readers to be aroused to action. His relentless list of threats—to rivers, to sand dunes and seashores, to forests—represented the significance and breadth of the menace of modern society to wilderness values. Douglas wanted his readers to know that nature stood in jeopardy.[3]

His was not just a negative message; the justice did not simply leave readers with a ghastly list of polluted rivers, endangered parks, and hopelessly degraded ecosystems. Believing that "[u]gliness is not an inevitable cost of modernity," Douglas suggested ways Americans could slow, halt, or even reverse these devastating trends. Instead of "fighting rear-guard actions," those who loved unspoiled nature needed "an overall plan ... [that] drives as deeply into law as can be driven guarantees that precise areas will be kept as wilderness exhibits, now and forever." Douglas pushed even further to advocate for constitutional guarantees to preserve wilderness, knowing such assurances would last longer.[4]

It was a momentous time for the wilderness movement. Just a few short months after "America's Vanishing Wilderness" appeared, Congress passed and President Lyndon B. Johnson signed the Wilderness Act. As Douglas had desired, the law instantly protected 9.1 million acres from roads and automobiles and vastly constricted or prohibited economic activities there; moreover, the act instituted a review process that would allow new wilderness areas to be added to the National Wilderness Preservation System, a system that today contains over 106 million acres. Moreover, even though the Wilderness Act empowered Congress to reverse wild designations, the cumbersome process made it far more difficult for wildlands to be desecrated by clear-cuts, subdivisions, or automobiles. The legislation represented the culmination of advocacy begun in the interwar era and intensely fought for since 1956. The new law grew out of a national, coordinated effort from the grassroots. Douglas had stood in the thick of these national wilderness politics for a decade, and he brought readers there with him.[5]

America's natural heritage belonged to the public, Douglas preached. "These remote valleys belong not to the lumber companies and the few loggers and road builders who will profit from their destruction," Douglas wrote, "but to all the people." The public's land, though, was vulnerable, because in July 1964 a government bureaucrat in Washington, D.C., could open up an existing roadless areas to all manner of despoliation, including logging, grazing, and construction. And even after the Wilderness Act passed in September which prevented those activities on millions of acres, bureaucrats controlled many millions more that could be opened to intensive extraction. To check those bureaucrats' power and to promote wilderness preservation, Douglas suggested a strategy:

> We need Committees of Correspondence to coordinate the efforts
> of diverse groups to keep America beautiful and to preserve the few
> wilderness alcoves we have left. We used such committees in the days of
> our Revolution, and through them helped bolster the efforts of people
> everywhere in the common cause. Our common cause today is to
> preserve our country's natural beauty and keep our wilderness areas

sacrosanct. The threats are everywhere; and the most serious ones are often made in unobtrusive beginnings under the banner of "progress." Local groups need national assistance; and that means joining hands in an overall effort to keep our land bright and shining.

For Douglas, the struggle for wilderness compared to the historic revolutionary struggle. His call for new Committees of Correspondence to coordinate local activists, who knew wilderness threats best, and national organizations like the Sierra Club and the Wilderness Society, who knew lobbying best, announced an important, effective, and common strategy. Only together, Douglas seemed to say, could conservationists stop wanton destruction of the nation's natural heritage.[6] He proved prescient in many ways, for ensuring that local organizations and populations, and not just national groups, support wilderness designations has become a virtual prerequisite in modern environmental politics.[7]

Douglas ended "America's Vanishing Wilderness" with a final, poignant plea. "We inherited the loveliest of all the continents," he celebrated. "We should bequeath it to our grandchildren as a land where the majority is disciplined to respect the values even of a minority." As he worked to protect a natural inheritance for future generations, Douglas expressed another deeply held conviction—that minority interests in the United States must be protected, as mandated by the Constitution. In this case, the minority was those whose "values are aesthetic or spiritual, and … reflect the principle that beauty is an end in itself and that man will find relaxation, renewed strength and inspiration in the wildness of the earth." Few Americans in the twentieth century could surpass Douglas's record in favor of protecting the interest of minority groups, and so this perspective—so common in other elements of the American postwar liberal tradition—merited attention from a large audience in this new context of conservation.[8]

The article in *Ladies' Home Journal* perfectly fit a pattern for Douglas concerning conservation issues—both in substance and style. Douglas sustained the core of this argument through his conservation work from the 1950s through the 1970s: wilderness and other environmental problems needed national solutions that included public involvement and protections of minority interests because the issues were nationally important and the forces against preservation were too strong. In myriad situations—whether writing a legal opinion, leading a high-profile public hike, writing politicians or federal bureaucrats, penning articles for mass-circulation magazines and books, or speaking to civic groups—Douglas promoted democratic action for conservation, public monitoring of government and business activities, and stronger laws to insure environmental and political integrity. As a sitting Supreme Court justice, Douglas brought prestige to the conservation crusades of the time and enormous symbolic power of legal authority at a time when the nation's laws did not favor environmental protection.

Perhaps even greater than the substance of his argument—which was consistent with that of many national conservationists at the time such as Howard Zahniser or Olaus Murie—Douglas's position as a Supreme Court justice marked him as a singular individual for the movement. Thus, while representative of a generation of conservationists, he was distinguished by his unique experiences, priorities, and qualifications. Having made a prominent name for himself outside the conservation field, the justice strategically used his public standing to promote an environmental agenda and to explain complex scientific, legal, and political issues to the public.[9] In short, Douglas was a public intellectual for conservation.

The public intellectual is a slippery concept, not altogether easy to define. Intellectuals serve necessary roles for societies to both legitimate and challenge authorities. Douglas embodied this very contradiction by being an ultimate political insider but one who consistently railed against government and other authorities. An intellectual's role was to "speak truth to power," as scholar Edward Said explained employing a common phrase. Said further characterized the intellectual as "an individual endowed with a faculty for representing, embodying, articulating a message, a view, an attitude, philosophy or opinion to ... a public." Similarly, writer and Circuit Judge Richard A. Posner classified public intellectuals variously, but included public figures—such as government officials like Douglas—writing for a general audience. Posner maintained, "a public intellectual expresses himself in a way that is accessible to the public, and the focus of his expression is on matters of general public concern of (or inflected by) a political or ideological cast." Such definitions certainly fit Douglas and his conservation work, as he reached beyond his professional audience to focus on a contemporary issue with an often defiant tone. Others recognized Douglas's capacity for taking concepts—from conservation to international relations to liberty—ruminating on them, and presenting them as a "public philosopher" or "national teacher" to the public. Most often, as with conservation, his public intellectual role took the form of castigating the existing system. In criticizing current problems and promoting alternatives, Douglas used his public intellectual role as a reformer.[10]

Douglas took conservation to the public in ways perhaps no one else could have done, or in a combination of ways that could not be duplicated by others. The forums available to Douglas, as a Supreme Court justice, included not only halls of government, ears of politicians or administrators, and the pages of the legal opinions, but also popular magazines, books, and coverage by the day's media. No one else in conservation circles could marshal this attention. More of the public paid attention when a Supreme Court justice wrote a letter to a newspaper editor on a conservation topic than when the leader of the Wilderness Society or local Audubon Society did. After all, such organizations were supposed to advocate conservation. If Justice Douglas led a hike or rafting trip to publicize a threat by a road or a dam, it seemingly had a different value and reached a different audience than if only the Sierra Club arranged it. Douglas thrived on this sort of public engagement and used it masterfully to not only expose particular issues and to advocate for solutions, but also to educate. His speeches, articles, and books included lessons on everything from predator-prey ecology to the workings of federal agencies and laws. Even in his Supreme Court opinions, Douglas often wrote as much for a public audience as he did for legal colleagues, putting complex legal arguments into terms more comprehensible for an educated layperson or sometimes eschewing legalities altogether. In all of his work, Douglas demanded of himself that he engage an expansive public. For conservation, this approach allowed him to build on an already-strong public image to reach larger numbers of Americans than conservationists alone could do, drawing the public into controversies while educating them about the importance of protection for ecological or political reasons.[11]

Key to understanding Douglas's conservation career, then, is the public. He interacted with the public in deliberate ways. For example, he crafted an image of himself for public consumption that emphasized his youthful western roots and challenging experiences in the rugged outdoors. Douglas routinely employed that public persona for conservation, using it to bolster his moral authority to speak for a variety of places and causes. In 1954, he first used that persona in a significant public campaign, the fight to stop the National Park Service from building a road along the scenic Chesapeake and Ohio Canal. Douglas challenged editors in the pages of the *Washington Post* and ultimately led a group of hikers on a nearly two-hundred-mile hike that generated much publicity and allowed Douglas to explain to an absorbed public the value of walking over driving. His activism built from this key event.

But the public was not simply an audience. Douglas advocated reforms primarily to increase the public's involvement in environmental management. The failure to incorporate public opinion and values in managing public resources demonstrated to him the necessity of conservation reform. Through much of Douglas's career, for example, he sounded a consistent drumbeat of the necessity of public hearings; they would allow the public a role in shaping resource management and a method to challenge the dominant ethos of commercial development. To Douglas, it was imperative to allow a national public to be informed of—and to inform—resource management, since public resources had for too long been exploited for the economic gain of a small number of local interests. Ultimately, Douglas and the larger conservation movement succeeded in getting public hearings written into various environmental laws, including the Wilderness Act and the National Environmental Policy Act (1970). As such, they democratized conservation; this was part of a larger reform process to open up the process of governing and among the most significant achievements of activism like Douglas's in the two decades when the wilderness movement and environmentalism generally matured. Additionally, a significant portion of conservationists' work in the 1950s through 1970s focused on public resources—whether clean water and air or national forests and parks—and their regulation. Making sure the public enjoyed a healthy and aesthetically pleasing environment and that public resources were not squandered for private gain remained Douglas's overriding concern.[12]

As important and admirable as many of these actions were, Douglas had an unsavory side that attracted critics who focused on personal and political shortcomings. Privately, Douglas was more flawed than most. His autobiographies are full of misdirection, half-truths, and outright lies. His notorious womanizing ruined his four marriages, although his fourth survived it. His children did not remember him fondly. He treated his staff, including his law clerks, shabbily. His colleagues, though sometimes admiring of his intellect, often bore the brunt of a cold, hostile personality. For example, Douglas engaged in near-legendary personal and professional battles with fellow President Franklin D. Roosevelt appointee Felix Frankfurter for years. Many, especially political conservatives, found and continue to find Douglas's brand of judicial activism to be anathema to the proper role of a judge. And his extra-judicial activism and writings certainly strike some as lacking proper dispassion and distance.[13]

A leading Douglas scholar explained that he "could be and often was petty, mean-spirited and arrogant." Such a man could be hard to like, and it seems that many who traveled in Douglas's political circles disliked him intensely. However, a near-consensus exists that outside that realm Douglas was a charming man willing to work tirelessly on behalf of nature. Few, if any, of his colleagues from conservation circles complained about Douglas's deep personality flaws. Charles A. Reich, Douglas's friend and author of the countercultural manifesto *The Greening of America*, knew of Douglas's personal demons well, but Reich also recognized that on the hiking trail those demons disappeared in perhaps the only place where the justice could relax and be authentically himself. Rather than charges of pettiness or arrogance, comments from conservationists were more appreciative and admiring. Typical is the comment from pioneering environmental journalist Michael Frome: "I picked my own heroes, like William O. Douglas, the Supreme Court justice whose entire life stands as a record of courage and willingness to hold fast against odds. ... For a while it seemed that whenever I went to some hot spot of conservation controversy he had already been there hiking, camping, and communing with people who cared." To conservationists like Frome, Douglas stood as a beacon, a ubiquitous activist who could be counted on to unselfishly lend support in myriad environmental confrontations for three decades. He was neither lazy nor mean in their eyes.[14] For scholars and writers, it has been difficult to avoid the dark side of Douglas's personality—such a temptingly large and sensational topic—but it has kept us from focusing on this other, critical area in his life.[15]

Douglas's conservationism was not without its problems, especially as seen in the context of concerns that have become more prominent in environmental circles since 1970. A significant part of his conservation focused on wilderness preservation, an environmental emphasis much maligned over the past decade. Among other things, critics have charged the wilderness idea with being ethnocentric, sexist, and imperialist. Moreover, they have maintained that stressing wilderness preservation of distant lands distracted conservationists from addressing issues closer to home, issues that disproportionately affected poor Americans and people of color—causes that Douglas did confront by the end of his career. These indictments of wilderness have merit but can be taken too far in Douglas's case. Douglas did not favor excluding anyone from wilderness areas, except extractive industry and mass recreationists. Advocates from this latter group occasionally called conservationists of Douglas's ilk elitist, for not desiring the largest possible number to participate in outdoor activities in easy ways.[16] Similarly, Douglas can be accused of practicing a form of NIMBY-ism, applying himself most steadfastly in efforts to preserve areas close to his residences.[17] Both the elitist and NIMBY characteristics of Douglas's conservation are associated with his all-too-human tendency to believe he possessed *the* answer to a problem. In this respect, Douglas certainly was guilty of a healthy ego that alienated his opponents and can sound moralistic today.

Despite these legitimate criticisms, Douglas's efforts and those of his generation sought as much as anything to reform the process by which environmental resources and values were protected. With the legal safeguards Douglas's generation of conservationists instituted, they ensured that the political system could be used to protect wilderness or to challenge the siting of a toxic waste dump or to bring suit against polluters. Moreover, as conservationists like Douglas expanded ethical boundaries to incorporate nature to an unprecedented degree, Americans would build into their culture a greater awareness of and sensitivity to nature. Douglas's vision had blind spots, but he and others shone bright lights in areas heretofore hidden or obscured, lighting the way for further reform.

To understand wilderness and modern conservation, some scholars have focused on specific places and struggles over designating wilderness, while others have taken a cultural or ideological approach, and still others have grounded their analysis in the structure of American politics.[18] The approach taken here combines all those perspectives and views them through the prism of a prominent individual. Douglas was a product of and heavily invested in particular landscapes, articulated specific personal and cultural values of wilderness, and negotiated the ever-shifting political system. Such an individualistic approach is appropriate, for the encounter with wilderness, after all, is typically an individual encounter, mediated by one's culture and politics. Because Douglas was equally adept at explaining legal issues, penning celebratory nature writing, advocating political reforms, and engaging the public on the hiking trail, his story is an ideal vehicle to see how conservation worked at this time when it was growing, transforming, and achieving so much.

When reading "America's Vanishing Wilderness" in 1964, readers were invited by a leading participant to take part in an important movement at a critical moment. Time was running out for America's wilderness heritage. The costs of inaction were mounting. "Commercial interests unrestrained by biologists, botanists, ornithologists, artists and others, who see the spiritual values in the outdoors, can in time convert *every* acre of America into a money-making scheme," the author warned.[19] But William O. Douglas—the environmental justice—envisioned a different future if readers would only involve themselves and serve in Committees of Correspondence to keep the nation apprised of threats and to organize against further despoliation. He would tell them why and show them how.

CHAPTER ONE:

Roots and Reputation

The boy makes a deep imprint on the man. My young
experiences in the high Cascades have placed the heavy mark of
the mountains on me.

William O. Douglas, *Of Men and Mountains*[1]

In October 1949, William O. Douglas and a childhood friend, Elon Gilbert, started on a horseback trip near Mount Rainier just as the "mountain [was] gathering itself together for the winter's assault." Douglas and his horse, Kendall, were climbing a hillside when the horse "reared and whirled, his front feet pawing the steep slope." Douglas described what happened next:

> *I dismounted by slipping off his tail. I landed in shale rock, lost my*
> *footing and rolled some thirty yards. I ended on a narrow ledge lying on*
> *my stomach, uninjured. I started to rise. I glanced up. I looked into the*
> *face of an avalanche. Kendall had slipped, and fallen, too. He had come*
> *rolling down over the same thirty precipitous yards I had traversed.*
> *There was no possibility of escape. Kendall was right on me. I had only*
> *time to duck my head. The great horse hit me. Sixteen hundred pounds*
> *of solid horseflesh rolled me flat. I could hear my own bones break in*
> *a sickening crescendo. Then Kendall dropped over the ledge and rolled*
> *heavily down the mountain to end up without a scratch. I lay paralyzed*
> *with pain—twenty-three of twenty-four ribs broken.*

Douglas was in agony. "First I feared I would die," he complained; "then, as the pain continued unabated from the broken ribs, I feared I would not." The accident produced thirty-eight fractures in twenty-three ribs and punctured his right lung. Gilbert found his friend several minutes later, and a rescue party managed to get him out of the mountains, into an ambulance, and down to a hospital in Yakima, Washington. He spent seven weeks in the hospital and then transferred to a guest ranch in Tucson, Arizona, for further recuperation.[2]

Each element of this vignette reflected central characteristics of Douglas's life and image. It occurred in the great outdoors of the Pacific Northwest, his home in spirit if not always in fact. The accident forced him to struggle to recover physically, as he had done previously in these very mountains.

The overall scene portrayed a rugged setting with towering mountains, no mechanized conveniences, horses, and men. From these fundamentals, Douglas forged his identity and constructed a public image. He was a tough outdoorsman at home in the mountains, away from cities. He embraced the strenuous life Theodore Roosevelt had evangelized years before. Douglas lived a vital, vigorous existence with his character built in the Pacific Northwest environment, just as other conservationists identified with specific landscapes such as John Muir in the Sierra Nevadas or Sigurd Olson in the Boundary Waters. The riding accident reflected all these things. Moreover, his convalescence furnished Douglas an opportunity to reflect on his life, and he ultimately used it to confirm and further his public identity, a persona crucial to how he worked for conservation.

Childhood Tragedies and Mountain Salvation

The childhood Douglas remembered was marked by ongoing personal tragedies and challenges that he met by taking to the mountains. Scholars have long known that Douglas exaggerated his youthful deprivation. Yet few writers have considered seriously why he told the stories he did about growing up. And virtually all have neglected to consider the ways in which his youth functioned in his subsequent conservation career. Douglas understood himself and presented his life to the public as linked intimately with the Northwestern mountains he called home, even though he was born far from them.[3]

Douglas's parents met in the flatland of the upper Midwest. In 1895, Julia Fisk became acquainted with William Douglas when the pastor-in-training arrived for fieldwork at the Maine, Minnesota, church where she played the organ. They married the following year and soon had two children—Martha was born in 1897 and William Orville in 1898. Douglas remembered his home town by its natural features. "My first memories of Minnesota," Douglas said in a 1962 speech before the Minnesota Historical Society, "were stinging spits of snow in an ice cold wind in Winter. Then came memories of melting snows and a warming sun and the first flowers of Spring." It was typical for Douglas to record his memories in terms of nature and the seasons, but that environment was a short-lived home. Trying to relieve the minister's chronic stomach pains, the family moved to Estrella, California, where the last child, Arthur, was born in 1902. Estrella instilled in Douglas a love of home in the "dry, rolling hills dotted with oaks" so characteristic of much of California. Unfortunately, the move failed to improve his father's health, and so the Douglas family soon moved north to Cleveland, Washington.[4]

Resting in south-central Washington State's agricultural heartland, Cleveland was home to "wheat farmers and cattlemen. Their farms were large units, running from 600 to 6000 acres. ... [T]hey were neighborly folks." While the elder Douglas ministered to these parishioners, the younger Douglas explored the area and first glimpsed the two principal natural features of the Pacific Northwest that would ultimately prove so important in his upbringing and identity—the Cascade Mountains forty miles to the west and the Columbia River thirty miles to the south. For example, on a ferry crossing the Columbia River in those early years, Douglas "saw strange flashes below [the water's] surface—quick movements of salmon or steelhead or sturgeon that excited me." Contact with nature in a rural and wild form thus began early to create a strong sense of place for Douglas. He formed emotional, even spiritual, bonds with the river and especially the mountains, forged in a crucible of pain.[5]

A tragedy in the family deepened Douglas's attachment to the landscape. Despite this region's natural bounty and beauty, it could not cure the minister's persistent stomach ulcers. In summer 1904, he traveled to Portland for surgery that proved unsuccessful. He died on August 12. "He was present one day and then he was gone—forever," Douglas remembered the trauma. "There would never be another to lift me high in the air, to squeeze my hand and give me masculine praise." Orville, as he was called as a child, keenly felt the loss, especially the end of a strong male influence. At his father's memorial service, he longed to escape the "meaningless and melancholy" funeral and church. But later, at the cemetery, the melancholy gave way to lonesomeness and then fear. "I became afraid— afraid of being left alone, afraid because the grave held my defender and protector," Douglas wrote years later. His fears intensified when he realized his mother shared them. As he began to cry, the presiding minister counseled the five-year-old, "You must now be a man, sonny." Then came a revelation, a transformative vision rooted in the western landscape. He lifted his gaze to the mountains, and Mount Adams stood prominently in the western sky—"a giant whose head touched the sky." "As I looked," Douglas reflected, "I stopped sobbing. My eyes dried. Adams stood cool and calm, unperturbed by an event that had stirred us so deeply that Mother was crushed for years. Adams suddenly seemed to be a friend. Adams subtly became a force for me to tie to, a symbol of stability and strength."[6]

Almost half a century after the fact, he wrote with a clarity and sophistication obviously influenced by years of introspection. However idealized, the funeral scene described in his memoir *Of Men and Mountains*, and later recapitulated in another autobiography, *Go East, Young Man*, suggested that Douglas knew nature to be comforting.[7] The mountains were permanent and tangible. And since much of his life was unstable, the mountains' stability, immensity, and permanence consoled the fearful child and later the man. Mountains generally and the Cascades specifically remained an anchor for Douglas from that day forward. The mountains, he knew, would not fail him; they would remain sources of inspiration and eventually places he worked to protect. The bond with the mountains—a bond that succored Douglas in trying times—deepened when he turned to nature for other reasons.

As others have remarked, children often bond early with specific home landscapes, and throughout their lifetime, they will judge all other landscapes against that home place. For Douglas, that home was Yakima, Washington. After the death of her husband, Julia Douglas moved her family—three children under the age of seven—to Yakima. She chose the town because of family connections and the desire to be close to her husband's grave. Yakima, its inhabitants, and its natural history formed a deep impression on Douglas that remained with him throughout his lifetime. "Early associations control the nostalgic urges of every person," Douglas explained. "My love is for what many would put down as the dreariest aspects of the dry foothills of the West—sagebrush and lava rock." That love did not come from passive observation but from deliberate immersion in the landscape.[8]

While still in Minnesota, a few months before he reached his second birthday, Douglas had contracted a serious illness that confined him to bed for weeks. Although it was apparently undiagnosed at the time, Douglas later claimed it was a case of polio.[9] Despite his mother's near-constant attention, including massaging the child's legs every two hours and praying constantly for weeks, his young legs remained weak. Douglas eventually regained the use of his legs. Still, his mother made excuses for his lingering weakness into his teenage years. "He's not as strong as other boys," Douglas remembered his mother saying to others; "he has to be careful what he does—you know, his legs were almost paralyzed." Predictably, as any child would be, he was afraid of "being publicly recognized as a puny person—a weakling." On the way to school, classmates teased: "Look at that kid's skinny legs. … Did you ever see anything as funny?" At a loss, Douglas cried, confirming at least in his own mind his weakling status. Always determined, even as a child, he resolved first to rise above his peers in academics, which he did. But, especially in the American West just past the turn of the twentieth century, a boy's world required strength, and as Douglas recalled, "By boyhood standards I was a failure."[10]

Douglas keenly understood the implications of his shortcomings. Drawing a parallel with the natural world, Douglas explained his fears, laced heavily with Darwinian language: "[T]he physical world loomed large in my mind. I read what happened to cripples in the wilds. They were the weak strain that nature did not protect. They were cast aside, discarded for hardier types. ... Man was the same, I thought. Only men can do the work of the world—operating trains, felling trees, digging ditches, managing farms. Only robust men can be heroes of a war." Whether it was the martial heroism of war or the more prosaic heroism of work, Douglas knew he fell short. The western world in which he wished to live and that was enshrined in popular culture had no room for the weak. Because American culture demanded it, he sought an individualist, even masculine, resolution.[11]

Douglas came of age at a time when white men faced a masculinity crisis. At the turn of the twentieth century, women's challenge to men's economic and political hegemony threatened many men's understanding of their place in society. They turned to organized athletics, bodybuilding, and organizations like the Boy Scouts to bolster their strength and validate their masculinity. Indeed, Douglas served for a time as scoutmaster in Yakima as a young adult. Many men feared that industrialization and urbanization threatened to feminize male workers now that more middle-class men worked in offices, not on farms, in the woods, in mines, or other traditional Western locales and occupations.[12]

Douglas's predicament was one an earlier leader—Theodore Roosevelt— would have understood. In his autobiography, the president recalled his own asthmatic youth. Like Douglas, Roosevelt was "a sickly boy, with no natural bodily prowess," whom other boys ridiculed. His heroes—mostly military—"could hold their own in the world, and I had a great desire to be like them." In response, Roosevelt learned to box and pursued outdoor activities, most famously hunting, especially during his frequent removes to a North Dakota ranch. Physical activity would lead to "bodily vigor," Roosevelt thought, a prerequisite for a worthwhile life. His concern about a strong body reflected similar contemporary anxieties among white middle-class men. Recent scholarship underscores the contested and dynamic nature of gender, masculinity in particular, in response to turn-of-the-twentieth-century concerns over economic concentration, massive urbanization, and devastating assaults on Western natural resources. As Roosevelt remarked, "The dweller in cities has less chance than the dweller in the country to keep his body sound and vigorous." Indeed, men like Roosevelt derided the United States' newly urban cast and longed for the recently vanished frontier where men might prove themselves by conquering the wilderness. Roosevelt celebrated such a life, "the strenuous life" as he called it in a notable 1900 speech and "the vigor of life," as he termed it

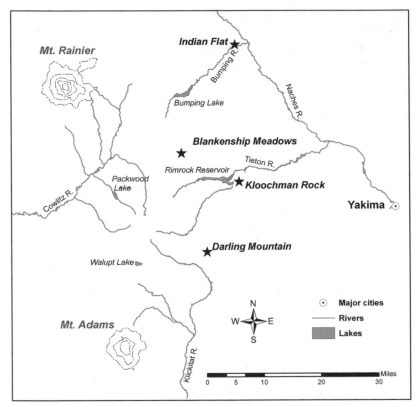

William O. Douglas's tramping grounds in the Cascade Mountains

in his autobiography. Roosevelt was but the most influential figure who rejoiced in the American westering spirit, and although Douglas expressed some ambivalence about Roosevelt's politics, he certainly inculcated many of Roosevelt's masculine values.[13]

Just as Roosevelt had learned to box and became an adept outdoorsman, Douglas too worked to develop strength and took to nature to prove himself, and the parallels with Roosevelt's own recovery were not accidental. In a fashion to be repeated time and again, Douglas set out to meet a challenge and conquer a fear, for Douglas had concluded that "man is not ready for adventure unless he is rid of fear." And perhaps as much as wanting to prove his strength, Douglas longed for adventure. Fortunately, the foothills north of Yakima provided an ideal testing ground. After meeting a Sunday-school classmate who had been climbing those hills under a doctor's orders, Douglas knew instinctively that he would strengthen his legs similarly. "First I tried to go up the hills without stopping," the justice explained his restorative regimen. "When I conquered that, I tried to go up without

A youthful William O. Douglas in the backcountry

change of pace. When that was achieved, I practiced going up not only without a change of pace but whistling as I went." After several seasons of this invigorating hiking, Douglas's "legs were filling out. They were getting stronger." He eventually sought greater challenges.[14]

Two youthful hikes with his brother, Art, stood out to Douglas for their challenging nature and the personal meditation they triggered. Carrying packs between thirty and sixty pounds, the Douglas brothers explored the area near Cougar Lakes—an important place in Douglas's later activism. They saw magnificent vistas of Mount Rainer while gorging themselves on huckleberries. "It is easy to see the delicate handiwork of the Creator in any meadow," Douglas explained. "But perhaps it takes these startling views to remind of us His omnipotence. Perhaps it takes such a view to make us realize that vain, cocky, aggressive, selfish man never conquers the mountains in spite of all his boasting and bustling and exertion. He conquers only himself." Douglas sounded much like John Muir, whose turn-of-the-twentieth-century writings equated communing with nature with communing with God and whose tracts did much to entice others into the wild to find God's presence. Moreover, the theme of nature as evidence of God's beneficence and humans' profaneness had been popular since the eighteenth century and became a mainstay of twentieth-century nature writing. Also, one could certainly see the preacher's son in such passages. But if the area the Douglases hiked was site to God's handiwork and a place above human society, Douglas had other messages to teach.[15]

This day the brothers hiked in places they believed had never been seen by people before. Such a wilderness provoked feelings of cyclical time: "This forest was primeval, untouched, unseen. Trees fell and in a generation or more were turned into duff. New trees sprang from fallen seed, reached with their thin tips through a colonnade of evergreens for a slit in the sky, pushed lesser trees aside, and in time were reclaimed, as man is reclaimed, by Mother Earth." Attuned to evolution, Douglas recognized the changeability of nature and the necessity of struggle—much like his own successful struggle against weakness—to survive and thrive. In the end, of course, people were subsumed by the earth, emphasizing again nature's primacy. Eventually, Douglas's reverie broke as the brothers came upon a trail. Although they had hiked a full day and were tired, Douglas decided to push them to reach a distant destination, Indian Flat. Exhausted and "on the edge of hunger," the older Douglas pushed his little brother. Finally, after twenty-five miles, they arrived and collapsed with fatigue. But Douglas was elated: "My legs had stood up. I had conquered my doubts. So far as my legs were concerned, I knew that I was now free to roam these mountains at will, to go on foot where any man could go, to enter any forest without hesitation." He had tested himself and passed with flying colors. That success ensured freedom in the mountains, for Douglas had proved himself able to compete.[16]

Never one to leave any doubt, Douglas recounted another, even more strenuous, hike from his teenage years. This time hiking with a friend, Douglas missed a branching trail and decided to explore new ground, climbing 3,500 feet to reach Darling Mountain's summit. In his account, Douglas deeply anthropomorphized the landscape and even the plants he encountered in the now-familiar Darwinian trope. The avalanche lily, for instance, only "grows in a rugged environment; there and there alone it thrives. Like man, it needs a challenge to reach its full fruition." Similarly, from Darling Mountain's high vista, Douglas felt heightened and somewhat mixed emotions. At first, the landscape inspired his explorer's inclinations and also connected him to the frontier tradition that so pleased him: "I feel a challenge to explore each ridge and valley, to climb each snow-capped peak, to sleep in each high basin, to sample the berries and fish and all

CHAPTER ONE: Roots and Reputation ꜘ 17

the other rich produce of the wilderness. It is the feeling that he who first topped the Blue Ridge Mountains or the Rockies must have had when he looked west and saw valleys untouched by the plow and a primeval forest that had never known an ax." In such places, Douglas clearly imagined himself a Daniel Boone or Lewis and Clark figure and connected himself to the frontier tradition popularized at the turn of the century by Theodore Roosevelt, Frederick Jackson Turner, Buffalo Bill Cody, and others. Douglas offered both an anthropocentric view of nature being made for humans, but then he shifted to a view that minimized humans' place in the scheme of the universe :

> These peaks and meadows were made for man, and man for them. They are man's habitat. He has eyes, ears, nose, and brain to understand them. He has legs and lungs to take him anywhere and everywhere through them. Man must explore them and come to know them. They belong to him; yet they will eventually reclaim him and rule beyond his day as they ruled long before he appeared on the earth, long before he stood erect and faced the sun.

This vacillation and transition in thinking was evident within the larger conservation movement at the time, with Aldo Leopold articulating an ecocentric land ethic contemporaneously to Douglas's writing these words. Then, figuratively merging with the elements, Douglas claimed, "When one stands on Darling Mountain, he is not remote and apart from the wilderness; he is an intimate part of it." This peaceful attitude of being at one with nature proved a common one in American environmental culture, marking Douglas's experience as certainly culturally familiar. He valued nature, as others before him like Henry David Thoreau or John Muir had, as a place to find solitude, a place where one can listen to oneself without civilized distractions. Furthermore, Douglas treasured nature for its repository of time. That is, wilderness provided evidence of deep time and humanity's connection to it, an evolutionary link inherent to the species. On this hike to Darling Mountain, Douglas found all those things and wanted his readers to understand the closeness to God, the historic importance, and the blessings of solitude abundantly found in the wilderness.[17]

However, never far beneath the humble surface was Douglas's desire to show off his ability to accomplish great feats in the mountains, a type of conquest typical in male mountaineering narratives and reminiscent of Bob Marshall's famed long-distance forays in the West's wildlands. On the last night of his hike, Douglas and his companion sat down in camp and readied themselves for an evening meal. Abruptly, they decided to head for home right then. So, as the evening's darkness arrived, they descended the mountains, crossed rivers, avoided snakes, and sidestepped drop-offs into deep canyons. "We were on a treadmill, plodding on and on but standing still," Douglas described his feelings of the long hike. By dawn, they had covered forty miles, and Douglas "had walked the whole night through. I was proud of my legs. I wanted to shout 'Look at my legs! Hear what I have done!' Remember, I was a boy. I wanted to laugh at the guys that said I had puny legs. I wanted to take them to the hills for a contest—an endurance contest, if you please." The forty-mile hike banished any lingering doubts and assured him of his strength. Douglas was healed, his body strong.[18]

Douglas's recovery narrative connects well-worn historical themes, such as the West as a place for health and recovery, the West as a testing ground, and the West as site of individualistic conquests. Many Americans since the nineteenth century migrated to the West for its healthful attributes.[19] Writers have long praised individualism and associated it with the American West; indeed, two of the earliest popularizers of western frontier histories, Roosevelt and Frederick Jackson Turner, framed much of their understanding of the West along these lines—individuals moving into the West, conquering the people and the environment they encountered.[20] Historians today recognize the myriad shortcomings of such interpretations of the western past, yet often popular images and mythologies of the region continue to reinforce, if not embrace, such notions. Buffalo Bill Cody pioneered ways to deploy western images for middle-class consumption at the turn of the twentieth century. And similar popular interpretations have long been available for people like Douglas to exploit. By framing his story with these traditions, Douglas ensured readers would recognize his position within a long line of American outdoor adventurers, a twentieth-century Daniel Boone. This approach proved a common and effective one for Douglas; he commonly wrote in ways familiar to his American audience, introducing new ideas but through recognizable tropes.[21]

For Douglas, his youthful times exploring the Cascade Range served a critical role, especially for the public persona he constructed. He defeated his weakness, learned to appreciate nature in the mountains, and developed a passion for hiking in magnificent landscapes. The same could be said for Roosevelt, who went west to help strengthen himself from a sickly childhood, and John Muir, whose thousand-mile walk to the Gulf of Mexico as a prelude to his relocation to California furnished his own conversion to a type of wilderness religion and helped him recover from near-blindness. Douglas absorbed other important lessons concerning his recovery. One might achieve mastery over one's difficulties by directly confronting the challenge and diligently working to overcome it. As his treks lengthened and

Douglas's confidence grew, he "felt an increasing flow of health in my legs and a growing sense of contentment in my heart." Through hiking, Douglas learned that nature offered spiritual and physical salvation, making him sensitive to the importance of maintaining wild areas so that others could enjoy the opportunities nature furnished for personal growth.[22]

The western environment represented home, provided solitude and strength, and connected Douglas to forces—environmental and historical—larger than himself. Such experiences depended on preserving wilderness as a source of American greatness. While in the mountains, he strengthened himself, often alone, and that lesson in independence and solitude always stayed with him. Most of all, he felt at ease there, for he was part of the mountains and the larger environment. All of these factors coalesced: "Every trail leads beyond the frontier. Every ridge, every valley, every peak offers a solitude deeper even than that of the sea. It offers the peace that comes only from solitude. It is in solitude that man can come to know both his heart and his mind."[23] The mountains of the Pacific Northwest held Douglas's imagination and desire. This place—as home and as the site of his recovery—made lasting imprints on a young man destined for a life that led him away from his beloved sage-covered hills near the Cascade Mountains.

Away from Home and To the Court

Douglas worked hard in high school, earning valedictorian honors and a scholarship to Whitman College. As classes began in the fall of 1916, he determinedly made his way from Yakima to Walla Walla, riding his bicycle the 165 miles. Douglas needed to pay for all his living expenses in addition to sending home twenty dollars a month. Accordingly, he worked his way through college at a Norwegian immigrant's jewelry store as a janitor and as an agricultural worker during summertime. At Whitman, Douglas met influential science and literature professors, who taught him that the earth, not dogma or creeds, was eternal and that literature mirrored the historical, economic, and political culture of a given period. These lessons, no doubt, enlarged Douglas's perspective of the world and led him to rebel against all types of dogmatism. This recollection may well be idealized, but it helped Douglas build on his public image as an iconoclast who went his own way on the Court and life rather than follow anyone else's path.[24]

Following graduation in May 1920, Douglas first went back to Yakima to teach, and then moved on to Columbia Law School in 1922. "Ideas were not congenial in Yakima," Douglas remarked as his reason for leaving. His years at Whitman had broadened his mind and encouraged him to seek new challenges. So he set out for Columbia Law School, not by bicycle but by freight train, shepherding two thousand sheep from Wenatchee, Washington, to Chicago, Illinois, along the Great Northern Railroad. In Chicago, after delivering the sheep, Douglas was thrown off the train for not paying his fare. Still he persisted, arriving in New York with only six cents in his pockets, or so he claimed in a likely exaggeration designed to emphasize the many hardships he overcame and the Horatio Alger rags-to-riches story he wove about his young life.[25]

Over the next several years, Douglas's life took several storybook turns. He graduated from Columbia and made the law review. While teaching courses in the morning at Columbia, he worked at the prestigious Wall Street firm of Cravath, deGersdorff, Swaine, and Wood. It did not take long in private practice for Douglas to grow complacent. The men who surrounded him were not like him. "I looked around at the older men in my profession and I knew I did not want to be like *any* of them," Douglas professed. He continued with what he meant to be a most devastating assessment: "They couldn't climb a mountain, couldn't tie a dry fly; they knew nothing about the world that was closest to me, the real world, the natural world." He left the New York City practice and went back to Washington, only to return to New York to teach full-time at Columbia. Then he moved to Yale Law School because it was the center of legal realism, a legal philosophy and methodology that inspired Douglas's legal work. Unmistakably, Douglas possessed deep ambition, along with ample talent, that facilitated his rapid rise.[26]

Douglas specialized in bankruptcy, a timely interest in the late 1920s and early 1930s. When Joseph P. Kennedy, chair of the New Deal's Securities and Exchange Commission (SEC), searched for someone to produce a study of corporate reorganization and how it affected investors, Douglas emerged as the logical choice. He soon moved into an SEC commissioner's seat and then took over as chair himself in 1936, a rather young man to preside over such a powerful federal agency. At the SEC, he took part in what he described as a "revolution" in government by applying social science to the act of governing, an approach he continued once in the judicial branch. Douglas earned a reputation as a fine administrator who never shied from a fight, even with the powerful New York Stock Exchange. His hard work, stunning success, faithful support of New Deal policies, and active sociability paid large dividends. What already had been an almost-mythical American success story, took a rather unpredictable turn in 1939.[27]

Early that year, Louis Brandeis, U.S. Supreme Court Associate Justice, as well as hero and mentor to Douglas, announced his plans to retire. President Franklin D. Roosevelt made no secret of the fact that he wished to appoint a westerner to the nation's highest tribunal to balance the Court's regional representation. A front-runner for the position seemed to be a senator from Washington State named Lewis Schwellenbach, a loyal New Dealer who even faithfully supported Roosevelt's ill-advised Court-packing plan. As a prominent New Dealer himself, Douglas was also a possibility, but Roosevelt initially dismissed him as an easterner. To borrow Schwellenbach's characterization, Douglas "was anything but a 'technical' Westerner." It may have been true that Douglas had grown up in Washington State, but since the 1920s he had been a member of the eastern intelligentsia as a Wall Street attorney, law professor at Columbia and Yale, and a commissioner and eventually the chair of the SEC. Clearly an individual who had spent his entire professional life on the East Coast would not fit Roosevelt's bill.[28]

Despite those strikes against him, Douglas and his allies maneuvered to emphasize his western background, experience, and sensibilities, as well as to demonstrate regional support. The campaign worked, especially when the well-known William Borah, a maverick Republican senator from Idaho, announced that Douglas would make a fine representative of the West on the Court. In March, Roosevelt sent Douglas's name to the Senate for confirmation, which he received with a vote of sixty-two to four. Douglas became the second-youngest person ever appointed to the Court.[29]

A National, Regional Reputation

As Douglas made his meteoric rise from "the outstanding professor of law in the nation," as one commentator claimed, to SEC commissioner to SEC chair to Supreme Court Justice in just a few years, he garnered national media attention, and the portraits were flattering. This attention fixed prominently on his previous western life and the "Horatio Alger" aspects to his rise. Richard L. Neuberger, an Oregon journalist and eventual U.S. senator, wrote a feature on "Mr. Justice Douglas" in the August 1942 edition of *Harper's*, depicting the young justice with "the five-gallon Western hat he invariably wears." Neuberger maintained that everyone called Douglas "Bill," emphasized the marked informality cultivated from his western background, and recalled that in a speech given to Wall Street Douglas "looked something like Gary Cooper playing a hayseed role." Neuberger's was an apt description, and Douglas consciously played up that hayseed image. Finally, the journalist explained the political appeal of Douglas drawn unmistakably from his humble Yakima roots: "He has a grassroots personality, a homespun Lincolnesque appearance, and the nearest thing to a log-cabin background there is in American politics today." The poverty in his background (even if exaggerated), the almost frontier heritage, and the identification with common citizens combined to make Douglas an appealing, if slightly unusual, associate justice.[30]

Neuberger presented a Supreme Court Justice unlike any other before or since.[31] Douglas seemed too undignified to sit on the Court according to a woman who once saw him light a match by scratching it on the seat of his pants. He also spoke in language colored by his experiences with the rough-and-tumble workers in the western woods, farms, ranches, and railroads. Those who encountered Douglas in the West invariably were surprised at his august profession. For example, Neuberger told of Douglas's meeting with railroad workers in La Grande, Oregon: "[A] leathery engineer on No. 26, the Pacific Limited, said: 'He looks and acts a hell of a lot more like my fireman than a Supreme Court judge.' " According to the *Harper's* article, a Forest Service ranger also reported that Douglas was "the best woodsman ever to camp in his district, even including a troupe of movie heroes noted for outdoor roles." Clearly, Douglas's public image was firmly tied to a western outdoor life, and it was an image of admiration.[32]

At the time Neuberger's article appeared, rumors that President Roosevelt might shuffle his cabinet for World War II led to conjectures that Douglas might receive a cabinet appointment. Neuberger actively promoted Douglas for such positions as director of the War Production Board or Secretary of War. Western liberals and progressives also readily praised Douglas's qualities and urged his reassignment. "The west has an especial regard for Justice Douglas," stated an editorial from southern Oregon's *Coos Bay Times*. "The northwest has found Justice Douglas, as has the east, a man of intellectual vigor, of impeccable honesty, with a *restless physical verve* so necessary for high offices in conduct of war. Douglas gets things done. ... This area knows he would make a valuable addition to any reconstituted cabinet the president may select." This image of a Rooseveltian man of action resonated well with Douglas's own self-perception and self-promotion. In a similar endorsement, the *Oregon Labor Press* offered even higher praise. After complaining that there were "too few Westerners" in the war program, an editorial announced, "the common people of the country—and especially the common people of the West—know that Mr. Douglas understands their problems." These Northwestern newspapers sanctioned Douglas's westernness and accepted Douglas as an able regional representative, even if the cabinet appointment was never forthcoming. If these editorials at all reflected their readers' opinions, then western communities, especially the liberal constituencies, happily claimed Douglas as one of their own.[33]

After World War II, Douglas became an even more prominent member of the liberal wing of American politics. He was rumored to be a vice-presidential contender in 1940 and more seriously in 1944. Harry S Truman offered him the position in 1948, and many liberals pushed him to run in 1952. Throughout such promotional efforts, his liberal qualifications and his western roots were reported faithfully. Writing in the *American Mercury*, Fred Rodell, a law professor at Yale University and friend of Douglas, wrote about "Bill Douglas, American." Sounding much like Neuberger, Rodell praised the justice's "homespun background and his fabulous rise from rags to fame." Despite stating that Douglas had not wanted the 1944 vice-presidential nomination, Rodell used his article to herald his friend's qualifications and even stump for his nomination in 1948 or 1952. Never far from the surface, though, is the image of Justice Douglas, the western liberal. Rodell quoted Douglas at the end of the article: "The average American is an independent, rough and ready kind of fellow who wants to take a swing on his own." Rodell suggested that the description fit Douglas best of all. Douglas certainly appreciated this attention and promoted similar images as he hoped for continued national prominence. In truth, Douglas adored the media's positive attention.[34]

Increasingly, observers connected Douglas's brand of liberalism with the outdoor life commonly associated with the West. As was made clear in a 1946 letter to the editor of the *American Mercury* in response to Rodell's article, the public identified the justice with the outdoors: "Douglas suggests the strength and ruggedness of the giant oaks of his own Wallowa Mountains of Oregon." This characterization surely would have pleased Douglas, even though he knew that oaks were relatively rare in the pine-dominated Wallowas where he spent his summers in these years.[35]

Douglas's journey from Yakima to the Court marked a tremendous achievement. By the late 1940s, Douglas no longer needed any more friends touting his abilities or western credentials; his national reputation as a westerner was secure. Nevertheless, he accelerated his own concerted effort to assemble an indelible public persona of himself as a rugged outdoorsman. In 1949, the horseback-riding accident in the Cascade Mountains helped immeasurably. Not only did it show him nearing his fifty-first birthday as someone who still courted danger in the backwoods, but the recovery allowed him to finish *Of Men and Mountains*, a book that ensured his name would remain synonymous with the outdoor life of the West.

Of Men and Mountains

Almost immediately, Douglas's popular image radiated strength through his valiant recovery from the near-fatal accident. An Associated Press account reported, "The stamina gained from an active, outdoor life away from his judicial duties stood him in good stead." So, despite the severity of his injuries, Douglas's prognosis looked positive. Letters of concern flooded into the hospital. To his friend, E. Palmer Hoyt, the editor of the *Denver Post* and erstwhile editor of Portland's *Oregonian*, Douglas reported his daily strain but ultimately remained optimistic:

> *Thanks for your letters and messages. I'm doing as well as can be expected from one of our vintage. Ribs are pretty important. They move with every breath and burp. They go into violent action on a cough and sneeze. They are in constant movement. That's why it's hell to break them. Be good to yours, Ep. ... I'm sitting up a bit each day and that helps. But the day when I can swagger down a corridor seems far distant. ... Meanwhile it will be a pretty low vitality, so I'm going to stay way [sic] from those Wash. D.C. flu and pneumonia bugs until I can meet them on equal terms.*

In spite of his pain, Douglas remained light-hearted. Moreover, he looked forward to a full recovery.[36]

William O. Douglas with Kendall, the horse who rolled over the justice, crushing his ribs

At least since 1947, Douglas had been working on a book about his life, and he used his recovery time in Arizona to finish it. As early as September 1948, the *Seattle Times* reported that the "rugged" justice was researching his book while in the area on summer recess and was "more interested in mountains and streams, in fishing, camping, and hiking than … weighty national and international problems." That was, indeed, the focus. Writing to the president of Harper & Row, Douglas assured him that his book project was "not about my recollections of Roosevelt or the workings of the New Deal" as so many others were producing in the immediate post-Roosevelt era. About six months before his horse accident, Douglas sent a copy of a manuscript he tentatively titled "Men and Mountains" to several publishers. Eventually, he published *Of Men and Mountains* with Harper & Row after putting the finishing touches on the book while recuperating outside Tucson. The setting furnished all a press agent could ask for: the prominent author of a book of outdoor adventures, replete with characters who seemingly just stepped out of the frontier West, was kept from his duties as a Supreme Court Justice because of a horseback-riding accident. In spring 1950, Douglas held a press conference, mentioning his recovery and his forthcoming book. The book he wrote matched and even exceeded the image others had painted in national magazines. Now, Douglas introduced himself to the country in the way he most desired. He had survived the accident, and the mythic qualities of his life grew even bigger.[37]

Of Men and Mountains proved a notable success. Douglas had written a good adventure story, or more accurately, a series of adventure stories. *Of Men and Mountains* contained vivid characters for whom outdoor living in the western woods was a natural way of life. The frontier feel of the book's setting could not be mistaken, and the rags-to-riches genre always held appeal to American audiences. In his study of Douglas's writing, James C. Duram correctly called it the justice's "seminal work."[38]

Predictably, Douglas located the roots of his identity in the Cascade Mountains and the local foothills near Yakima. "My love of the mountains, my interest in conservation, my longing for the wilderness—all these were lifetime concerns that were established in my boyhood in the hills around Yakima and in the mountains to the west of it," Douglas wrote. Those hikes up the sagebrush-covered hills two miles north of his home instilled the first seed of affection for nature in the Yakima boy. He explained, "These early hikes put me on intimate terms with the hills." Such intimacy gave Douglas a sense of the region's geological, natural, and human history. He filled *Of Men and Mountains* with geological facts, botanical observations, American Indian legends, and explorers' accounts. This knowledge made

Douglas especially sensitive to a sense of place, a sensitivity evident in later writings about the many mountains he climbed, rivers he rafted, and forests he hiked.[39]

Of Men and Mountains revealed Douglas's observant eyes and reflective thought. He appreciated the desert-like foothills because of their scarcity: "I do not envy those whose introduction to nature was lush meadows, lakes, and swamps where life abounds."

> *The desert hills of Yakima had a poverty that sharpened perception. ... Where nature is more bountiful, even the tender bitterroot might go unnoticed. Yet when a lone plant is seen in bloom on scabland between batches of bunchgrass and sage, it can transform the spot as completely as only a whole bank of flowers could do in a more lush environment. It is the old relationship between scarcity and value.*
>
> *These are the botanical lessons of the desert which the foothills of Yakima taught me.*

A plant, or person, singled out among the others might affect the landscape, or history, to a greater degree than in a crowd. Here were individualism and nonconformity in nature. These were lessons from the environment that Douglas could embrace, because they conformed well to the social vision that was emerging from his judicial opinions in these years. Douglas valued these singular traits that derived from the landscape of his home.[40]

Additionally, that home landscape revealed broader truths to Douglas. One spring evening Douglas walked into the foothills. He gazed at the stars and mused that they were the same stars that had hung over the valley from time immemorial, witnessing the evolution of the landscape, the passing of various human cultures, and the travels of Lewis and Clark. "On the foothills that night I think I got my first sense of Time," Douglas reflected. "In the great parade of events that this region unfolded, man was indeed insignificant." But although long expanses of time and an indifference to humanity might mark nature, other values were also present.[41]

As Douglas continued hiking, he drew deeper conclusions. A chinook blew. These warm and damp winds from the southwest usually brought with them needed rains for the dry interior Northwest. When the chinook came, Douglas felt "a measure of the kindliness of the universe to man, a token of the hospitality that awaits man when he puts foot on this earth." Reflecting a long tradition, begun with Plateau Indians stories, about the beneficence of chinook winds, Douglas saw the winds as nature's promise to the inhabitants of the dry interior. "That night I felt at peace," he continued. "I felt that I was part of the universe, a companion to the friendly chinook that brought the promise of life and adventure. That night, I think, there first came to me the germ of a philosophy of life: that man's best measure of the universe is in his hopes and his dreams, not his fears; that man is a part of a plan, only a fraction of which he, perhaps, can ever comprehend." So, while humans may be insignificant, the universe was not indifferent, not simply a meaningless struggle for existence. Nature, in fact, had a beneficent plan, including profound meaning for humanity. This is what Duram meant when claiming that *Of Men and Mountains* was "philosophical in the sense that it illustrates the discoveries Douglas made about the meaning of life." Indeed, that spring night in the Yakima foothills, Douglas explored the ultimate significance of nature, ideas he would adjust, elaborate, and articulate in various ways for the next twenty-five years.[42]

Meanwhile, throughout *Of Men and Mountains*, Douglas contrasted his two Washingtons—DC and the state—implicitly and explicitly. For instance, the book opens with Douglas daydreaming from the bench while a lawyer droned on with "accumulating monotony." He dreamt he was fishing for trout in the Big Klickitat of the Cascades with Hallock killer and No. 12 flies. In his reverie, he had had "wonderful luck." Such was the lure of the rivers and streams of the Pacific Northwest.[43]

Mountains were the same. From the time when Mount Adams comforted Douglas at his father's funeral, mountains represented a tangible force for him. Douglas compared law and the mountains. He was in a "dusty" law library searching "for the elusive thing called law. High in an office building on New York's Wall Street I would be lost in the maze of a legal problem, forgetful of my bearings, and then suddenly look from the window to the west, thinking for a second that I might see Mount Adams, somber in its purplish snow at sunset." This longing for western landscapes, never sated while in the East, drove Douglas west at every opportunity. Despite how well Douglas maneuvered through the East Coast establishment, he never cared much for the place. He recalled frequently feeling "an almost irresistible urge to go West. It was the call of the Cascade Mountains." To answer that call, Douglas maintained summer cabins at various places throughout the Northwest where he escaped from Washington, DC, as soon as the court recessed (and sometimes even before). As a Yakima friend recalled, "I always felt that Bill's residence in Washington [State] was terminated each summer in the way a man might be held by an elastic band. Just as soon as he could, he came back. It was remarkable not that he came back, but that he stayed in the East. He was more one of us."[44]

On one of his summer trips west in 1948, Douglas climbed a favorite rock in the Cascade's Teiton Basin, Kloochman Rock. That summer, nearing his fiftieth birthday, he enjoyed a "leisurely" climb and the magnificent views Kloochman afforded, but he recalled a different experience, a harrowing climb in 1913 with his friend Douglas Corpron. His reverie—*Of Men and Mountains'* denouement—describes a near-fatal ascent of the 4,500-foot rock. Choosing the southeast face, which Douglas believed had never been climbed, the young companions scrambled up only to find themselves stranded on a disappearing ledge. After Corpron nearly fell twice, saved once with Douglas's help, they moved determinedly to the northwest wall, which offered better routes for climbing. Soon, having climbed much higher, Douglas faced a crisis as the ledge he was on gave way. He "grabbed for a hold above me. ... [T]here I was, hanging by my hands 200 feet in the air, my feet pawing the rock." Douglas waited as Corpron moved to assist. Meantime, fatigue set in his fingers, then wrists, then arms. Facing certain death, he thought, Douglas prayed for strength. With Corpron's help, he found new toeholds, and together the youthful friends reached the summit. "[B]oth Doug and I valued life more because death had passed so close," Douglas recalled. "It was wonderful to be alive, breathing, using our muscles, shouting, seeing." Historian Susan R. Schrepfer used Douglas's account to illustrate what she termed the "masculine sublime" that men's mountaineering tales often deployed, depicting male climbers conquering a feminine nature. Such an interpretation is valid, but limited, for it only recognizes one cultural element at work in Douglas and neglects the more important personal and the political elements in play.[45]

This final adventure, synecdoche for the book and metaphor for Douglas's early life, represented ultimate triumph. But not just for Douglas. Meeting such challenges would make America strong. In the book's final pages, Douglas reasoned:

> *If throughout time the youth of the nation accept the challenge the mountains offer, they will help keep alive in our people the spirit of adventure. That spirit is a measure of the vitality of both nations and men. A people who climb the ridges and sleep under the stars in high mountain meadows, who enter the forest and scale the peaks, who explore glaciers and walk ridges buried deep in snow—these people will give their country some of the indomitable spirit of the mountains.*

And all of this depended on access to wild nature; the stakes could not be higher—for the nation, for individuals, for nature.[46]

Conclusion

By the end of *Of Men and Mountains*, Douglas had created a strong portrait of himself that endured. He had struggled mightily to achieve success and mastery of his body and nature. Moreover, his story was of a largely individual effort to overcome the many obstacles that stood in his way. Douglas had interpreted many of his companions and supportive family right out of his story to emphasize his independent accomplishments. The path to his achievements ran deep through western mountains, for there nature leveled the playing field, eliminating social distinctions of birth and allowing merit and determination alone to decide.[47] He learned that, given an equal opportunity, he could surpass his peers, even those who had most troubled him with their condescension and harsh teasing. Such an attitude pervaded his jurisprudence and personal philosophy. Most of all, he learned that the mountains were home, provided solitude, and connected him to forces larger than himself and the problems he faced, bigger in fact than the time in which he lived. While in the mountains, he healed, and that lesson always guided him. He believed those with far fewer problems than his own would benefit immensely from a few days in the wilds of his Cascade Mountains; indeed, this became a common rationale for his and others' subsequent conservation efforts. Perhaps most significant, Douglas made certain that others identified him as the rugged individualist comfortable above the timberline with a pack on his back.

Elements of Douglas's story resonate with others who made names for themselves as conservationists. The sickly childhood that transformed into a vigorous adulthood is reminiscent of Teddy Roosevelt. Locating God in nature and realizing the humility of humanity strikes one as Muir-esque. The long, rugged hikes to test one's ability to withstand nature's test seem like a page out of Bob Marshall's book. The close identification with a particular landscape is like many—John Muir's Sierra Nevadas, Howard Zahniser's Adirondacks, Edward Abbey's Arches. Yet despite these similarities, Douglas occupied a different place for American conservation. With the exception of Roosevelt, no one associated with conservation was positioned so highly in the realms of national power.

Douglas succeeded. Americans, already in the 1940s wont to associate Douglas with the outdoors, began writing to him, asking his advice. In an answer to a letter from a Seattle girl, Douglas explained the lessons of the mountains. "A person's experience on a mountainside turns so much on his own personality," Douglas wrote to Sharon Fairley in 1954. "For myself it is a testing ground of my strength and endurance, a pitting of finite man against one of the great rigors of the universe. It is an interesting testing ground. A man—or a girl—can get to know himself—or herself—on the mountain. He gets to know his inner strength—the power of the soul to add to the power of the legs and lungs."[48] The themes were common ones, rooted in American environmental culture and ubiquitous in *Of Men and Mountains*. He evangelized them the rest of his life. Douglas had become, arguably, the country's best-known outdoorsman. By the 1950s, he had occupied a seat on the nation's highest court for more than a decade and had been offered the vice-presidency once. Here was a man, politically talented and ambitious, who turned his reputation increasingly to the conservation cause. Quite simply, by mid-century, no one in the nation brought such a high profile to conservation. Douglas bridged the movement and political power in ways no one else could.

CHAPTER TWO

Roads to Protest

When roads supplant trails, the precious, unique values of
God's wilderness disappear.

William O. Douglas, *My Wilderness: The Pacific West.*[1]

It was an automobile age and a time of widespread conformity. In the 1950s, most Americans did not expect people to protest the building of roads. And certainly they did not anticipate a Supreme Court Justice walking nearly two hundred miles on one occasion and almost thirty miles of rugged wilderness beach on another to rally support against highway construction. But in 1954 and 1958, William O. Douglas took his reputation to the public through two notable protest hikes, one on each coast. He acted on his conviction that roads destroyed something special about a place. Although not a new idea or a particularly radical position, that Douglas took the issue to the public suggested a new day was dawning both in his own activism and in the conservation movement at large. If his carefully crafted image created the public identity of a rugged outdoorsman, then these hikes formally launched Douglas on his path as a public intellectual and activist for conservation.

Wilderness politics transformed in the 1950s from a struggling and quiet movement to a nationally important and conspicuous one. Justice Douglas advanced that transformation with two protests that captured media attention and made the need for wilderness apparent and public. The hikes targeted roads, those most sacred symbols of the automobile age and the constant bane of wilderness advocates.[2] Along the Chesapeake and Ohio (C&O) Canal in suburban Washington, DC, and the Pacific Beach in Washington State's Olympic National Park, Douglas led groups of hikers who favored trails over roads, hiking over driving, and the unique values of wilderness over mass recreation. In the process, the justice made his outdoor pastime a political act and became a leading public spokesperson for wilderness.

Prelude to Protests

Douglas certainly did not start from scratch; prominent environmental protests enjoyed a history going back at least five decades in the United States. The justice and his allies learned lessons from earlier protests, employing successful strategies and adapting to changing political structures and circumstances. Although seldom acknowledging these roots, Douglas acted within an evolving tradition of conservation activism. From the turn of the twentieth century to the 1950s, American conservationists evolved in myriad ways in how they challenged and shaped official policies. Understanding that critical context improves our understanding of these early Douglas hikes.

Despite deep nineteenth-century roots, conservation achieved its first real institutional success at the turn of the twentieth century. Historian Samuel P. Hays has argued that the conservation movement represents an exemplary case of modernization in which centralization gradually triumphed over localism with decisions made further from the grassroots by a limited number of experts. As American politics and economics became more specialized, government gained greater control over the structures of American life, a tendency toward a more closed political system. As part of the progressive strain of liberalism, conservation sought to regulate. The conservation movement's heart lay in efficient management of resources and that meant reducing economically wasteful practices, developing natural resources for profit, and establishing government agencies to safeguard public resources. Gifford Pinchot, the nation's chief forester and most noted conservationist, famously characterized conservation as working for "the greatest good for the greatest number for the longest time." Such a perspective left room for critics who found much missing in such a materialist philosophy or who wished to define the greatest good or the greatest number in alternative ways. Whereas the U.S. Forest Service might manage forests or the Reclamation Service might tap rivers for irrigation, some conservation critics thought certain lands deserved less intensive management or development. For them, nature's best use sometimes was simply to be enjoyed in a wild state or with recreation as the chief economic use.[3]

These differences collided famously in Hetch Hetchy Valley, a portion of Yosemite National Park. San Francisco wanted a source of public water that would supplant that of the city's private water supplier and cast its eyes on the Tuolumne River running through Hetch Hetchy Valley. Led by famed naturalist John Muir, many citizens criticized the choice as anathema to the park's higher purposes. Favoring the valley undammed on aesthetic grounds, Muir and his allies, often called preservationists, mobilized the public as best they could to stop the dam plans. Advocates also envisioned Hetch Hetchy Valley as a premier tourist ground and often suggested hotels, campgrounds, and other developments to encourage vacationers' use.

Hardly a pure wilderness position, this approach demonstrated the need to show public interest and economic benefits in leaving the Tuolumne River running. Besides encouraging recreational use, activists like Muir took their cause to the national public and political circles through articles in mass-circulation magazines and letter-writing campaigns targeting politicians and opinion leaders. With San Francisco interests entrenched in favor of the dam, preservationists understood that only a national campaign could save their valley. Theirs was the first national campaign of its sort.[4]

And they lost. Although Muir and his followers generated tremendous publicity, gathered many converts to their cause, and delayed the ultimate decision for several years, Congress authorized the dam in 1913. Many legacies come from defeat, however. While they were unsuccessful this time, advocates recognized that their near-success depended on convincing a national constituency to voice their support. When faced with similar circumstances in the future, activists appealed broadly. Part of that, too, meant encouraging more Americans to experience nature firsthand, so they would be more likely to care when a proposal for a dam or a mine or a timber sale resurfaced. In addition, many who found development in Yosemite National Park distasteful successfully convinced Congress in 1916 to authorize the National Park Service so that there would be an organization within the federal bureaucracy to manage and advocate for the parks. Finally, the sense of defeat left the preservationists embittered. Hetch Hetchy became a rallying cry that continues to resonate with wilderness activists.[5]

As the consumer economy of the 1920s accelerated, automobiles reached the masses who demanded roads that punched into wilderness. Mass recreation created a growing constituency for outdoor activities, such as camping, a development preservationists like Muir desired. Yet it produced unanticipated problems. Overcrowded campgrounds, ubiquitous roads, and fractured environments compromised wilderness experiences and prevented the sort of rugged outdoor adventures that many outdoor enthusiasts like Aldo Leopold—and Douglas—believed were what forged American character. The threat to wilderness, then, came not just from economic developments such as dams or mines, but from excessive recreational developments that precluded certain experiences and challenges nature provided.[6]

By the 1930s, several additional concerns about conservation coalesced and shaped the structure of conservation policy and politics. During the Depression, President Franklin D. Roosevelt's New Deal program initiated far-reaching changes in the American political system and on the landscape, transformations that conservationists of Douglas's generation inherited in later decades. The Civilian Conservation Corps best exemplifies these changes. One of the New Deal's most popular programs, the CCC put young men to work on conservation projects, such as reforestation, soil-erosion control, and trail building. Influenced by the standard arguments that contact with nature would improve one's character, the CCC set out to jointly transform men and the landscape, regenerating each from their depressed and degraded states. The program was wildly successful in both endeavors, but it also attracted critics like Aldo Leopold, who condemned CCC activities for doing ecological damage, and Bob Marshall, who found CCC road-building efforts invasive to wilderness areas. In 1935, Leopold, Marshall, and several others joined together to form the Wilderness Society to lobby for wilderness.[7]

While some CCC work on the ground inspired conservation conflict, its efforts along with many other New Deal initiatives also helped change American politics in ways that facilitated that very opposition. The CCC made conservation visible to local communities that welcomed and resisted, supported and debated the Corps' employees and aims. Regardless, a national conservation conversation occurred in part because of the CCC, and it opened up conservation politics to larger communities just as the New Deal as a whole opened up a new brand of liberalism dependent on, and beholden to, interest groups more than simply elite experts. In the post-New Deal era, such organizations as labor unions or the Wilderness Society operated within a structure that favored organized interest groups, allowing a space for grassroots political lobbying to an unprecedented degree.[8]

After World War II, when Douglas entered the public fray in various environmental protests, he crossed onto ground well prepared by earlier leaders. Conservationists had favored strategies (e.g., nationalizing issues) and targets (e.g., roads), and they were prepared for the shifting political system where a closed system of elites was opening to grassroots politics. Furthermore, changing values and economics made the postwar years ripe for new conservation protests.[9] Douglas understood well the value of these precedents, and he could not help but be influenced by them as he stood ready to take his outdoor image to the trails to mobilize the American public for wilderness.

The Chesapeake & Ohio Canal Hike (1954)

The Chesapeake & Ohio Canal was an important place to Douglas. In his months in Washington, DC, the canal with its abundant flora and fauna became a frequent respite for him, an escape from urban pressures. "My wilderness, though small and confined, was real," he wrote. Hiking along the canal one winter day,

The din of the city, the roar of its traffic, was behind me. So was the
squalor of its slums. The schemes and machinations of the little men
who possess the place seemed far away. I did not have to go far this
winter morning to reach this wilderness of solitude and quiet. Only
a few miles. That's what the cities need, I found myself saying. A
wilderness at their back door, where a man can go and once more find
harmony and peace in his inner being.

Modern Americans required this, and Douglas recognized such places were increasingly besieged, especially near growing metropolitan areas, an urban focus relatively unusual in conservation circles at the time. The C&O Canal was a prime example of such threatened landscapes because the National Park Service planned to develop the canal for mass tourism. So, it is unsurprising that Douglas's first foray into public activism occurred on the canal's behalf.[10]

The canal's history reached back to America's founding generation. On Independence Day, 1828, President John Quincy Adams broke ground on the C&O Canal. The canal fulfilled a dream of George Washington who in 1785 helped organize the Potomac Company, which began building canals on the Potomac River with the ultimate goal of connecting inland Cumberland, Maryland, to Washington, DC, and the tidewater. Completed in 1850, the canal ran 184.5 miles, used seventy-four lift locks, and featured two notable engineering feats: the Monocacy Aqueduct spanning 560 feet atop seven arches and the 3,117-foot Paw Paw Tunnel. Barges pulled by mules traveled along the canal and brought coal, agricultural goods, and building materials to the nation's capital. Competition from railroads and later automobiles, along with several damaging floods, forced the canal out of use by 1924. Within two years, federal departments expressed interest in purchasing the canal right-of-way. The federal government's interest peaked under President Franklin D. Roosevelt. Correspondence in 1934-35 indicates that President Roosevelt, Secretary of Interior Harold L. Ickes, and others wanted to acquire the canal for transportation and recreational purposes. By September 1938, the federal government obtained title to the canal. The Public Works Administration planned a parkway along the canal towpath as relief work for some of the Depression's unemployed. Soon, the National Park Service offered barge trips for tourists and worked to improve the fish population to increase fishing opportunities. World War II postponed these and other developments on the canal.[11]

Following the war, parkway proposals resurfaced, proponents hoping to capitalize on increased automobile tourism. Modeled after the Blue Ridge Parkway and the Natchez Trace Parkway established in 1938, a renewed proposal appeared that would construct a scenic byway to highlight the canal's natural and cultural heritage, while developing possibilities for mass recreation. Road proponents partially pitched the idea by using the canal's scenery as a selling point. Reflecting the growing interest in outdoor recreation, a 1950 Congressional report enthused:

> *The scenery runs the full cycle from tranquil wide waters and pastoral river slopes to the greater excitement of the winding, twisting river palisades and ultimately the scale of the mountain valley. This retinue of interests holds attraction for the tourist camper, the sportsman and the day outing party in all degrees from the novice to the sophisticated.*
>
> *The environment of the canal and river immediately generates in one an enthusiasm to see these 170 miles of delightful scenery unfolded on parkway terms.*

Parkway advocates envisioned the scenery through automobiles' windshields, "on parkway terms." Moreover, they promoted opportunities for recreation, tapping into the postwar desire for access to developed recreational facilities. With enthusiastic support, in September 1950 and without dissent, Congress authorized a parkway bill supported by the National Park Service and the Bureau of Roads.[12]

Beginning that fall and increasing in the next few years, local conservation organizations publicly and privately argued against constructing the parkway. Representatives from the Izaak Walton League, the National Parks Association, and the Audubon Society all voiced concerns, which focused on diminished natural qualities after road construction. Besides this opposition from private conservation groups, state conservation officials voiced concerns about loss of control to the federal government over fish and wildlife management. In face of this pressure, the Maryland General Assembly asked several agencies—the State Planning Commission, the State Roads Commission, and the Board of Natural Resources—to reexamine the proposal. Eventually, the Maryland committee recommended a much shorter road of about sixty miles.[13]

In addition to the state government's objections, concerned members of the public voiced their concerns. Irston R. Barnes, the president of the DC area Audubon Society and writer for the *Washington Post*, emphatically urged the NPS to restore the canal to nineteenth-century specifications and add simple recreational facilities, "small camp sites at intervals of a few miles, equipped with safe drinking water, Adirondack shelters, fireplaces, and simple sanitation facilities." Such development shifted away from mechanized use. Most of all, Barnes wanted to keep road access to a minimum so that "the motorist [could] … escape from traffic and enjoy, but not destroy, the quiet beauty of the river country." While Barnes railed against roads in the *Post* and later in *National Parks Magazine*, Retired Navy Rear Admiral Neill Phillips, an Audubon Society activist, drafted a letter urging members of the Maryland legislature to vote against the road. Somewhat paradoxically, Phillips suggested that preserving the canal without the road would make the "C. & O. Canal Park one of the most intensively used … National Parks." Later in the spring of 1953, the DC Audubon Society met at the home of Cornelia Bryce Pinchot, the widow of pioneering forester Gifford Pinchot, with nearly fifty people opposed to the parkway development. In addition to Audubon activists, members of the National Parks Association and the Wilderness Society, including Howard Zahniser, the society's executive secretary, attended and all objected to the road.[14]

Even though conservationists were rallying against the Park Service's parkway, others found it a good idea. In January 1954, the *Washington Post*'s editorial page jumped into the debate. The editors favored a road that would "open up the greatest scenic asset in this area … to wider public enjoyment." It would "enable more people to enjoy beauties now seen by very few. … [while l]arge areas of wilderness would be left out to be protected permanently against further encroachment." In addition, with more people using the Potomac River along the parkway, the *Post* hoped the area would be cleaned up. In short, automobile access would encourage mass recreation and give positive attention to an underused resource easily within the capital's reach. The *Post* tapped into a critical tension that runs through American conservation. In favoring easy access, the *Post* hoped to expand public outdoor-recreation activities, a seemingly democratic position that would potentially expand nature's constituency. Seen this way, conservationists who preferred more primitive recreation opportunities seemed elitist and anti-democratic. Such criticisms followed Douglas and his allies for decades, although he did his best to counter them.[15]

When he read the editorial, Douglas immediately felt his sanctuary threatened. He wrote to the *Post* on January 15, 1954. Many were upset by the prospect of a road, he explained. "Fishermen, hunters, hikers, campers, ornithologists, and others who like to get acquainted with nature first-hand and on their own," Douglas informed the *Post* editors, "are opposed to making a highway out of this Sanctuary." The canal and the nearly two hundred miles between the capital and Cumberland, Maryland, occupy some of the "most fascinating and picturesque" landscapes in the country. The C&O Canal served as a "Sanctuary," a "refuge," a "retreat," a "long stretch of quiet and peace at the Capital's back door," a "place not yet marred by the roar of wheels and the sound of horns." The haste of urban life in the capital required a place to unwind; the canal furnished "a wilderness area where man can be alone with his thoughts, a sanctuary where he can commune with God and with nature." A two-lane highway, thus, would utterly destroy this "Sanctuary for everyone who loves woods."[16]

Douglas couched his letter in ways that would resonate with the public. Most obviously, he celebrated God in nature and the solitude one could find outside of the city. By using these themes, Douglas wrote in a language many Americans already recognized from Henry David Thoreau's or John Muir's nineteenth-century paeans to nature and individualism. Douglas's contemporaries like Howard Zahniser or Sigurd Olson also employed such rhetoric. Referring to the canal as a "Sanctuary" or urging the editors to go there to "commune with God and with nature" also made the canal area a part of God's creation, so the idea of a paved road through it seemed sacrilegious.[17]

After celebrating the canal as a wilderness sanctuary, Douglas cleverly and publicly challenged the *Post* editors. "I wish the man who wrote your editorial of January 3, 1954, approving the Parkway would take time off and come with me," Douglas urged.

> We would go with packs on our backs and walk the 185 miles to Cumberland. I feel that if your editor did, he would return a new man and use the power of your great editorial page to help keep this Sanctuary untouched.
>
> One who walked the canal its full length could plead that cause with the eloquence of a John Muir. He would get to know muskrats, badgers, and fox; he would hear the roar of wind in thickets; he would see strange islands and promontories through the fantasy of fog; he would discover the glory there is in the first flower of spring, the glory there is even in a blade of grass; the whistling wings of ducks would make silence have new values for him. Certain it is that he could never acquire that understanding going 60, or even 25, miles an hour.

He appealed the best way he knew how—from familiarity and intimacy. Douglas remained convinced throughout his career that if people could experience wilderness firsthand, then they would want to protect it and work toward that goal. The letter revealed this strategy so clearly. He implored the *Post* writers—and readers—to walk slowly along the canal and learn its intimate natural secrets of flora and fauna. Once one knew a landscape at an ecological level, then one would not allow such a place to be paved over. Furthermore, Douglas invited not just the editor to take a hike; he implicitly invited the public to participate in the debate, to reconsider mechanized mass recreation.[18]

Despite several years of protest from the Audubon Society or the Izaak Walton League, the matter had received relatively little publicity. That all changed with Douglas's letter and the editorial response. After throwing down the gauntlet, Douglas did not have to wait long. Merlo John Pusey, who wrote the original editorial, and Robert Estabrook, the *Post*'s editorial page editor, accepted the justice's challenge. In a second column published on January 21, they labeled accessibility as the paramount value. They reminded their readers that they "directed attention to this delightful wilderness at the Capital's back door and supported the plan to build a parkway along the canal so that the people might enjoy it." The road would bring more people into greater contact with nature along the Potomac, the desired but paradoxical goal of mass recreation in nature. Conservationists themselves were divided over the place of recreation in their program. Indeed, the roots of modern wilderness politics grew out of many conservationists' criticism of the expanding recreational landscape. Thus, the editors' position favoring more recreation touched the heart of a critical and ongoing conservation debate. Nevertheless, the editors were:

> pleased to accept Justice Douglas's invitation to walk the towpath of
> the old canal—the entire 185 miles of it between Washington and
> Cumberland, if that meets with his pleasure. He has only to name
> the time and the starting point of the journey and to prescribe the
> equipment to be taken along. But it is only fair to warn the Justice that
> we are already familiar with some parts of the beautiful country that
> will be traversed. We are sufficiently enthusiastic about it to wear some
> blisters on our feet, but we do not believe this back-yard wilderness so
> near to Washington should be kept closed to those who cannot hike 15
> or 20 miles a day.

The journalists remained skeptical that any hike could change their minds and reiterated their belief that a road embraced democratic goals better than developing the towpath and canal with non-motorized recreational facilities. As they had in the original editorial, they compared the canal parkway with the Skyline Drive in Shenandoah National Park. That latter Park Service road, however, helped inspire several committed conservationists to start the Wilderness Society in 1935 to protest what they perceived as rampant road building that ruined wilderness values. It is doubtful the *Post* recognized that irony. Perhaps most important, though, the *Post* editors' favorable response to Douglas's challenge generated publicity.[19]

"Washington, D.C., area residents visibly perked up and took notice," *American Forests* proclaimed. "This was something novel and refreshing." Clearly, the C&O Canal issue resonated with readers who wrote to the *Post*. One explained: "When the editor of the Nation's most influential newspaper and a Justice from our country's highest court take time out from the cares of the day to undertake such an unmaterialistic, unorthodox, and unheard of thing as a walk in the woods, we have a little less apprehension about the fate of man that we read so much about." A couple weeks later, another letter appeared in the *Post*, keeping the cause alive in the newspaper. With obvious joy, the writer suspected that "Justice Douglas, himself, will have an opportunity of pointing out at length the error of your collective ways along the C&O towpath." The "complete wildness ... and the absence of crowds" along the canal made it a particularly valuable place for wilderness enthusiasts. With pointed criticism, the writer accused the editors of claiming "that this river should be made more available to persons too lazy or unenterprising to walk the few hundred yards from the road to the river bank." The letter pleaded that the *Post* ought to do more to respect "the claims of a small minority, to whom the river is a continuing tonic. ... There is still a place in America for wilderness." This notion of minority rights was becoming an important one in several contemporary political struggles, including conservation. For conservationists, protecting minority interests became a common refrain to the frequent charges of elitism, a perspective pioneered by Bob Marshall and one that Douglas employed frequently. The letter exchanges in the *Post* pages prompted by Douglas built up anticipation and in so doing he had in important ways succeeded even before the hike occurred.[20]

Douglas lent the C&O Canal cause legitimacy and provided needed exposure to the issue. These were roles he relished and would continue for numerous conservation causes for two more decades. In a February 11, 1954, letter to Douglas, Wilderness Society Executive Secretary Howard Zahniser praised the justice's public stance: "I should like to say once again that in focussing [sic] broad attention upon the recreation and other values of this historic strip of countryside, you are performing a signal service to the cause of conservation in the Nation's capital as well as in the United States." Zahniser recognized the importance of Douglas's participation and hoped the justice's example would influence others across the nation. Zahniser also wrote to several members of the country's conservation elite, including Sigurd F. Olson, president of the National Parks Association, and Harvey Broome, co-founder of the Wilderness Society, informing them that Douglas had "authorized us to invite you to join him on this trip." As this roster demonstrated, Douglas was becoming well connected with the nation's preeminent conservationists. Zahniser explained the purpose and context: "Thus with representative preservationists from all parts of the country we can hope not only to call deserved national attention to this C and O Canal and national-capital-area parks but also to arouse interest in the values that such areas have." Zahniser knew that the hike could achieve much if activists put forth a strong front at the canal. His organizational acumen proved critical in this and many other instances, including the passage of the Wilderness Act a decade later. Justice Douglas's involvement was a windfall to the causes conservationists like Zahniser held dear.[21]

The clamor for the hike grew. *Time* covered the preparations, calling Douglas "woods-wise" and "mountain-loving." As the justice recalled some years later, "about 600 applications [came] in from people who wanted to go along." Unable and unwilling to have such a flock of hikers, Douglas and Estabrook set out to establish criteria. Douglas explained without elaboration: "First, we eliminated all women; second, we eliminated all publicists; third, we tried to select only those who had some real, legitimate interest in the outdoors." After Douglas and Estabrook winnowed the group down, thirty-seven remained, including Olaus J. Murie, Harvey Broome, Bernard Frank, and Howard Zahniser, all ranking members of the Wilderness Society; Sigurd F. Olson and Anthony Wayne Smith, both of whom held high positions in the National Parks Association; and several others from the DC Audubon Society, the Potomac Appalachian Trail Club, the U.S. Geological Survey, and some journalists. Undeniably, it constituted an influential group.[22]

The party of thirty-seven headed down the towpath toward Washington from Cumberland, Maryland, on March 20, 1954. The *Washington Post* placed on the front page a photo of Douglas arriving at Union Station on his way to Cumberland; "The Challenger Arrives," it proclaimed. The night before the hike, the group ate steaks at the Cumberland Country Club and heard various politicians pontificate. Republican Senator J. Glenn Beall of Maryland forecasted the group's defection to the parkway cause, and former state senator William A. Gunter put the hike's stakes in sharp relief: "the question is 'whether this long strip of land should be converted into a runway for goldplated Cadillacs in a Machine Age, or be reserved as a foot path for the pleasure of nature-loving pedestrians of the Paleolithic Age,' such as Douglas and his fellow nature lovers." These locals clearly saw Douglas's cause as backward-looking and did not expect it to succeed. But Douglas and allies plunged forward, walking twenty-two miles the first day, a distance that gave more than one journalist blisters. Although

William O. Douglas leading a band of hikers along the Chesapeake & Ohio Canal towpath in 1954

some took packs—Douglas's was a reported forty pounds—there was automotive support: "A six-ton truck is hauling much of the duffle for the less professional members of the party. And there's a fellow in charge of cuisine who'll sell a breakfast, lunch or dinner to any softie who doesn't want to bother cooking his own." The hike was an efficient operation, even if it was not exactly roughing it for most. Still, as the article suggested, a masculine premium was placed on those men who lugged their own packs and cooked their own food. Over the next week, the hikers and the papers debated the virtues of unspoiled nature and hiking as Douglas hoped to convince the public of saving the canal from pavement.[23]

Even though the group covered between twenty-one and twenty-seven miles daily, all participants paid close attention to the landscape through which they passed. Harvey Broome claimed portions of the canal comprised "perhaps the most beautiful river scenery in America." He waxed poetic about the river, rocks and stones, plants, the "innumberable waterfowl," giant trees, and even the "grandeur" of cliffs along the Potomac River. With a parkway, however, "The intimacy, the sense of an on-and-on-and-on-ness which must have beckoned to our forefathers, would be gone forever." Sigurd Olson made a similar point. "Only by walking, paddling a canoe, or by riding a horse," Olson maintained, "can one go slowly enough to become a part of the scene and really appreciate it." The deliberate pace and distance of a hike worked as a stroke of genius. Walking the entire 189 miles forced each individual to become intimately acquainted with the canal's ecology. After only a day, the *Post* editors could even praise "the call of birds, the quiet flow of the river, the chatter of carefree men." The long hike embedded particular scenes on the minds of these men not easily erased and not duplicable by driving or a shorter, easier hike.[24]

Despite the daily rain, the hikers deeply enjoyed the camaraderie. Broome, for instance, recalled the hike fondly because of the companionship of Zahniser, Murie, Olson, "the Judge," and others. Olson told Douglas "that in a lifetime of expeditions of various kinds this one will always stand out," a distinct compliment from one so prominent in outdoor circles. Even Pusey wrote to Douglas immediately following the hike, explaining, "It was an experience that I shall always prize not only because of its novelty but also because of the fine companionship that it afforded. … I count myself very fortunate to have shared this adventure with you, and I feel certain that every member of the party feels the same way." Pusey not only recognized the historic nature of the event, but he experienced Douglas's renowned trailside charm. Along the way, the hikers were regaled with stories, such as Douglas's recounting of "lassoing mountain lions" in Arizona. They met an elementary school band, old canal workers, and even a fourteen-year-old *Post* paperboy hiking the trail with his father in the reverse direction. Midway through the hike a sign of support greeted the party: "Justice Douglas, keep to right. Booby traps to left are for Post editors." Other signs were less supportive, including one that pointed out, "Jackasses have traveled this trail before."[25]

Such signs did not dampen the spirits of the inveterate hikers, who composed "The C&O Canal Song," putting their own adventures to light-hearted verse. Led by Olson, the hikers composed at least thirty-one stanzas. The song began:

> *From Cumberland to Washington*
> *Is one-eight-nine they say;*
> *That doesn't faze this dauntless band,*
> *It's down hill all the way.*

Some stanzas indicated some mild frustration with the journalists from Washington, DC, but the words were clearly tongue in cheek since publicity was crucial:

> *The blisters are a'burning*
> *And the tendon's getting sore,*
> *While the shutter-boys from Washington*
> *Keep yelling 'Just one more!'*
> …

The towpath's winding on ahead,
It goes God knows how far,
We'll never know how far we've come
'Til we read it in the "Star."

Most of the "Immortal Nine," who walked the entire 189 miles, were memorialized in one stanza or another. The one dedicated to Justice Douglas reflected his well-earned reputation for being a quick and able hiker at age fifty-five:

The duffers climbed aboard the truck
With many a groan and sigh,
But something faster passed them up
The Judge was whizzing by.

The song was a big hit. According to Olson, Douglas "was so tickled with them he was singing them all the time." The final two stanzas captured the essence of their success and accomplishments.

Glory to the immortal Nine,
The waiting thousans [sic] roared,
The conquering heroes hit Lock 5,
And hurled themselves on board.

And now our journey's ended,
Our aches and troubles gone;
"But blisters heal," so says the Post,
And memories linger on.

The fun and companionship reflected in the song represented an important aspect of the trip. After eight days of walking more than twenty miles a day, the band knew each other well and forged, if not unanimity for the cause, at least a series of intimate memories and mutual respect.[26]

By March 25, only nine hikers remained who had walked the entire way— "bona fide 14-carat hoofers," as the *Post* called them, or the "Immortal Nine" as they called themselves. Conspicuously absent from this stalwart group were Robert Estabrook and Merlo Pusey, the *Post* editors, who took to horses or trucks for forty or fifty miles along the way. When the party, back to a full thirty-seven, reached Washington, Secretary of the Interior Douglas McKay met them with others who gave the group a "roaring welcome." Once the hike ended, the work began. The C&O Canal Committee, formed along the way with Douglas serving as chair, tried to organize appropriate action that now seemed within their grasp given the television, radio, and newspaper coverage and a public captivated by the event.[27]

Douglas invited responses from the hikers. Many hikers expressed their gratitude for Douglas's involvement, underscoring the consensus that his stature as a public figure made a decided difference. One who did not make it the entire way wrote to the justice with confident expectation: "The preservation fight is never ended, but I feel you have reversed the course in this great effort." Zahniser, who had done much of the organizing for the hike, echoed similar sentiments in a letter to Douglas. "It has indeed been a joy to be associated with you and the other members of this fine group," Zahniser wrote, "and the resulting prospects for the preservation of the great values that the C&O Canal has for us are a great encouragement and inspiration." All recognized the important role the justice played in the hike and were thankful for it. Because of Douglas, the prospects of preservation were much greater than they had been in the previous several years when only local and comparatively anonymous preservationists worked to stop the parkway plans.[28]

And what about the *Washington Post*? "In one important respect we have changed our minds," the editors acknowledged. They no longer could advocate the Park Service parkway plan. "We ... believe that many semi-wilderness stretches along the old canal ought not to be disturbed. There are the habitats of deer, fox, raccoon and birds without number." Still, Estabrook and Pusey did not entirely acquiesce to Douglas's vision. They maintained their original reasoning: "[T]here are a number of scenic sectors where a parkway would do little harm and would be an attraction for persons who do not have the stamina for long hikes." Despite their continued insistence on some roads, the *Post* writers had altered their position. They advocated a new NPS plan that would be "substantially modified to avoid encroachment on the best of the natural areas, to preserve as much as possible of the towpath and canal bed." Although they did not embrace a full wilderness perspective, their change of heart certainly revealed "at least a partial victory," as *American Forests* reported. Subsequent letters to the *Post* indicated, too, that the Douglas hike had changed some minds and kept the discussion in the public square for weeks following the hike.[29]

In April 1954, Douglas wrote Interior Secretary Douglas McKay with the C&O Canal Committee's recommendations. Predictably, Douglas concluded no parkway should be built on or immediately adjacent to the canal bed or towpath. He urged its preservation "as a recreational and historical entity" and its inclusion in the national park system. He believed the existing system of roads might provide an acceptable alternative to a new highway. "The area is rich in history," Douglas concluded his letter to McKay. "It has great charm and beauty. In some of its western-most reaches it is as pretty as any country one will find east of the Rocky Mountains. It can be made an attractive tourist area, where people can come by car with their families and spend a week-end, or for a few dollars have a real vacation." Besides its chauvinism for western landscapes, Douglas's letter reflected the justice's encouragement of use, as had the *Post*. Both believed urban Americans needed to get outdoors and experience nature firsthand. Maintaining wild areas near population centers would facilitate this essential experience. Douglas explained, "I am in favor of access roads and outdoor shelters along the canal to entice more city folks into the wilderness." Douglas understood the need for access. Since people tended to support wilderness areas they knew, wilderness advocates needed to get others to the places they loved. But Douglas believed a parkway would do more than provide access; it would fundamentally change the nature of the place, rendering a wilderness experience impossible. Even the *Post* editors recognized this potential in their follow-up editorial.[30]

The C&O Canal functioned perfectly for this need given its closeness to the nation's capital, and Douglas's hike served ideally to raise awareness at a time when wilderness preservation did not rank high among Americans' priorities. The C&O Canal hike helped change that. As historian Mark Harvey has explained, no longer were conservationists seen just as "flower pickers" or "bird watchers." Douglas lent "credibility" and gave a "stamp of legitimacy" to the movement heretofore lacking. Moreover, Douglas's involvement symbolized "[i]mportant people in high places had taken notice. Wilderness protection was no longer just the dream of a few but an aspiration of the powerful and influential in American life." No other public figure had been forthcoming for this cause. Douglas jumped in and made a difference and not just for the C&O Canal.[31]

Two years later, Interior Secretary McKay approved the idea of the C&O Canal National Historical Park and pursued enabling legislation. Douglas and the C&O Canal Committee endorsed the idea enthusiastically. By April 1956, Douglas informed Zahniser, Pusey, Broome, and others that McKay and the Park Service officials "decided not to build a highway on the old canal. ... This was very good news. I think we should celebrate by getting together again." With the reunion hike idea submitted, the group made it an annual event enjoyed by an ever-widening group of outdoor enthusiasts. Reunion hikers usually just walked along a portion of the canal, not the entire 189 miles again. Douglas continued to be involved for decades; he was the public face, after all. Even with a pacemaker and in his seventies, he barely slowed his pace to three miles an hour.[32]

At the time of the initial hike, *American Forests* reported: "Chief interest seemed to center around the fact that a group of hardy souls were hiking 189 miles in eight days in what has become a decidedly automotive age."

This was certainly true. Yet a broader context makes the C&O Canal hike more momentous than simply several individuals hiking when the masses preferred driving. Americans of all stripes were reconsidering their relationship to nature at this time. Unlike the earlier conservation focus on efficient use and management of resources, now Americans were more concerned with quality of life and environmental amenities. They sought, in the words of historian Samuel P. Hays, "beauty, health, and permanence." The Park Service, the federal agency perhaps most readily identified with conservationists' concerns, tried to capture this growing demand. Indeed, the parkway proposal was part of its continued program of trying to promote tourism. Two years after the hike, the Park Service announced its new development program called Mission 66. Under Director Conrad Wirth, the NPS planned to improve existing or build additional roads, trails, and facilities to accommodate eighty million park visitors by 1966. This ambitious program, however, faced some hostility from the wilderness movement. Although Douglas, Zahniser, and others wanted Americans to get to the wilderness and experience the life-changing powers nature offered, they feared overdevelopment. As at the C&O Canal, they feared promotion would ruin the very qualities preserved in parks. The 1954 canal hike and the prominent fight against the Echo Park dam in which the wilderness activists

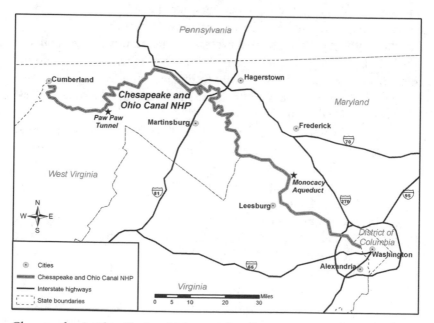

Chesapeake & Ohio National Historical Park

emerged victorious two years later demonstrated that conservationists were gaining power, experience, and maturity in environmental politicking. That success, though, required dedicated organizers, such as Zahniser, and prominent spokespersons, such as Douglas. Following the canal hike, Douglas found himself called on frequently to serve this role, and he went willingly.[33]

The Olympic Beach Hike (1958)

Douglas enlisted in his next major public activism just four years after the first C&O Canal hike, when he led another protest hike of conservation's luminaries. This controversy in Olympic National Park erupted in the mid-1950s, as Olympic Peninsula business interests urged a willing Park Service to build a new road that would wind along the park's ocean beach. The road promised to make automobile travel for commercial and tourist purposes easier within the remote peninsula and to promote park visitation along the Pacific coast section. Local boosters looked enviously south to the Oregon coast's booming tourist industry and coveted tourists' fuel, food, and lodging dollars for the local economy. In addition, proponents argued that national parks ought to be "made available to everyone, including old folks and children who can't hike along the ocean." Such arguments concerning access became increasingly common in the postwar period. Improving access and developing recreational facilities in national parks became a renewed emphasis for the National Park Service in the 1950s and 1960s. When conservationists protested these trends on the peninsula and elsewhere, locals reacted against what they perceived as economic colonialism, elitism, and insensitivity to local economies. The road issue epitomized these key issues and continued the tradition of roadlessness being the principal quality of wilderness.[34]

Douglas knew the Olympic Peninsula well from his outdoor activities in the mountains, along the coast, and on the rivers. In 1952, he wrote to the former superintendent of Olympic National Park, Preston Macy, inquiring about "good camping grounds high on the range." With Macy's recommendations, Douglas planned a summer trip "in some high basin remote from all points of civilization where I can set up a camp and settle down to enjoyment of the beauties of that mountain range." He also used a cabin on the Quillayute River near Rialto Beach from which he set out on a number of outdoor adventures described in a July 1952 article for *The American Magazine*. One could rough it in varying degrees, Douglas explained, from auto camps and inns to campgrounds and shelters to "trails for those who want to press beyond the limits of civilization." The justice sought wilderness experiences and urged others to do the same.

Understandably, when the proposed road threatened the sanctity of this wilderness, Douglas reacted.[35]

As early as 1956, Douglas expressed his outrage. Calling the beach "wild, raw, and beautiful," he informed a correspondent of the plans for a highway that would "drive the wild animals away; and would fill the place with automobiles." The next year, the justice wrote Conrad Wirth, director of the NPS, expressing concern. As usual, Douglas wrote a personal testimony. "I have hiked this primitive beach," he explained. "As a result of that hike I fell in love with that primitive beach and its great charm and beauty, and its abundant wildlife." He worried that if a road were allowed, the traffic would "drive out the game and we'd end up with just another ordinary beach." The justice wanted to maintain the beach as something other than ordinary. According to Polly Dyer of the Federation of Western Outdoor Clubs (FWOC), Howard Zahniser proposed inviting Douglas to participate in a field trip along the beach in conjunction with the society's planned annual meeting in 1958 at Stehekin in the North Cascades. Dyer ultimately organized the three-day, twenty-two-mile hike to bring attention to the road proposal and to underscore the superiority of hiking over driving, and Douglas happily led it. Besides interested local residents, the hikers included high-profile national conservationists from the Wilderness Society, the Sierra Club, and the NPS, such as Harvey Broome, Olaus J. Murie, Zahniser, and Wirth. Douglas told Wirth that he "would consider it a great personal pleasure if you yourself could be on hand" for the hike. Ultimately, the group included some of the most important members of the postwar wilderness movement, suggesting the importance of the event and confirming the esteem in which they held the justice.[36]

Douglas and the others favored preserving the beach undeveloped for several reasons. Not completely insensitive to local economic needs, they acknowledged the need for a road on the peninsula, but maintained it should not cross national park land. Their preferred notions of wilderness held that designated national park land ought to remain sacred; in the recent battle over the proposed Echo Park Dam in Dinosaur National Monument wilderness advocates succeeded in keeping a dam out of the national park system while acceding to a dam outside of it. Earlier, in the late 1930s in Olympic National Park, the NPS had struck a compromise position. They designed the famed Hurricane Ridge Road to concentrate visitors along one avenue that brought them to the edge of wilderness rather than to its heart. Increasingly, this pioneering type of limited access became common for national parks, and Douglas urged the NPS to add no more roads in Olympic National Park, to keep it "a wilderness park autos would never cross," in the words of historian David Louter. "Wilderness all over America is diminishing. Let's not put roads everywhere," pleaded Douglas. "Let's leave some of the state, some of the country, free from roads and from the effects of civilization that roads always bring." The beach was "a place of haunting beauty, of deep solitude," he wrote. The undisturbed processes of nature, the abundance of fauna and flora, the power of marine storms, "the music of the beaches," all overwhelmed Douglas on the Pacific beach. "I like to lose myself in the solitude of this beach," he reflected, "the solitude that no automobile can puncture." Douglas's experiences there shaped his protest, as did prevailing conservationist views of national parks as inviolate space.[37]

The hikers, along with the justice, cited other reasons that the road ought not to be built. Development especially threatened America's coastlines, making the primitive Ocean Strip portion of Olympic National Park particularly uncommon and thus especially valuable as wilderness. Excluding Alaska, only fifty miles of the 4,840 miles of U. S. coastline remained in public land and still roadless, newspapers reported at the time. Geology and geography, they also charged, made the proposed road too expensive and downright unsafe. Unlike the popular Oregon coast, the Washington shoreline consisted of "sliding bluffs" unable to hold a highway. A firm that surveyed the land in the early 1950s cautioned against the "high costs of both construction and maintenance." Estimates placed the costs for the twenty-mile section the protest hike covered at between $2.75 and $3.8 million even without the bridges needed to cross two rivers. Thus, armed with practical arguments and philosophical predilections against the road, the hike went forth to publicize the importance of remaining wilderness.[38]

The sponsors and Douglas designed the hike to garner attention. Louis R. Huber, a *Christian Science Monitor* writer and filmmaker in charge of publicity for the hike, invited journalists to "come fully prepared to spend three days in a wilderness area." The group also invited supporters of the road; none accepted, although some apparently canceled only at the last minute. The leaders of the hike hoped to engage the issues that permeated postwar society. Indeed, Polly Dyer, the president of the FWOC, called it a "walking national town meeting." Douglas functioned perfectly in such a setting as a representative from the highest court in the nation and in his role as a public intellectual for conservation. As he wrote to Director Wirth, "The purpose of the hike is to acquaint more of the conservationists with the exact character of the beach and to educate the public as to its more favorable features, and in general to awaken people to the potentialities of that area as a recreational wilderness." So, the event was designed to create greater awareness and concern among conservationists while engaging

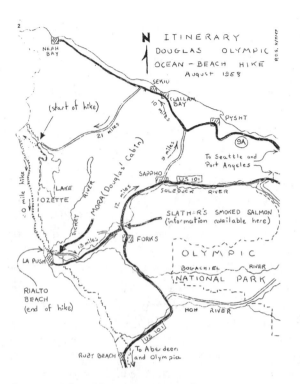

Olympic Beach Hike map, part of the publicity for the 1958 hike. From John Osseward Papers, Acc. 3818, box 5, University of Washington Libraries, Special Collections Division. Courtesy of John Osseward Papers.

the general public. In a "fact sheet" marked for release on August 21, 1958, during the hike, organizers explained that the hike's purpose was "to provide an opportunity for all now concerned, as trustees for this wilderness treasure which can be inherited by succeeding generations, to see the wisdom of retaining this small portion of primitive ocean shore which is still undisturbed by man. [The sponsors of the hike] want to encourage walking to beauty that *is*, rather than motoring to beauty that *was*." Douglas, the Wilderness Society, and the FWOC thus pitched themselves as legitimate spokespersons for the future of the public's wilderness. Moreover, they transcended local commercial interests by appealing to a national public, a necessary strategy in many rural areas concerned primarily with economic development and one honed from experience in campaigns such as Hetch Hetchy and Echo Park. This strategy of appealing to a national audience elicited understandable charges of elitism and anti-democratic methods. However, from Douglas's and others' perspectives, public lands required a public conversation concerning management and development. The Olympic Strip was not the peninsula residents' private domain but a treasure for the entire nation. The "primitive" Olympic Strip in Olympic National Park constituted a rare remnant of America's natural heritage needing protection. After all, they argued, the beach "can never be imitated by the labor and invention of man."[39]

The night before the hike began the hikers gathered for a salmon barbecue at Douglas's cabin. Douglas welcomed the group and set the tone for the event. He instructed them to travel together to minimize their impact on the wildlife. Finally, he beseeched them: "I hope you are friends of the wilderness and will pass this word along to others, because this wilderness needs friends." Douglas's remarks attested to the importance of publicity and far-reaching networks necessary for political success, and the justice remained vital in attracting attention to the cause and in facilitating the national networks of conservationists necessary to mobilize support. The following day the hikers drove north to leave from Lake Ozette. By the time of its departure, the group had grown to seventy individuals, "safari proportions," according to the *Seattle Times*.[40]

A particularly poignant scene met the hikers as they traveled to the trailhead. Clayton Fox recorded the landscape for the *Olympic Tribune*: "On the drive we passed through some completely logged-off land, with all the rubble which follows such logging. ... This[,] perhaps, heightened the group's desire to save the Ocean Strip from a road, since they could picture similar devastation following construction of a road." Fox drew the conclusion Douglas and organizers desired: roads equaled environmental degradation and ruined wilderness experiences.[41]

Participants responded well to the hike and its underlying message. Mrs. Lincoln Morse, proudly reporting that women comprised about one-quarter of the party, told the *Seattle Times*: "I'm not a politician and I don't know what good we may have done in the way of preserving the coastline beauty, but I think everyone had a good time in spite of heavy packs. Lots of people learned a lot of things from this hike." She continued, "[A]ll of us agreed that the country up there is worth keeping as it is whether it's for scientific or scenic reasons." Most of the publicity had not emphasized scientific justifications for stopping the road, but clearly hikers discussed that during their time on the beach. Scientific rationales for wilderness preservation were becoming much more significant. Others confirmed Morse's attitudes. For Harvey Broome, a co-founder of the Wilderness Society and one of the Immortal Nine from the C&O Canal hike, the beach made him ponder "the ultimate meaning of life." It was an overwhelming experience for him, being perched at "the meeting place of earth and sea—wild, untamed, and tremendous." Broome also expressed what was surely true for other hikers: Douglas's "consuming interest" in the place and his presence on the hike, prodding the hikers along, made the trip especially

William O. Douglas along the Pacific Coast beach where he helped lead a hike in 1958 protesting a potential road

memorable. This personal connection represented an indefinable quality that Douglas's authority furnished similar to what he had offered on the C&O Canal hike.[42]

On the hike's last night, the group met to assess the event's importance, to validate wilderness values, and to plan for the future. Employing the common frontier argument, Broome connected this local wilderness area to a larger role in American heritage. The nation's greatness in the past, Broome maintained, was reflected from and forged in the rugged environment and in the struggle of individuals with that environment. Wild, rugged land ought to be preserved, then, "to keep America from softness"—to keep Americans themselves wild and rugged. Douglas concurred and urged everyone to return and hike the beach again. The consequences of failing to keep the beach in a "primitive" state were clear and the stakes high: nothing less than American greatness depended on it, for the American character depended on it. The group appointed an Olympic Park-Pacific Ocean Committee to keep the issue in the forefront of the public's attention. As he had with the C&O Canal Committee, Douglas served as chair. Much of the importance of the hike, however, derived from the way Douglas and the beach affected individuals, reflecting the importance of personal experience with wilderness that remained common to the emerging environmental movement and central to Douglas's activism throughout his career. Thus, Douglas's presence as a knowledgeable and seasonal local remained crucial.[43]

The hike did not proceed without challenges, however, and those challenges revealed critical dynamics in the postwar conservation movement. Fox interviewed one disgruntled woman who spoke on condition of anonymity: "If I ever saw a place without a road that needed a road, this is it. As far as I'm concerned they can build it down the cotton-pickin' beach." In addition, during the hike, Fox questioned Douglas's reasoning for preserving the beach. He cautiously hinted that the hikers who wanted to keep the land for a special few who could hike smacked of the "aristocratic ideas of Alexander Hamilton" that Douglas, "a great liberal justice," ought to abhor. Douglas proceeded to give Fox a civics and history lesson about the rights of individuals and minorities and the government's promise to protect those rights in the American republic. In this instance, wilderness enthusiasts comprised the minority requiring and deserving federal protection. Fox conceded: "Since I did not believe a single college course in American History qualified me to talk Constitutional Law with a Justice of the Supreme Court, I retired very quickly."[44]

Perhaps the hike's defining moment came at trail's end when a single protester with his young son met the group. His presence highlighted the underlying tensions that pervaded the peninsula and hinted at Fox's muted criticism. L. V. Venable, the Port Angeles manager of the Black Ball Freight Service and a director of the Automobile Club of Washington, met the group led by Douglas as they emerged from the wooded beach trail with four signs:

WE OWN THIS PARK, TOO. WE WANT A SHORE LINE ROAD
FIFTY MILLION U.S. AUTO OWNERS AND THEIR FAMILIES LIKE
    SCENERY, TOO!
SUPER HIGHWAYS FOR 47 STATES BUT PRIMITIVE AREAS FOR
    US
BIRD WATCHER GO HOME

Despite the acrimony Venable presented, Douglas offered a friendly greeting. "Sorry you weren't on the hike with us," Douglas ventured. Although Venable agreed the beach was beautiful, he remained steadfast in his support for the road, primarily for the sake of the peninsula's economy. In a parting plea, Douglas proffered a compromise to Venable: "We'll settle for a road east of Lake Ozette. We'll give you 99 percent of the U. S. but save us the other 1 percent, please." The justice then moved on, unleashing the rest of the hiking group to argue with the Port Angeles man. However, the confrontation, captured by several photographers, symbolized important disagreements, and, even more importantly, it provided a dramatic moment perfect for media attention. Indeed, Dyer reminisced that Venable "made our day. He made our story legitimate for the press. We couldn't have hoped for a better opportunity for spreading our story—that the Olympic Coast *had to remain roadless.*"[45]

In his four signs, Venable succinctly captured local opponents' position. As members of the public, the locals wanted easy access to the park as public land. Indeed, fifty million auto owners surely constituted a majority. In addition, Venable asserted the hikers were primitive, even anti-modern, in their preference for walking over driving. He feared Washington was going to be left behind. But most damning was the final sign, suggesting both outside interference and effeminate interests in wildlife watching. None of these arguments was original; indeed, they constituted quite common refrains for half a century.

Douglas's strategy here angered Venable and some other locals, but it mapped well onto existing and effective conservationist approaches. In his response to Venable, Douglas offered a significant alternative. He and the hikers would accept a road routed east of the Ocean Strip portion of Olympic National Park that would not cross NPS land. They held to a dichotomy of sacred and profane lands. The legacy of the sanctity of parks, inherited from the Hetch Hetchy dam controversy down through the Echo Park Dam debate, remained engrained. The strategy, too, had much in common with those earlier fights, for Douglas and his allies took their position to audiences beyond local constituencies. Since local boosters like Venable tended to promote economic development, conservationists, from the 1910s to today, have worked successfully to garner national support and link it with notable local conservationists to overwhelm local opposition. Their strategy was politically astute, often effective, and deeply frustrating to local economic powers. In addition to Venable's sign, local news coverage and letters to the editor on the Olympic Peninsula complained about "outsiders" coming to the peninsula and preventing economic development. Such arguments about the loss of local control in environmental matters remain central in western political controversies. Yet the dynamics of localism here were more complex than Venable allowed. Peninsula residents may have seen these conservationists as simply outsiders who needed to go home. To the national conservation community, however, Douglas's larger regional identification as a Pacific Northwesterner and his peninsula summer cabin constituted sufficient local connections and legitimacy, and of course, not all peninsula residents did favor the road.[46]

The 1958 beach hike portended several aspects of the post-World War II conservation movement. It reinforced the significance of national parks among wilderness advocates. In addition, the beach hike affirmed public protest as an effective method for wilderness advocates in these days before substantial legislative protections; few mechanisms existed to challenge or slow development plans, so public campaigns were necessary. Although their hike did not compare with the protests of the next decade, it generated enough attention. With Douglas in the midst of this early wilderness confrontation, the protesters' odds improved, for as a local with a national reputation he helped legitimize their cause much as he had with the canal hike. Most importantly, journalists and citizens took notice. In this instance, Douglas and the road's opponents ultimately emerged triumphant; no road has been built.[47]

Conclusion

After germinating in the interwar period and then suffering wartime dormancy, the wilderness movement reasserted itself in the 1950s to become a nationally important and visible social and political force by decade's end. Along with other developments, Douglas's public protests advanced that transformation by capturing media attention at a time when the movement needed publicity. More than the organizational acumen of the Wilderness Society's Howard Zahinser or the blistering Congressional testimony of the Sierra Club's David Brower, Douglas's presence made the wilderness cause widely visible to audiences beyond the relatively small circle of conservationists. The early postwar fights for wilderness required this public exposure; indeed, the challenge of saving threatened wilderness seemed to demand spectacle in both the form of natural beauty and crowds of protesters because legislative remedies did not yet exist. Sigurd Olson recognized this after the Olympic Beach hike when he explained, "Without this *dramatic* effort we would no doubt have lost the battle by default." Even if it were staged and somewhat artificial, drama mattered in this age of minimal legal protection for wilderness. In this context, Douglas was uniquely positioned to help create a stir in the wilderness given his public image that relied on his outdoors background and his prominence as a Supreme Court justice.[48]

The problems that spawned these hiking protests centered on important and increasingly urgent concerns for conservationists: What was appropriate for outdoor recreation? How do managers balance the need for access with wilderness preservation? How do advocates best argue for protecting imperiled landscapes? Conservationists struggled in answering these questions satisfactorily, but they certainly engaged them in the 1950s.

Environmental historians have long identified the controversy over a proposed dam in Echo Park, part of Dinosaur National Monument, as the "birth of the modern wilderness movement." Beginning in 1949 and lasting until 1956, this campaign mobilized wilderness forces around the country and remarkably succeeded in stopping the dam in 1956. Wilderness forces succeeded because of a carefully crafted strategy that had important legacies that shaped contemporaneous and subsequent activism, including that at the C&O Canal and Olympic Beach. Conservation organizations and their friends, like writers Bernard DeVoto and Wallace Stegner, recognized that publicity would be central to their success. Moreover, they understood that they must reach a national audience, for comparatively few Americans in the 1950s, especially westerners perhaps, argued against more hydropower and what seemed to be inevitable economic growth and prosperity. In other words, wilderness required a *national* constituency. The C&O Canal and Olympic Beach hikes must be understood in this context, and Douglas contributed essential recognizability and national prominence at this crucial moment of transformation for conservation.[49]

In addition, these protests reveal the wide diversity of wilderness struggles in the postwar era. They spanned the continent and were not focused only on the mountainous West, as is so often the image associated with the dawn of environmentalism. They were not even always remote; the C&O Canal was, after all, "a wilderness at their back door," as Douglas wrote. The canal also could not be interpreted as a pristine landscape without human modifications. Thus, wilderness did not require purity as some have maintained. Given the hardened political lines that have emerged in wilderness politics, it is easy to forget that the movement in the 1950s stood at a moment of self-definition when ideas were in flux. The wilderness cause remained a small and marginalized movement, limited to a group of relatively unknown scientists, mountain climbers, and bird and wildlife watchers. Through his public commitment, Douglas helped transform conservation. In the future, he would seldom have such public dramas played out as he did on these hikes, but Douglas continued to work as a public intellectual for conservation. But drama was not the only way to reach the American public. The roads to protest, thus, changed as the 1960s dawned.

CHAPTER THREE

Toward a Wilderness Bill of Rights

The wilderness cannot be preserved against the pressures of population and "progress" unless the guarantees are explicit and severely enforced, unless wilderness values become a crusade.

William O. Douglas, *A Wilderness Bill of Rights*[1]

In the late 1940s and early 1950s, William O. Douglas became a world-famous traveler, writing accounts of "strange lands and friendly people" while commenting on social and political themes.[2] By the late 1950s, he was traveling more at home, concentrating on wild areas and writing about conservation. In 1960, he published *My Wilderness: The Pacific West*, a book with profiles of eleven locales special to him that he had visited in recent years. From Alaska's Brooks Range to Washington's Glacier Peak to California's Sierra Nevada, Douglas reported on his adventures, the natural history of each place, the threats to their ecology from economic activities like grazing and mining, and the beautiful delicacy of unspoiled nature. *My Wilderness'* opening epigraph came from John Muir and declared: "In God's wildness lies the hope of the world—the great fresh unblighted, unredeemed wilderness. The galling harness of civilization drops off, and the wounds heal ere we are aware." Five years later, *A Wilderness Bill of Rights* appeared. Rather than a celebration of natural beauty, this book chronicled a plethora of environmental problems and mismanagement by federal agencies. Justice Douglas ended the book with a call for a "wilderness bill of rights" that would promote an ethical relationship between people and nature through a massive reform of the legal structure. Instead of Muir, Douglas this time quoted President Lyndon B. Johnson in his epigraph:

> *For over three centuries the beauty of America has sustained our spirit and enlarged our vision. We must act now to protect this heritage.*
>
> *In a fruitful new partnership with the states and cities the next decade should be a conservation milestone. We must make a massive effort to save the countryside and establish—as a green legacy for tomorrow—more large and small parks, more seashores and open spaces than have been created during any period in our history. ...*
>
> *We will seek legal power to prevent pollution of our air and water before it happens.*

The differences between the two volumes and their epigraphs were emblematic of the changing nature of American conservation in the early 1960s and Douglas's position within that transformation. From a preservationist's hopeful celebration of the wild to a president's focus on immediate threats and legal protections, these books—and the movement—evolved toward concerted and consistent calls for political action, responding to both continuing threats and a shifting American polity. More than any national figure, Douglas conveyed these changes to a public eager to work for nature.[3]

The first few years of the 1960s were a dizzying time for the emerging environmental movement and for Douglas. Both accelerated their efforts at building a strong national constituency who sought permanent legislative changes to protect nature. To a remarkable degree, they succeeded. The wilderness movement coordinated a national campaign to secure passage of the Wilderness Act in 1964 after eight years of near-constant lobbying and negotiating. In the meantime, Rachel Carson shocked readers by publishing *Silent Spring* in 1962, an exposé warning the public of science run amok and poisons ubiquitous in the world. And civil rights advocates and student activists riveted the nation's attention, calling for an end to discrimination and greater participation in civic life for all Americans. So, along with the many other reform discussions filling the air in the decade, environmental protection occupied a notable place—not least because Douglas took seriously his role as a public intellectual for conservation, his reputation furthered by his recent hikes for the Chesapeake & Ohio Canal and Olympic Beach. In his numerous speeches, articles, and books, he engaged and educated the public about ecology, threats to special places, and the importance of reforming political and administrative processes. Rather than adhering to any strict ideological approach to wilderness or other environmental concerns, Douglas embraced a flexible, pragmatic, and evolving perspective on environmental protection, a position that mirrored much environmental activism at this time.[4]

My Wilderness: Nature Celebration, Ecology Lessons, and Wilderness Politics

When Douglas walked off the Olympic Beach in 1958, the secretary of agriculture could have stricken every last acre of designated wilderness or primitive areas within the national forest system with a single signature. However unlikely such a drastic measure would have been, its mere specter motivated wilderness advocates to move toward permanency. By 1964, not only had the legislative landscape transformed dramatically to strip the agriculture secretary of that power, but a broader wilderness movement had emerged with strong popular national support. And from that basis of success in wilderness preservation, the movement expanded to focus on other environmental matters, applying its methods of activism and encouraging other administrative reforms.[5]

Wilderness politics flourished and were transformed because of the momentum generated in the 1950s and because of new threats. After wilderness advocates faced down reclamation fever at Echo Park, they kept their coalition together and mobilized to pursue a permanently protected wilderness system. Meanwhile, the Forest Service, the agency that oversaw the vast majority of roadless areas in the nation, set about reclassifying its wild lands with an eye to opening many of the roadless areas to timber production. This vulnerability prompted local conservationists to organize and oppose the Forest Service, and they called on national conservationists and their organizations to lend help to local causes. This coordination was essential to success, as was the focus on specific places under threat. Rather than an ideological movement to protect idealized wilderness landscapes, the wilderness movement through the 1960s remained focused on specific locations important to active citizen groups. This strategy of protecting particular places under specific threats with a coordinated local and national effort sowed success and kept the movement popular among a sizable portion of Americans whose changing social values appreciated the amenities of wilderness in addition to or instead of the commodity values such areas embodied. Douglas advocated this precise strategy.[6]

To stop administrative threats to local wilderness, grassroots activists focused attention on besieged places. Already a veteran of such publicity campaigns, Douglas generated necessary attention through his writing and publicized visits to myriad landscapes. Moreover, as conservationists confronted intransigent agencies and administrators, they articulated political, legal, and ecological arguments to counter managers' and industries' perspectives. Given his august position, Douglas brought great symbolic power to this aspect of the movement. Through it all, Douglas facilitated a public education campaign, as he remained conservation's public intellectual *par excellence.*

Readers of *Of Men and Mountains* could recognize Douglas's interest in land, but that interest served mostly as a backdrop for his adventures in the mountains. With the publication of *My Wilderness: The Pacific West* (1960) and its companion, *My Wilderness: East to Katahdin* (1961), Douglas made the environment more than a setting for personal transformations. The books served important political purposes for Douglas and reflected his deepening connection to conservation circles. To be sure, the books continued to celebrate magnificent landscapes. But they moved in new directions, too, articulating his environmental values to a greater degree, values that deepened each passing year. More than simply describing personal experiences and philosophies forged in the outdoors, Douglas used these books to educate the public about little-known places facing little-known, but ubiquitous, threats. The chapters blended celebration in the tradition of Henry David Thoreau and John Muir with the ecological analysis of Aldo Leopold and a political analysis that incorporated all of the above with his own perspective and ideals. His approach was thus broadly cultural and deeply personal.

In emphasizing certain familiar themes, Douglas drew on the long tradition of American nature writing. Wilderness inspired him, as it had so many others, in part because of its isolation. After visiting the famed conservationists and biologists Olaus and Margaret Murie in Alaska, Douglas eloquently described the deep seclusion of the Brooks Range: "The Arctic has strange stillness that no other wilderness knows. It has loneliness too—a feeling of isolation and remoteness born of vast spaces, the rolling tundra, and the barren domes of limestone mountains. This is a loneliness that is joyous and exhilarating. All the noises of civilization have been left behind; now the music of the wilderness can be heard." Like others before him, Douglas recognized that the beautiful northern wilderness sharpened his perceptions. Without distractions, in deep solitude, the justice experienced nature with all his senses.[7]

Such solitude produced two responses in Douglas—a harder and a softer one. In wild places where one could find isolation, adventure often followed. Just as he had described in *Of Men and Mountains,* Douglas valued nature as a place to test himself and be rewarded by the struggle of climbing a high mountain or walking a strenuous hike. Without the challenge of getting to them, summits, high meadows, or mountain lakes were pedestrian. Recalling frontier ideology, in Douglas's thinking, those who met the challenge deserved wilderness rewards, but those who did not work for it deserved only disdain. Writing about Bird Creek Meadows near his beloved Mount Adams, Douglas praised the meadows as a fine reward after a long day hiking and climbing. It was an ideal "place to stay for days, searching out beds of dainty phlox on the slopes above the lake, fishing from an old raft, or just lying on the shore watching fleecy clouds race by." One summer afternoon in the 1950s Douglas returned to Bird Creek Meadows from his summer home, then in Glenwood, Washington. He discovered a road now climbed further up the mountain than before. Twenty-seven cars preceded his own up the mountainside. The "alpine meadow that I used to reach only after days of hiking," Douglas complained, "was now accessible to everyone *without effort*. It had been desecrated by the automobile. This high shoulder of Mount Adams now had all the amenities of Rock Creek Park in Washington, D.C., and Central Park in New York City." Even worse, "[p]otbellied men, smoking black cigars, who never could climb a hundred feet, were now in the sacred precincts of a great mountain. Part of the charm of Bird Creek Meadows had been their remoteness and the struggle to reach them." The meadows no longer impressed Douglas with their beauty. Without the challenge of hiking to the place, without the experience of the strenuous life, the wilderness sense no longer existed. If one could drive to it, Douglas complained, the mountain meadow became "merely another spot on a busy highway." For Douglas, then, wilderness was not the simple existence of meadows or flowers. Instead, wilderness required a challenge, for without a challenge one's character, especially one's masculinity, would not be tested and changed for the better in the wilderness crucible.[8]

Douglas feared that the modern age dulled freedom and individuals' senses. "Nature builds strength and character competitively," Douglas believed. In earlier times, the frontier had provided that opportunity for such character building. Now, "[s]oft and flabby" Americans had lost their independence and strong qualities. Earlier, the outdoor life had demanded ingenuity with survival as the reward. Americans in Douglas's time were "apartment-born" and never experienced the challenges that wilderness demanded. "Men need testing grounds," sounded Douglas, once again employing this theme while considering Glacier Peak in the Cascades. "Men need to know the elemental challenges that sea and mountains present." After confronting the danger of river rapids on the Quinault River in the Olympic Mountains, Douglas celebrated the rewards of such encounters with nature. One matched one's strength and cunning against a relentless natural force, and for that individual, "[a]ll that matters is his skill, and his alone." Encounters with wilderness, thus, strengthened individualism, just as Theodore Roosevelt and frontier historians had argued half a century before. Without such direct knowledge and firsthand experience, Douglas fearfully imagined a future without vitality, progressive-era anxiety remaining a palpable force.[9]

After returning from a hike along the Virgin River in Utah, Douglas relished the adventure he had experienced. Near Zion National Park, the Virgin River attracted many tourists "by car to the edge of adventure" and no further. They missed the beauty of the "symphony of the wilderness" that Douglas had experienced. Soft tourists, "traveling on rubber tires," would never know the lessons nature brought; a return to the elements,

Beside campfires, William O. Douglas felt most comfortable and articulated his evolving ideas of the value of nature

to adventure, to the wild could educate and revitalize them. But Douglas recognized that "[o]nly those who choose to get lost in it, cutting all ties with civilization, can know what I mean." With challenge and risk, one might comprehend fundamental relationships in the world. These would not be revealed in the city or an automobile, only in the wilderness.[10]

In New England, Douglas met others who disgusted him by their unfitness. On one occasion, the justice had climbed slowly and deliberately up Mount Washington and wrote knowledgeably about grasses, fruits, trees, insects, and weather, demonstrating intimate familiarity with the region. After the 4000-foot climb to the summit, Douglas burst out of the woods to a scene that troubled him: "A man who was fifty pounds overweight and smoking a cigar greeted me and cast aspersions on my character for walking up, when there were commercial enterprises which, for a fee, could have saved me the effort." Hundreds of people milled around oblivious to the diverse flora and fauna thriving around them. "These people," Douglas thought, "represent the America that had grown soft and flabby and overfed and perhaps a bit callous." The scene so discouraged him, he would not return for years.[11]

The anxieties about manhood embedded in Douglas's writing reflected early twentieth-century concerns about closing frontiers. However, they also elucidated new concerns for American men. While Douglas grew up during a time when masculine roles faced challenges, he wrote *My Wilderness* at another time when manliness was being redefined. In the early Cold War era, a new crisis in gender emerged. Some historians have located this crisis in fears of the "flabby American," a concern Douglas certainly understood, embodied, for example, in John F. Kennedy's advocacy of physical fitness. American men learned that strength, competition, and hard bodies were prerequisites for Cold War victory. In addition, the increasing assault on western public lands represented the latest threat to America's remnant frontier. The era's rampant dam building and the rapid acceleration of timber cutting in the national forests mobilized Americans to environmental causes in part because of these fears of disappearing opportunities for Americans, especially men, to prove themselves against the elements and by extension to external enemies—real and imagined. Massive suburbanization consumed rural areas, transforming the land and recasting Americans' relationship with the outdoors. Postwar booms in highway and home construction threatened American lands, as the deepened commitment to a consumer economy increased the sedentary nature of American work. Just as it had at the turn of the twentieth century, then, this postwar era found men like Douglas struggling against trends that imperiled their prospects of meeting the wilderness on its own terms and proving their abilities, and the Cold War lurked ominously in the background.[12]

If Douglas reveled in individualistic endeavors that tested one's mental and physical strength, he also enjoyed quieter, easier elements in nature. His second response to solitude, then, led him to contemplate the role of the sacred in nature. Perhaps not surprising in a minister's son, his writing was laced with discussions of God. Frequently, he simply praised God's handiwork, as he had in Alaska: "Never, I believe, had God worked more wondrously than in the creation of this beautiful, delicate alcove in the remoteness of the Sheenjek Valley." But beyond such natural acclaim, Douglas argued that sacred creation demanded special treatment. At a lake in the Olympic Mountains, Douglas approached "a quiet alcove … reverently. It is a sanctuary where voices above a whisper seem almost sacrilegious." Wilderness isolation, thus, promoted a sense of divine presence. Nature inspired Douglas, and he encouraged others to "learn to worship God where pointed spires of balsam fir turn a mountain meadow into a cathedral." In ways reminiscent of Muir, Howard Zahniser, and others who found wilderness charged with spirituality, Douglas encouraged his readers to recognize the importance of caring for creation. "We look to the heavens for help and uplift," he wrote, "but it is from the earth that we must find our sustenance; it is on the earth that we must find solutions to the problems that promise to destroy all life here." At a time when the threat of nuclear fallout and chemical contamination were ubiquitous, sustaining a divinely made earth must be a priority. Douglas urged a spiritual solution that included embracing creation and recognizing that "to be whole and harmonious, man must also know the music of the beaches and the woods. He must find the thing of which he is only an infinitesimal part and nurture it and love it, if he is to live." Douglas thus created a balancing act. Humans must recognize that the spiritual realm supersedes them and their needs, rendering individuals powerless in the long term. However, in perceiving nature's wonder as God's creation and treating it appropriately, one might improve, even save, the present. Both immediate needs and the afterlife, then, were protected when people redefined their relationship with the natural world.[13]

A significant foundation of Douglas's spirituality toward nature lay in the relationships it supported. Specifically, he connected his own solitude in nature with God's universe and plan. The simplicity and beauty of wilderness places and moments gave Douglas insight into infinite spiritual possibilities. The Cascades' Bird Creek Meadows inspired wonderment and worship as human problems dissipated in the awe of the Creator. Maine's Allagash River taught individuals humility in the face of God's sacred creation. At the same time, mining in the Glacier Peak area elicited calls of sacrilege. God made glorious places that inspired reverence, and callously using such places for human needs profaned them.[14]

The relationship between Douglas and God, mediated through nature, was not the only association that mattered. Indeed, some of the most powerful passages Douglas wrote at this time concerned ecological relationships. The *My Wilderness* books appeared just before Rachel Carson's *Silent Spring* (1962) dramatically changed Americans' awareness of ecology.[15] Douglas found himself in a position in which he thrived—that of the teacher with a purpose. He enjoyed being able to educate the public, and the justice found ecological lessons among his favorite tutorials. Implicit in his didactic prose, too, were criticisms about management.

Douglas wrote lessons about diverse ecologies. In Alaska's Sheenjek Valley, he observed a busy arctic ground squirrel trying to collect enough food before hibernation. The squirrel, Douglas explained, "is essential in the food chain." Bears, foxes, wolverines, and eagles all hunted the small animal. In addition, lemmings and voles in the region experienced "cycles of life with periods when the population reaches crash proportions and times when it is at low ebb." Scarce food generated stress in the animals causing "inflammation or ulceration of the digestive tract and a permanent metabolic derangement that directly or indirectly causes death. … In lemmings this tension becomes so great that it leads to mass migration … which amounts to mass suicide." Such images demonstrate Douglas's attention to detail and knowledge of current natural history research. In this case, his ecological understanding certainly came from his contact with Olaus and Margaret Murie whom he visited in the Brooks Range in 1956.[16]

Squirrels and lemmings, though, were hardly the height of drama, so Douglas included wolves—always glorious or notorious—to highlight broader ecological points. As predators, wolves occupied an important niche in the Arctic ecosystem, Douglas taught, not only by culling caribou herds but by indirectly providing carrion for lesser predators like the lynx. They acted "as a curb on the destructive overuse of the national range." In this region of northeast Alaska, wolves remained central to a functioning ecosystem, and Douglas implored that it must remain so. And that required protection:

> This is—and must forever remain—a roadless, primitive area where all food chains are unbroken, where the ancient ecological balance provided by nature is maintained. The wolf helps in that regard. He has, moreover, a charm that is wild and exciting. In this, our last great sanctuary, there should be a place for him. His very being puts life in new dimensions. The sight of a wolf loping across a hillside is as moving as a symphony.

This passage typified Douglas's approach. Following an ecological description (wolf as key predator), he connects to a political argument (need for preservation) and a cultural need (beauty of wild nature). In this way, Douglas educated and advocated.[17]

The theme of balance pervaded more of Douglas's concerns than just predator-prey relationships. In the Everglades, for instance, much of the focus on balance centered on water. "The balance between drought and wetness, between fresh water and salt, was always delicate," Douglas explained, and people "tampered dangerously with this delicate balance" through various draining efforts. Diverting water from the Everglades changed the habitat severely, so severely that some birds like the wood ibis virtually stopped breeding in the region. By emphasizing nature's fragility here, Douglas asserted a model of nature that was decidedly vulnerable; ecosystems were not inherently stable and strong, but complex and susceptible to small perturbations, natural and especially anthropogenic. Meanwhile, bald eagles were declining. Anticipating *Silent Spring*'s indictment that would appear the following year, Douglas reported that "many people suspect the DDT that is used in spraying for mosquitoes and that eventually enters the fish that the bald eagle eats" as the main culprit to the eagle's decline. An interdependent web of life depended on an equilibrium of freshwater and saltwater. The diverse system, Douglas revealed in myriad examples, required all species—from the lowly gambusia fish to the mighty alligator. Disruptions to one affected the others.[18]

These and many other examples of his ecology lessons showed Douglas relying on arguably the most common concept used to describe the natural world—the balance of nature. This metaphor proved irresistible to nature writers and environmental advocates in Douglas's time and since. Inspired in part by the work of early-twentieth-century ecologists like Frederic L. Clements, the balance of nature idea suggested that in a given environment a balanced, self-sustaining community, or ecosystem, would evolve. This climax community, as Clements called it, would continue forever provided no disturbance—human or natural—upset the balance. Ecologists gradually challenged the idea that a particular location had one potential climax community, seeing contingency and change as much more important. By the 1950s, ecologists began rejecting this idea of a stable nature, identifying fragmentation as the more important characteristic of natural communities. By the 1960s and 1970s, chaos became another way of understanding nature's inherent instability. More recently, one study synthesized modern ecology and characterized nature as made of "discordant harmonies." Change, rather than balance, has become a defining characteristic in ecosystem science today. It should not surprise us that ecologists have changed their models of nature, but none of the new models have been able to supplant the balance of nature for its rhetorical power. And Douglas employed the expression to great effect.[19]

As others had, Douglas used the concept of balance of nature because of its power to frame the landscape and the issues involved in managing it. If nature existed in a balance, any action that disrupted that stability violated the natural order of things and demanded condemnation and rectification. For example, Douglas reported on efforts by cattle interests to burn or spray sagebrush on eastern Oregon's Hart Mountain to improve grazing resources, a practice that would upset the balance that antelope—"as distinctively American as anything our wilderness offers"—and sagebrush had established. According to Douglas, then, "If we are to give antelope the preference they deserve, sagebrush and the other browse on which they are dependent must be allowed to flourish." Farmers and ranchers, land and water managers must protect, not disturb, natural processes. No matter how slippery an ecological concept it was, Douglas taught the lesson time and again.[20]

Clearly Douglas laced his nature portraits with celebrations of place and lessons of ecology. But also sneaking into his writing also was a political agenda—part praise, but mostly critique. For wilderness advocates, the Forest Service was arguably the most important agency for its history of recreation planning and wilderness protection, as well as the significant reforms it was confronting from the 1950s to the 1970s. The Forest Service began recreational planning in the 1910s responding to new consumer demands and as a reaction to the creation in 1916 of the National Park Service. Aldo Leopold and Arthur Carhart pioneered the wilderness idea within the Forest Service, and the agency adopted its first recreation regulations in 1929 for preserving wilderness, called primitive areas. A decade later new regulations appeared, furnishing more opportunities to preserve wild areas. The power to create or dissolve—or in Forest Service terms, to classify or declassify—wilderness rested with agency administrators, making preserved areas vulnerable to administrators' change of will and subjecting these foresters to intense pressure.[21]

Throughout the early postwar era, the agency evolved slowly to accommodate consumers who demanded more recreational opportunities, as well as better forest management practices. Of course, because of historical precedent and profit motives, the agency responded more readily to timber interests' demands. However, the last half of the 1950s found Congress debating the Forest Service over the direction of its policy. The initial result of these debates was the Multiple Use-Sustained Yield Act of 1960 (MUSY). Although it articulated multiple use and sustained harvesting as its goal, the law did not compel the agency to stop managing for maximum production. Despite its shortcomings, MUSY was the first law to purposefully put outdoor recreation alongside the more traditional range, timber, watershed, and wildlife and fish management priorities, a slight but notable change that wilderness advocates like Douglas used to castigate the Forest Service in coming years.[22]

Conservationists like Douglas confronted an important paradox in their dealings with the Forest Service. They were quick to challenge the agency's application of the multiple-use concept. Yet, the Forest Service also controlled the most land set aside in wild areas and millions more acres still in a roadless state. As such, the Forest Service was the largest stakeholder and theoretically offered the best protection against economic encroachments like grazing and timber cutting. Moreover, as Douglas described the relentless American tradition of transforming wilderness into farms and cities, he worried about the possibility that national forests might simply be turned into commercial space—a process into which he thought it would be easy to slip. In the Maroon Bells area of Colorado, for instance, grazers built up their cattle and sheep herds to the maximum allowable size. Then, the ranchers pressured the Forest Service to maintain the level, for reductions would mean adversity or poverty, at least psychologically. From the ranchers' perspective, an administrator who ordered herd reductions for range improvements "seems to be a man without conscience," Douglas wrote. But the Maroon Bells and other western rangelands were turning to dust under innumerable hooves. However, the Forest Service was the best, if imperfect, guardian to prevent further despoliation, and Douglas praised them for doing this challenging job.[23]

This proved to be a rare commendation. More common was condemnation, such as Douglas's description, only twenty pages later, of the Wind River Mountains of Wyoming:

> I had long suspected that "multiple" use was semantics for making cattlemen, sheepmen, lumbermen, miners the main beneficiaries. After they gutted and ruined the forests, then the rest of us could use them—to find campsites among stumps, to look for fish in waters heavy with silt from erosion, to search for game on ridges pounded to dust by sheep. On Piñon Ridge, I realized that the pretense of "multiple" use as applied in this area in Wyoming was an awful wrong.

New England's White Mountains faced even greater pressures because they sat within a day's drive of forty million people. Industry had already cut over the White Mountains and was eager to cut the returning forest. The Forest Service would ultimately decide. "Dedication of each section of land to as many uses as possible is a constructive policy so far as many areas go," Douglas acknowledged. "But if applied to some sections it means the end of the woodland wilderness." Multiple use must have limits, especially when new logging technologies like bulldozers could permanently alter the mountains.[24]

Multiple use, it seemed to Douglas, worked only as well as its administrators. And they were unprepared. "[T]heir education has emphasized, not conservation and recreation, but the conversion of God's wilderness into board feet of lumber," charged Douglas. Even if they were so inclined, though, Forest Service personnel could not prevent all incursions to wild areas. Mining was allowed. Hunting was unregulated. Dams and reservoirs could be built. The bureaucracy was powerless against these potential assaults, but it proved powerful enough to reclassify wild areas and open them to logging "if a few men in Washington, D.C., so decide." The system seemed doomed to fail. As with many of the landscapes he described, a delicate balance was needed. Douglas hoped his readers would take notice and call for change.[25]

Douglas explored the failure of the system most effectively in his portrait of his beloved Wallowa Mountains of northeastern Oregon. Douglas described a beautiful wilderness replete with fish, mountains, and aromatic balsam fir. This forest in the Minam River Canyon was threatened. The Forest Service planned to open it with a road for timber cutters. Not only would timber harvesting affect the clear mountain streams, but the road spelled myriad problems. Roads had long symbolized invasion to wilderness advocates, and Douglas, of course, had already developed a strong reputation against roads. "When roads supplant trails, the precious, unique values of God's wilderness disappear," he proclaimed. Furthermore, roads demonstrated "partial evidence of our great decline as a people. Without effort, struggle, and exertion, even high rewards turn to ashes." No longer would the high mountain meadows or streams be wild and rewarding if cars could get to them. The roads represented the "diabolic" nature of multiple-use management, according to an angry Douglas. "'[M]ultiple use' in practical operation means that every canyon is usually put to as many uses as possible," the justice lectured, "—lumber operations, roads, campsites, shelters, toilets, fireplaces, parking lots, and so on." Here again was prime evidence of the weaknesses in the agency's management.[26]

But Douglas took the critique further. Part of the Wallowas was designated as Forest Service wilderness. The borders, though, included mostly high country, excluding the valuable low-lying timber. This practice of boundary making was common and grounded much of the wilderness debate in the 1950s and 1960s. Those who determined the boundaries, Douglas pointed out, were not elected officials subject to the public's will. "Moreover, 'the law' under which they act is a set of regulations which they themselves drew. They can revise those regulations at will," he explained. Keeping these decisions about conservation out of reach of the public meant anti-democratic practices governed land use. A well-known champion of democratic principles in the face of economic or political power, Douglas asserted, "If the Minam is to be ravished, if roads are to pierce this wilderness, the people should decide it after a fair debate." Here was the crux of not only Douglas's argument but that of the wilderness movement as a whole. Agencies were largely unaccountable to the public. Wilderness advocates demanded a voice, accountability, and permanent protection.[27]

Douglas's *My Wilderness* books presented a striking account of environmental thinking as the 1960s dawned. Drawing on the deep roots of an American environmental tradition, he emphasized the beautiful landscapes that dotted the nation in seldom-explored corners, the important challenge of facing nature individually and with the struggle to achieve mental and physical mastery of it, and the sacred places where God revealed his creation's beneficent plan. Less common in the American tradition were the political barbs Douglas included; challenging Forest Service policy historically had not been a mainstay of most books in this genre. Douglas focused more on this sort of critique in the coming years, just as the wilderness movement gained crucial momentum toward the passage of the Wilderness Act in 1964. All his traveling in the 1950s and early 1960s took Douglas to diverse wild areas across the continent, and these places gave him firsthand experience to draw on while speaking and writing about these hotspots for conservation. This strategy gained him a greater sense of moral authority, for he could knowledgeably use personal experience with varying ecologies and management problems. Importantly and symbolically, Douglas spoke about many of the implications of a political system that failed to address environmental matters. A representative of the nation's highest legal authority, steeped in democratic philosophy, Douglas embodied legal and political authority and decided to speak for and teach about nature. It was an invaluable service.

Challenging the System

As the 1960s continued, Douglas kept to the themes developed in *My Wilderness* but significantly expanded the political arguments. This evolution certainly did not occur in a vacuum. Both the conservation movement and American society experienced fundamental changes in this period, transitions that Douglas reflected but in which he also participated and helped to advance.

The postwar era in the United States experienced explosive changes. The economic boom launched by World War II stimulated a massive expansion of urban and suburban growth with extensive environmental effects from increased energy consumption and septic tank pollution to heightened timber harvests and the draining of wetlands. Good economic times, along with increased automobility, also invigorated tourism, especially in the national parks, where the National Park Service sought to serve the growing number of visitors with new roads and more accommodations in an ambitious development program called Mission 66. In rural America, a chemical revolution spread in which synthetic chemicals promised greater agricultural harvests, even as they simultaneously produced harmful by-products damaging to land, water, soil, wildlife, fish, and people. With urban and rural America experiencing such physical changes and pressures, it is no surprise conservation-minded citizens stood up, took notice, and acted.[28]

The way they acted, though, derived in large part from other social and political currents. The mid-1950s found the nation gripped by a civil rights movement that became increasingly assertive over the coming decade. Civil rights activists mastered a variety of protest strategies, including direct action, Congressional lobbying, and litigation. Conservationists emulated these tactics as the 1960s unfolded.[29]

Connected centrally to these developments, of course, was mainstream liberalism, which underwent some important changes. Emerging from New Deal liberalism with its emphasis on bread-and-butter issues, such as better wages and shorter working hours, postwar liberals broadened their focus to include quality of life issues. Among the myriad items under the quality of life rubric was environmental protection, including wilderness preservation, pollution legislation, and highway beautification. This emphasis on amenities helped environmentalism branch into more directions than conservation's traditional emphasis on managing resources as efficiently as possible. In truth, the roots of that divergence ran back some decades, but for mainline liberals attention to these issues noticeably increased in the 1950s and set the stage for a full flourishing in the 1960s. Quality of life environmental concerns seem rooted primarily in postwar liberalism's emphasis on the public good, or reform liberalism as some have called it.[30]

However, another strand of liberalism was emerging strongly as the 1960s advanced, that of rights-based liberalism. In part, this rights-consciousness challenged reform liberalism through the rise of civil rights activism, New Left critiques, and eventually the counterculture's alternative social arrangements. In simple terms, these elements emphasized individual rights above the larger public good, distinguishing these competing brands of liberalism. So, for example, the civil rights movement battled for African Americans' undeniable individual rights to participate in public life, a right being violated by legal and extra-legal means throughout the nation.[31] Then, the New Left, whose leading activists had worked for civil rights in the South, called for participatory democracy as the best way to reform American society. In the New Left's 1962 manifesto, *The Port Huron Statement*, activists described a participatory democracy in which individuals would determine the direction of their lives and in which society would promote that individualism. New Leftists were small in number but influential in pushing forth reform agendas in the 1960s. The primacy of individual participation and rights thus took on an important role in liberal politics in the 1960s.[32]

Cross-fertilization occurred between these larger political and cultural currents and environmental concerns, as well as between reform liberalism and rights liberalism. For instance, scientists like Rachel Carson and Barry Commoner called for science to be less specialized and more open to public scrutiny, which certainly resembled the New Left's call for a participatory democracy. Carson's *Silent Spring* also called for the larger public good to be protected against indiscriminate poisoning, as well as the individual's right to experience nature in an unpoisoned state. As another example, *The Port Huron Statement* claimed in its introduction that "uncontrolled exploitation governs the sapping of the earth's physical resources," illustrating the importance of the environment to the early New Left. Douglas amplified these concerns.[33]

No one so prominent can better illustrate this mixture of anxieties and strategies than Douglas. In April 1961, he spoke at the Seventh Wilderness Conference, along with other luminaries like Ansel Adams, Sigurd Olson, Wallace Stegner, Stewart Udall, and Howard Zahniser. His speech, titled "The Wilderness and the New Frontier," or "Wilderness and Human Rights," was a powerful statement about the troubled state of modern society and its relationship to nature. "We have reached a new frontier where Science and Human Rights come increasingly into conflict," charged Douglas in his opening lines. He continued:

> *Science reflected in technological advances serves some needs of man. Yet technological advances often conflict with Human Rights. ...*
> *[W]e need not—we should not—take Science and its child, Technology—as our savior. For Science has no moral content; and no amoral approach to life can build an enduring society. ...*
>
> *Science produces machines that take their annual toll of human initiative. Man no longer walks. When he parks his car on the edge of woods, I notice he seldom gets more than a quarter mile from it. Science has produced instruments that make man lazier and less inclined to explore woods, valleys, ridges. The machine is almost a leash that keeps man from adventure.*

Sounding his familiar theme of striving for adventure in nature, Douglas also explored new ground by indicting science and technology as amoral forces that violated human rights by inserting machines everywhere—from the workplace to the wilderness—in ways that prevented people from enjoying their basic humanity. "Man was designed neither to be a *cog* in a machine as the communists conceive him," Douglas declared, "a *statistic* as Science conceives of him, nor a *consumer* as Madison Avenue views him." Continuing, Douglas chronicled numerous threats to wilderness and recreation resources: drained wetlands in Minnesota, overgrazed uplands in Washington, sewage contamination on the Potomac River, and polluted water in Lake Erie, as well as global examples from the Middle East and Africa. The portrait he drew was bleak indeed.[34]

This gloomy outlook troubled Douglas because he believed that the environment profoundly shaped individuals' characters. As much as anything, *Of Men and Mountains* had argued that the Cascades' ruggedness made Douglas a strong individual. With a degraded earth, people would be at risk. "Men born to apartments and confined to alleys and playgrounds for their relaxation seem either to become helpless, hopeless retiring people or to develop shrewdness and cunning with hardness, rancor, suspicion, or even bitterness," claimed Douglas. "This often leads, I feel, to juvenile delinquency and other forms of rebellion against authority." As a solution to this delinquency, Douglas asserted that young urban men in the 1930s joined the Civilian Conservation Corps and found themselves profoundly transformed and rejuvenated from their activity in nature, a transformation scholars have confirmed. "In the woods," he explained, "they seemed to get new bearings. ... The man who faces for the first time the wonders of a Douglas fir forest or the pileated woodpecker or the six-foot spread of the golden eagle, the person who hears the water ouzel above the roar of white water begins to undergo a transformation." What would occur if there were no uncontaminated places left to retreat to? Douglas shuddered to imagine. Clearly, much was at stake in wilderness for individuals, and then collectively for society.[35]

Deeply concerned about a rising population with great dependence on technology on the one hand and disappearing wilderness on the other, Douglas recognized that only systematic change—in politics and the public's thinking—would alleviate the threats. Douglas associated this need for protection with the Bill of Rights: "The right to pure water streams, virgin forests, the woodchuck and the antelope, and the other exciting wonders of the woods are as basic to our freedom as the special rights enshrined in our Bill of Rights." Similarly, the justice argued, "We need to expand our conception of man's liberty, enlarge his individual rights, and give them priority over Science. Those Human Rights include the right to put one's face in clear, pure water, to discover the wonders of sphagnum moss, and to hear the song of whippoorwills at dawn in a forest where the wilderness bowl is unbroken." As he emphasized rights, Douglas tapped into the growing importance of this element in the 1960's political agenda. These rights were basically anthropocentric; that is, Douglas did not advocate for the rights of wildlife per se but for human rights to have contact with wild places and things. But clearly he was moving in crucial new directions.[36]

In "The Wilderness and the New Frontier," Douglas firmly linked individual rights to a clean, healthy environment. By the next day, he had sketched out his ideas further and during a formal conference discussion included the phrase, "wilderness bill of rights" for the first time. This bill of rights included twelve principles to govern society's relationship to nature. Several measures suggested establishing proportions of recreation areas to population to ensure adequate places for wilderness activities. Others offered specific policies that would be universal, such as "[n]o raw sewage or industrial waste should be put into any of our rivers or lakes" and mandatory buffer zones around alpine meadows. Such proposals would be necessary "if mature integrated self-reliant people are to inherit this good American earth of ours," proclaimed Douglas. These substantive promises were meant to assure recreational resources to a growing population to ensure it remained a vigorous citizenry.[37]

The real heart of Douglas's proposal, though, rested in the procedural guarantees. No doubt his experience as a justice and a New Deal administrator influenced this approach. He advocated that the "decision-making tribunal in government should be as nearly judicial in its attitude as men can make it." This way, agencies could have some more objective standards and a more deliberative process by which to propose and promote resource projects, rather than the near-independence then granted to many administrators. Significantly, his proposal would divide authority within the bureaucracy, so that those who proposed a project would not be those who judged its ultimate merits. Engineers, after all, generally favored building another road or another dam, because that is what engineers did. Furthermore, Douglas argued that resource administrators needed to be treated more independently, like judges, so that they could be insulated from the pressure politics that seemed to drive decision making. Members of Congress or timber company lobbyists, for instance, would be prevented from pressuring administrators to make particular decisions concerning land use, just as judges were generally immune to politicians or lobbyists telling them how to decide a case. Douglas also recommended processes whereby citizens could petition and then open a public hearing to voice opinions about development projects. Finally, he believed that federal officials should not retire and then work for any group they previously had regulated, a rule that would limit potential conflicts of interest. Collectively, these substantive and procedural changes promised environmental management in new directions, changes that would create a more open deliberative process and protect myriad public perspectives. In this, it stood as an important step in the liberal reform traditions emerging out of the New Deal and the rights-based direction that liberalism was taking in the 1960s.[38]

This Wilderness Bill of Rights furnished, to Douglas's mind, necessary safeguards for the wilderness-loving public in the same way as the Bill of Rights defended freedom. The Bill of Rights constituted the centerpiece of Douglas's political values. Writing in 1962 to Edmond Nathaniel Cahn, a New York University law professor, Douglas explained that the Bill of Rights "do not generate the forces of freedom. They are merely designed to see to it that opportunities for freedom are not destroyed by the government." At another point, he explained to a group of young lawyers in 1976 that the founders adopted the Constitution and the Bill of Rights to "guarantee to us all the rights to personal and spiritual self-fulfillment." A Bill of Rights for nature fit perfectly in Douglas's expansive constitutional philosophy, even if it might make a strict constructionists squirm. Freedom must be allowed to flourish without restraints from government, businesses, or other individuals. His concept of freedom protected minority viewpoints, in particular, and that included those who wanted free-flowing rivers, wilderness areas, and an end to clear-cutting. Even though nature enthusiasts increased in their numbers and political power, they still were outmatched by extractive industries' power, and automobile tourists always outnumbered backpackers. Douglas built much of his judicial reputation on this idea that the Bill of Rights protects individuals from the government, so extending the concept to nature was a logical step. He believed that the founding political statement of the United States encouraged individuals to seek fulfillment. An untarnished natural heritage for new generations of Americans seemed central to achieving that.[39]

In the years after his wilderness conference speech and initial proposal of the Wilderness Bill of Rights in 1961, Douglas worked to refine his ideas and to accumulate numerous examples demonstrating the necessity for some legal guarantees for unspoiled land and water. The resulting book, *A Wilderness Bill of Rights* (1965), reflected Douglas's evolving perspective, as well as many contemporary concerns. The book mixed Douglas's vast knowledge of ecological problems with a call for political action. It cataloged numerous environmental issues, celebrated natural values, and chronicled the multitude of recreational resources available. All of these topics had found outlet in earlier Douglas writings, although seldom with such a heightened sense of crisis.

The core of this book lay in its extended political discussion. Douglas advocated a conservation "crusade" to protect the minority rights of wilderness enthusiasts from the "village, municipality, county, state and

*In the field, Douglas
constantly wrote
in his notebooks,
observing nature and
exploring ways to
enact environmental
protection*

on up to the federal government." He reminded his readers that a free
society protected minorities, and "[w]ilderness people are at the opposite
end of the spectrum from any standardized product of this machine age."
The pluralistic democracy of America demanded such protection. "When
it comes to wilderness," explained Douglas, "we need a ... Bill of Rights
to protect those whose spiritual values extend to the rivers and lakes, the
valleys and the ridges, and who find life in a mechanized society worth living
only because those splendid resources are not despoiled." Such statements
accentuated Douglas's penchant of individual rights, a direction consistent
with not only his constitutional philosophy but also the rights-consciousness
of the 1960s.[40]

Yet Douglas recognized deeper systemic problems with the relationship
of the government, the public, and the environment. So besides the
philosophical constitutional safeguards, Douglas argued for deeper reform
of the political and administrative system. Many environmental groups,
for instance, could not lobby Congress because of their tax-exempt status.
Thus, debates in Congress necessarily favored those who benefitted from
timber cutting, road building, or other destructive activities and who could
lobby freely. He proposed revising the tax codes to open up the political
process to reflect "a true picture of the national values." His Wilderness
Bill of Rights would include a "revision of these tax exemption laws to put

conservationists on a more equal footing with those who would destroy a sand dune or a river or a sanctuary or a high ridge for the Almighty Dollar." Sounding like John Muir in casting aspersions toward "the Almighty Dollar," Douglas worked to find practical solutions to a problem in the political system so that it was more truly representative and fair.[41]

Besides an unresponsive system, conservationists like Douglas worried about the impermanency of wild area designations. As Douglas had pointed out in his initial proposal, administrative agencies were not immune to political pressure. Administrators often decided when and whether to open a forest for timber cutting or to close a forest to road building, and such decisions were easily reversible with a change of heart, change of administrator, or change of political pressures. In many ways, conservationists' exasperation with the Forest Service's shifting administrative decisions was the leading impetus for the Wilderness Act, passed in 1964. The new law created wilderness areas that could only be changed by Congress. Ostensibly representing the American electorate, Congress should actively reserve wilderness by the legislative process and prevent politically aloof administrative agencies from running roughshod over democratic values. The Wilderness Act, thus, helped solve the impermanency issue and chastised Forest Service managers.[42]

Still, Douglas knew that conservationists could not always count on Congress to act with sufficient rigor. Consequently, he favored specific legal protections based on certain state models. Two years after *A Wilderness Bill of Rights* appeared, Maryland proposed a Conservation Bill of Rights to amend the state constitution. It provided for the state legislature to abate pollution, protect wetlands and shorelines, and acquire land for preservation purposes. In a nod to participatory democracy, then popular among New Left student activists, Maryland's constitutional proposal guaranteed that all parties affected by these conservation measures would have the opportunity to raise concerns. In another exemplary measure, New York had long ago protected part of the Adirondack forest through its constitution. Douglas praised the constitutional promise that the Adirondacks "shall be forever kept as wild forest lands." It was "far better protection than either an agency's regulations or a statute," because "[i]t takes much more time and effort to make a constitutional change; the process is deliberative; the people have a chance to be educated on the losses to be expected if wild areas are to be commercialized." Constitutional protections for wilderness in New York provided a model, and Douglas implored "[c]onservationists the country over" to visit the Adirondacks to learn how to protect nature constitutionally. Another law in California required that all road proposals be scrutinized with recreational, park, historical, and aesthetic values before being approved. In Oregon, lawmakers passed legislation allowing land to be assessed as open space to assign economic value to no development; accordingly, open space could be considered the highest use of the land. For Douglas, legal safeguards for environmental protection were best; the more permanent, the better, and he proved willing to look far and wide for models. That so many states were crafting significant reforms demonstrated how Douglas's ideas were part of a larger movement in American politics and culture.[43]

A Wilderness Bill of Rights stood as a testament to the seriousness of modern ecological problems, a call to protect minority interests, and a search for greater permanency in wilderness designation. Running through many of these topics was public involvement. The Administrative Procedures Act (1946) exempted agencies managing property from having to open decision- and rule-making processes to the public, an exemption that frustrated democracy in an open society and deeply troubled Douglas. Moreover, in the mid-1960s, wilderness all rested in public lands. Before 1964, none of that wilderness remained secure from administrative changes, and no public hearings were required for additions or deletions to wild areas or changes in management practices within them. After the Wilderness Act passed in 1964, Congress required, for the first time, public hearings when changes to those wild areas were proposed. But with so many areas still only receiving administrative protection and other roadless areas having none, not to mention the variety of other industrial activities that potentially harmed the environment, Douglas urged public hearings be required far more widely, effectively building on the momentum the Wilderness Act furnished. Only when federal agencies were held accountable by the public would ecologically destructive activities be scrutinized. Opening these lines of civic engagement helped democratize environmental management, and Douglas wanted it spread as far as possible. The strategy represented an environmental analogue to the liberal reforms of the 1960's social movements, and Douglas arguably became its best messenger, coming as he did from the august halls of the Supreme Court.[44]

Activists and friends of Douglas read the book enthusiastically. Sigurd Olson wrote to Douglas, "Many thanks for "the Wilderness Bill of Rights: It is *beautiful* and *significant* and will do more for wilderness preservation than anything I have ever read. Here is the essence of the whole problem; an analysis and a guide for all who are trying to help."[45] As a leading conservationist, Olson represented a powerful constituency, and his praise carried weight. Douglas had contributed an important and timely document. The numerous examples throughout the book illuminated current controversies, focused largely on pollution, development, and other threats to recreational resources. A reader would be able to understand the challenges to a healthful environment by reading Douglas's call to action and perhaps be inspired to act. Moreover, in its solutions, *A Wilderness Bill of Rights* gave form to the environmental mood in the country and expressed Douglas's political beliefs. A more revealing contemporary perspective is hard to find.

Conclusion

As he wrote about nature in the first half of the 1960s, Douglas shifted his emphasis. Part of this transition no doubt reflected his age and experience. Less and less interested in maintaining judicial niceties and a cloistered judge's life, Douglas felt little compunction about asserting increasingly political suggestions in his writing.[46] But more than life changes, it was the growing strength and new shape of the conservation movement that prompted Douglas to move toward a wilderness bill of rights, a move that both reflected and aided the movement's evolution. In the 1950s, Douglas provided a signal service to conservation by leading hikes designed to garner attention. He continued to hike and speak out about favored places to draw more of the public to the cause, and his *My Wilderness* books brought distant, wild places to the hands of anyone willing to spend $4.95. Meanwhile, the wilderness movement introduced, debated, and negotiated the Wilderness Act. Moving wilderness decisions out of the executive branch and into the legislative one, conservationists like Douglas hoped, would bring greater permanence to wilderness designation and more public involvement.

Published a year after the Wilderness Act became law, *A Wilderness Bill of Rights* stressed more than simply attention to threatened places. Douglas desired to continue moving toward a stronger and more institutionalized environmental ethic. This would require political and legal reforms to ensure adequate protection of environmental values. And it demanded that existing laws be enforced. For the next decade, until Douglas retired largely from public life, he worked consistently in myriad ways. He continued to bring attention to favorite places, hoping to either secure federal protection or improve existing protection. This approach enhanced his reputation as a public intellectual for conservation. Increasingly, too, Douglas labored behind the scenes to chastise federal resource managers, harangue politicians, and coordinate conservationists. Finally, Douglas used his official position on the Court to argue for his environmental values, a strategy that only occurred because Congress continued passing laws related to environmental management. By the mid-1960s, then, the stage was set for the next phase of Douglas's work pressing for environmental protection.

CHAPTER FOUR

Committees of Correspondence

We need Committees of Correspondence to coordinate the
efforts of diverse groups to keep America beautiful and to
preserve the few wilderness alcoves we have left.
William O. Douglas, "America's Vanishing Wilderness" (1964)[1]

The 1960s and early 1970s were a time of great symbiosis for Douglas. His evolving thinking influenced his actions on the ground in specific environmental campaigns, even as his experience in those contests shaped his ideas. More importantly, the conservation movement grew enormously and developed into a more diverse, complex environmental movement, providing a great deal of energy on which Douglas could draw.[2] He continued working for wilderness more than other environmental causes, although he did not avoid such issues as pollution and urban development. These various issues and the multiple ways to approach them—from creating administrative agencies to bolstering existing laws to promoting grassroots activism or watchdog groups—encouraged Douglas to work hard, but flexibly, for environmental protection. As he moved around the country and as the existing legal framework changed, he employed different strategies in different places. In the Cascade Mountains, Texas, and the Potomac Basin, Douglas used assorted methods of environmental activism to challenge management priorities. This shifting approach revealed critical elements of Douglas's ideas and his effectiveness, and it represents the larger movement's diversity.

Because of his roots, Douglas always took the greatest interest in Pacific Northwest landscapes. Not surprisingly, he developed the longest and most intimate relationship with these places, as well as with the regional activists, administrators, and politicians. An area of the Cascades known as Cougar Lakes kept Douglas's attention politically from 1959 until his death. His dire frustrations with local Forest Service administrators did more than anything to shift his thinking as conveyed in the previous chapter. His impression that Forest Service employees could run roughshod over public opinion in managing these mountainous forests compelled him to act. Douglas's actions demonstrated a number of political strategies common to conservationists. For instance, he worked to build a national constituency for this local place through his writings and networking. Better than anywhere else, Douglas facilitated the Committees of Correspondence he described in the early 1960s designed to bring local and national advocates together. Also, this activism illuminated the common desire to emphasize local support and firsthand experience in the places he hoped to save. Finally, because Douglas worked on behalf of Cougar Lakes so long, he bridged different legal and political circumstances. As those contexts changed, so did his strategy, demonstrating the ways he was politically adaptable, astute, and persistent.

Compared with either the West or East Coast, Texas was a relatively unknown environment to Douglas and other conservationists. So it was somewhat surprising to find Douglas agitating in Texas environmental politics. However, in the mid-1960s, he spent a fevered couple of years traveling through, advocating for, and writing about the issues pressing on various Texas landscapes. Here, Douglas confronted different historical and political dynamics, and once again, he responded to that specific context. A primary difference in Texas was its lack of existing public lands. Consequently, Douglas's and his allies' efforts had little to do with reforming federal agencies. Instead, they had to generate interest among federal officials in intervening in private land issues in the state, at a time when a Texan sat in the White House. Here, Douglas emphasized that certain American lands simply were too valuable to be left in private hands. They were the rightful inheritance of all the people, and thus the federal government needed to protect these special places. Thus, the shifting dynamics of local and national power and authority ran through Douglas's involvement in Texas.

In the Potomac Basin, Douglas confronted the public to a greater extent because of the burgeoning metropolis, a place that generated unique environmental and political problems and promises. Population pressures and outdated or insufficient facilities had produced a pollution problem that federal officials hoped to solve by damming the Potomac River. The Army Corps of Engineers proceeded to plan without adequate public input, a flawed process almost as bad to Douglas as the proposed solution. If the high population placed intense demands on the river system, it also created a sharp need for recreational resources as a relief or escape from humdrum urban lives. Douglas urged better management of the Chesapeake and Ohio Canal, primarily promoting the canal as a National Historical Park for most of the 1960s. He took this campaign to the public—through magazine articles, in speeches to civic groups, with his reunion hikes—in the hopes of creating a premier recreational space for the capital's residents. Although Douglas played a central role in Potomac Basin preservation from 1954 until his death, he interpreted the victory of preservationists at the C&O Canal as an achievement of dedicated civic action. Public scrutiny, public action, and public recreation coalesced near Washington, DC, and highlighted the importance of the public to Douglas's conservation work.

Assuredly, Douglas acted in other places.[3] But he spent longer periods and more energy in the Cascades, Texas, and the Potomac Basin. The lessons from these places demonstrate that local context—political, historical, legal—mattered in shaping the terms of the environmental debate, a group of differences that belies any notion of the environmental movement as monolithic. Douglas's varied responses showed his adaptability.

Cougar Lakes: Bridging Local and National Action

In his 1964 article for *Ladies' Home Journal*, Douglas explained the need to coordinate local and national conservationists in Committees of Correspondence as patriots had done during the American Revolution. He saw the stakes as enormously high and synchronizing efforts as a critical strategy. One of his central tasks in the Cascades from the late 1950s to the early 1970s was cultivating such relationships. Douglas used these networks to organize national conservation and political leaders with grassroots efforts. He and his allies called for public hearings where conservationists, particularly local people, would use the opportunity to argue against the proposed logging and road projects. In important ways, this exemplified in action the evolution of thought Douglas had undergone and illuminated the practical ways conservation functioned in the field.[4]

His efforts in the wilderness campaign for Cougar Lakes Limited Area in Washington's central Cascade Range was, in many ways, Douglas's most exemplary western environmental struggle. It lasted the longest, best demonstrated his political organizing skills, and accurately reflected regional and national conservation concerns and ideologies. The limited area designation made this area east of Mount Rainier National Park and west of the Yakima Valley weakly protected. The administrative classification, unique to Forest Service Region 6, could be changed by the regional forester, and indeed, the agency proposed to end the semi-protected status and to open the Cougar Lakes area to logging. Douglas and his allies spent much of the 1960s combating these proposals and, alternatively, proposing an official Cougar Lakes Wilderness Area. Thus, they operated defensively against timber sales and road building and offensively for wilderness status.[5]

A general pattern developed in Douglas's correspondence concerning Cougar Lakes that enacted his idea about Committees of Correspondence: he learned of a situation threatening the area, usually from his friends and

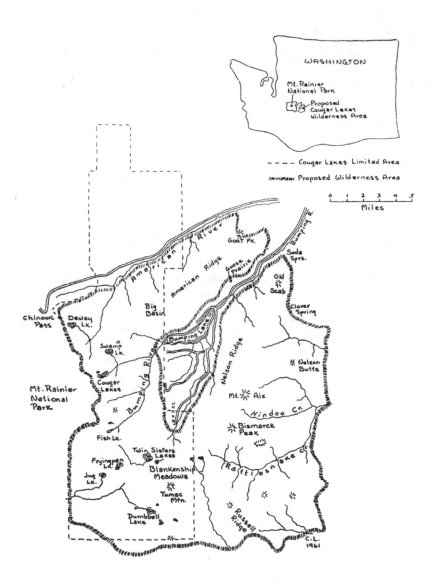

Proposed boundaries for the Cougar Lakes Wilderness Area in 1961.
From Cougar Lakes Wilderness Area folder, box 61, RG 95, United States
Forests Service, Region 6, Portland OR, Historical Collection, National
Archives and Records Administration, Pacific Alaska Region (Seattle, WA)

neighbors at his Goose Prairie residence in the Cascade Mountains, Kay Kershaw and Isabelle Lynn; contacted agency officials, typically Snoqualmie National Forest Supervisor Larry Barrett, U. S. Forest Service Chief Forester Ed Cliff, or Secretary of Agriculture Orville Freeman; lobbied power brokers in the nation's capital, most often Senator Henry "Scoop" Jackson of Washington; and alerted regional and national conservationists like John Osseward of the North Cascades Conservation Council and David Brower of the Sierra Club. He exhorted them all to protect nature's resources, specifically to halt timber sales and road-building plans and open up the decision-making process to the public.

Although Douglas fleetingly protested a road in this region in 1954, a timber sale proposed in the limited area near Copper City in 1959 roused him to sustained action through the 1960s.[6] This sale bothered Douglas for familiar reasons: a road would be built and would ruin wilderness qualities. On October 3, 1960, Douglas sent several letters enlisting the help of conservationists he knew, both regionally and nationally based. He emphasized several things objectionable about the prospect. For example, timber cutters would profit primarily from the road-building contract, not the timber. Indeed, Douglas claimed local loggers had reported that the timber was commercially worthless. More at the heart of the issue, the road would extend to the edge of Blankenship Meadow. Eventually, jeeps, as well as loggers, would invade the area, which Douglas noted had "been one of my favorite spots since I was a boy." He had seen evidence that jeeps already had surreptitiously entered Blankenship Meadows, and an extended road would only increase their destructive presence. Finally, the advancing road system threatened to eliminate the buffer zone between wilderness and developed lands.[7]

Since the threat seemed clear and significant, Douglas worked to stem the tide of development in the Cascades. He wrote to Barrett: "There is something terribly irrevocable about logging roads that put jeeps into the heart of a wilderness area. And the fact that there is no pressing need to get the lumber to the consumer seems to some of us to make a hearing to give all interests a chance to be heard the most appropriate course to take." In addition, he urged Senator Jackson to call on the "Regional Forester to see if a halt cannot be put to timber sales, including this one, until there is a chance to review the whole situation." The proposed development would permanently alter and eliminate the charm and beauty that Douglas associated with it from his long-standing relationship to the place and would prevent others from developing the same connection.[8]

In his initial strategy, Douglas encouraged a personal bond as he had by organizing the Olympic Beach or C&O Canal hikes. Recognizing the importance of knowing a wilderness firsthand, he invited Barrett to hike the region with him in the summer of 1961 to see the wilderness directly. In his invitation to the supervisor, Douglas confessed great concern for the Snoqualmie and Gifford Pinchot national forests derived from the "emotional hold" they had on him since "I tramped them as a boy." Believing in the power of place to affect individuals, Douglas thought Barrett might call off the timber sale after a two- or three-day backcountry trip with the justice. Douglas misplaced his hope; although they hiked together, Barrett pressed forward with the timber sale.[9]

Besides his fundamental concern over diminishing wilderness values that the timber sale and road building prompted, Douglas intimated that the Forest Service undermined democratic values in promoting timber sales on national forests without sufficient citizen input. He was convinced his solution—public hearings—would be a reliable way to serve the public interest. He pressed Barrett to hold hearings to encourage an open debate and to discover public sentiment before "a tragic stand was taken."[10] A hearing, Douglas implied, represented a fair way for public opinion to make itself known. Later, after the Forest Service finalized the timber sale, Douglas angrily claimed in a draft letter to Barrett that the only good thing to come of it was that when people traveled to the mountains "to escape civilization, [they would] see the destruction [he had] wrought, [and] they [would] insist on drastic changes in Forest Service procedures." Furthermore, Douglas suggested a yearly pilgrimage to Copper City on the anniversary of the timber sale to "be reminded of the monstrosities sometimes committed by an uncontrolled bureaucracy." These were harsh words, as Douglas recognized in a handwritten note on the draft to Kershaw: "Is this too strong?" It appears that the letter Douglas did send Barrett, dated over a month after this draft, did not include the statement about bureaucratic monstrosities, although he still called for procedural changes to the agency and an annual pilgrimage.[11]

Drawing from his experience both as a justice and in conservation, Douglas proposed several legal changes to require the Forest Service to open its decision making up to public scrutiny. Writing to David Brower in September 1961, Douglas urged two specific changes to Forest Service laws. Predictably, Douglas first proposed a public hearing before a timber sale or road construction. He suggested the hearing be conducted "before an independent board or panel which [did] not represent the men who drew up the plan and who [were] not beholden to the Regional Director." Douglas believed timber interests had captured Forest Service management, so his proposals attempted to wrest away decision-making power from a small group of agency administrators bent on what historian Paul W. Hirt termed a "conspiracy of optimism" that full-scale timber production could be managed in environmentally responsible ways. The sense of urgency Douglas felt was palpable: "We must get a bill introduced. We must start arousing the people. We must start writing and speaking and campaigning. Without these two basic protections we are lost. The remaining bits of wilderness in the U. S. Forests will be preserved or destroyed depending on the caprice of the Supervisor or Regional Director." Douglas focused on solving the impermanence of Forest Service wilderness. His comments proved not to be merely idle strategizing with a fellow conservationist. Soon, he spoke to the White House liaison to the Department of Agriculture, Myer Feldman, calling for similar rule changes. Of course, Douglas was not alone among those in conservation calling for public hearings; wilderness act advocates included this as part of their strategy and hearings were already held when new nuclear power plants were being sited. However, few were so well placed to convey conservationists' perspectives with White House liaisons, agency administrators, and legislators.[12]

Public hearings of the type Douglas proposed were eventually legislated in the Wilderness Act (1964). The act set aside over fifty wilderness areas amounting to over nine million acres drawn from Forest Service lands already designated as wilderness or wild areas. The act required the secretary of agriculture to review existing primitive areas and the secretary of interior to review roadless areas in national parks to determine their suitability as wilderness. In a victory for democracy and public involvement, the creation or destruction of a wilderness area henceforth required a public hearing for local citizens and government agencies to make their case. This was one of the wilderness movement's crowning achievements and a significant contribution to American democracy.[13]

When Congress passed the Wilderness Act in 1964, the political landscape of the Cascades changed, and Douglas and his Committee of Correspondence adjusted strategies. However, they confronted a significant challenge. No part of the act required any review or public hearing for limited areas, the unique administrative designation of Cougar Lakes. Thus, because of this rare Region 6 category, Cougar Lakes remained in a nebulous zone with few legal safeguards for its roadless state. Quickly after the passage of the Wilderness Act, Douglas and his allies proposed using the act to protect the area. Cougar Lakes, though, became a piece in the larger wilderness struggle in the Pacific Northwest. The North Cascades Study Team, a joint Department of Interior and Department of Agriculture committee, surveyed the Cascades to determine appropriate areas for wilderness preservation and to solve competing claims between the Forest Service and National Park Service in the region. Among other things, the team recommended four new wilderness areas (Alpine Lakes, Enchantment, Mount Aix, and Okanogan), extended boundaries in the existing Glacier Peak Wilderness, and advocated creating North Cascades National Park. Although much of this constituted good news for conservationists, the report also proposed declassifying the Cougar Lakes Limited Area to open up over one hundred thousand acres of commercial timber land, perhaps to placate the Forest Service, who stood to lose much land to the new national park in a significant rebuke to agency management. Thus, the new attention to wilderness did not achieve all Douglas had hoped.[14]

With *The North Cascades Study Report* offering a blueprint for Cascade wilderness without Cougar Lakes, Douglas reorganized and redoubled his efforts. A number of regional and national conservation groups, including the Wilderness Society, the North Cascades Conservation Council, the Sierra Club, the Federation of Western Outdoor Clubs, the Mountaineers, the National Parks Association, the Mazamas, the Cascadians, and the C&O Canal Association, publicly favored establishing a Cougar Lakes Wilderness Area, and this support bolstered Douglas. All of those groups submitted statements opposing declassification of the limited area and supporting a permanent wilderness area. Douglas and others used this strong existing constituency to show the widespread regional and national political support for wilderness designation and to slow the bureaucratic inertia of timber cutting so dominant in the Forest Service in the postwar era. By giving authority to Congress rather than to local administrators, the Wilderness Act had helped transform local national forest wilderness into a national concern, just as national parks had been since their inception.[15]

Later in 1965, before the Regional Office had finalized its report on Cougar Lakes, the Forest Service marked trees for cutting, prompting Douglas to write Secretary Freeman multiple times asking for a stay until more studies and hearings could be conducted, this time citing the authority of the Wilderness Act. Douglas also contacted members of the North Cascades Study Team, who had not personally visited Cougar Lakes, arguing that if they had seen it firsthand they would have enlarged it and recommended its preservation rather than declassifying it. His standby arguments—public hearings and firsthand experience—continued to shape Douglas's response to the politics of wilderness preservation.[16]

In addition, Douglas talked or wrote to Secretary Freeman, to the head of the Bureau of Outdoor Recreation Edward Crafts, and to Secretary of the Interior Stewart Udall. Locally, Douglas told Lynn that the only thing she could do, since the prime movers were ignoring Cougar Lakes, was to "get all the conservation groups hollering." But more needed to be done. To engage the broader public, Douglas wrote an article for *National Geographic* to bring attention to the environmental struggle in the Cascades. Unfortunately, the editors refused to print it, believing it too controversial. Incensed, Douglas wondered: "But what the hell isn't, that is worth talking about?"[17]

Finally, Douglas suggested a new tactic. Acknowledging the importance of local opinion, regional wilderness advocates might write a short, specific statement about the proposed wilderness area that local people could sign as a petition. He believed: "[W]e could use it both at the White House and at the Forest Service office here in Washington, DC and on the Hill." He thought it might serve as an effective lobbying tool and impetus to action. Douglas adapted the petition from a statement Lynn had written that included remarks by Frederic W. Braun from within the lumber industry, arguing that sometimes "the wilderness concept and use overrides all other facts." Furthermore, Braun argued that the timbered area in Cougar Lakes was marginal and could not be harvested on a sustained-yield basis. Douglas and allies hoped that using someone from within the timber industry would furnish some credibility that did not seem to exist when only conservationists were urging the protection of Cougar Lakes. Ever mindful of the need for local political support, the justice also pointed out that when the Interior Committee held hearings in Seattle, few objected to the establishment of the wilderness area. This support no doubt gratified Douglas, who had long been arguing that public hearings would reveal broad support for wilderness protection. Meanwhile, he worked to line up local support for the petition, demonstrating his role in a Committee of Correspondence constantly urging action. The informal letter-writing campaign, conservation group activism, and local citizen alerts continued the campaign and represented a broader and more coordinated approach than Douglas's earlier public efforts on behalf of the C&O Canal and Olympic Beach. He proved he would be present, oiling the political wheels and directing professional and amateur conservationists, national and grassroots, in their efforts to secure wilderness protection.[18]

In the meantime, in 1966 Supervisor Barrett encouraged the residents of Yakima to believe that the wilderness area proposal had already failed. Infuriated, Douglas wrote to Secretary Freeman "[I] plead with you, beg you, … implore you, not to cast the die against us conservationists by going ahead with development programs before we have had a chance for a hearing." Douglas reminded Freeman of the new statutory requirement for public hearings for wilderness areas. Furthermore, dismayed by Barrett's past management record, Douglas argued that with Barrett in charge locally, "the public will not even get due process and that is a thing that I know you and [Chief Forester] Ed Cliff would be the first to demand." The emphasis on due process reflected Douglas's concerns about procedural legalities and fundamental fairness. Freeman assured Douglas that nothing would be done in Cougar Lakes until every side had had an opportunity to air its views. But as Douglas continued for months to call for hearings, Secretary Freeman and the Forest Service rebuffed him, and the Cougar Lakes fight largely disappeared from the public and Douglas's work for several years.[19]

Nevertheless, by 1971, promising developments encouraged Douglas and his allies. Douglas's hometown paper, the *Yakima Herald Republic*, published an article in April explaining the new situation in relatively dispassionate terms. Republican Representative John P. Saylor of Pennsylvania, a key sponsor of the Wilderness Act, introduced a bill in the House of Representatives to create a wilderness area encompassing Cougar Lakes. That a Pennsylvanian proposed the Cougar Lakes Wilderness Area indicated the extent to which wilderness in national forests had become a nationalized concern. Senator Jackson would soon introduce a bill in the Senate. The district's new Representative, Democrat Mike McCormack, remained undecided in his position on the wilderness proposal. Douglas immediately wrote the editor of the *Yakima Herald Republic*, encouraging the paper's entire staff to visit Blankenship Meadows or another area in the proposed wilderness. He believed, then, they "would rise up in wrath at proposals to destroy it." This comment once again illustrated Douglas's tendency to privilege firsthand experience, believing that with personal experience one would naturally favor wilderness designation. In addition, he explained that he had hiked the area as a boy and felt like frontier folk hero Daniel Boone: "Does your paper want that to become impossible? Do you want all boys—as well as old folks—carried to the few sanctuaries we have left? Is there to be no place for the adventuresome lad? Should there be a funicular on Rainier to make it easy for your great-grandchildren?" The rhetorical questions revealed how Douglas valued wilderness challenges and feared the irrevocable loss when roads invaded such sanctuaries. To him, wilderness represented a necessary legacy to be protected for the nation's future.[20]

His long efforts on behalf of Cougar Lakes illuminated many things. Douglas used multiple connections with friends in Pacific Northwest conservationist circles and in the power circles of Washington, DC, to communicate strategies and developments. In essence, he served as the liaison between those groups, informing Senator Jackson or Secretary

Freeman of Pacific Northwest activists' perspectives on Cougar Lakes policy. In turn, he kept friends apprised of beltway politics. Through his activities, he worked to keep conservation politics open, asking for hearings and informing Freeman of errant forest supervisors. Moreover, as he explained to the editor of the *Yakima Herald Republic*, and by extension the region's public, the nation needed wilderness areas for the young and the old. Such areas were part of America's irreplaceable heritage and needed to be preserved. Eventually, the combination of his deep personal connection with the region and his long political advocacy for its preservation in a wilderness area, not to mention the tireless work of many other regional and national conservationists, bore fruit. In 1984, four years after Douglas's death, Congress set aside as a wilderness area much of the land he and others proposed in the early 1960s. It is fittingly called the William O. Douglas Wilderness Area.

Douglas's personality and long-standing identification with the region made a crucial difference in Cougar Lakes. Douglas could be accused of practicing a form of NIMBY activism, given that he owned a home near the area. Rather than reflecting the narrow self-interest characteristic of the charge against NIMBYism, the strategy Douglas and regional conservationists employed demonstrated a key reality of postwar conservation battles: people fought to protect the wildernesses they personally knew.[21] After all, it was no accident that the elegiac book the Sierra Club produced about the submergence of Glen Canyon beneath Lake Powell was titled *The Place No One Knew*.[22] With Douglas in the fray, newspapers, resource managers, and politicians took notice, helping wilderness causes in incalculable, but no doubt substantial, ways. By bringing national attention to regional causes, Douglas helped nationalize concerns for the Northwest's mountains. Simultaneously, by bringing western issues to the nation's capital, Douglas advanced a regional conservation agenda and created a trans-regional network of dedicated conservationists and their political champions. These grassroots Committees of Correspondence ensured local and national activists coordinated with national political figures during long-standing political struggles over specific western landscapes. These organizations and dynamics demonstrate how wilderness ideology and democratic politics interacted in practice.

Modern Ahabs in Texas: The Federal-Local Divide

In the Washington Cascades, Douglas faced a familiar foe and worked with familiar allies. In Texas, by contrast, he faced a different situation. By the mid-1960s, Douglas had floated the state's rivers, climbed its mountains, and hiked its forests. The environment he encountered in Texas included landscapes as fabulous as anywhere else, but the conservation politics he confronted there challenged his type of environmental values more powerfully perhaps than those anywhere in the nation. Consequently, his Texas work exuded a marked pessimism. Nevertheless, Douglas mounted a vigorous campaign for public environmental protection in the state. Douglas's activism in Texas reveals his ideas about nature and government in particularly powerful ways. Specifically, it illuminates him as a proponent of federal involvement to counter what he perceived as local obstacles—namely local government bending to local corporations' will—to environmental goals and protection for future generations.

Douglas constructed his 1967 book about Texas—*Farewell to Texas: A Vanishing Wilderness*—around an effective metaphor, employing the biblical parable of Ahab in Naboth's vineyard as described in I Kings, Chapter 21. Naboth had a vineyard next to Ahab's palace. Ahab said, "Give me your vineyard, that I may have it for a vegetable garden, because it is near my house; and I will give you a better vineyard for it; or, if it seems good to you, I will give you its value in money." However, Naboth replied, "The Lord forbid that I should give you the inheritance of my fathers." Ahab grew despondent until his wife, the infamous Jezebel, promised to give Ahab Naboth's vineyard. Jezebel set up Naboth on deceitful charges of blasphemy, and he was subsequently stoned to death. However, when Ahab went to take possession of Naboth's vineyard, God cursed him. Douglas likened Texas's natural resources to Naboth's vineyard and pointed to several deceitful "modern Ahabs," including public utilities, government agencies, stockmen, lumber barons, and oil companies. These special interests were destroying the state's natural heritage, and Douglas employed the metaphor of "modern Ahabs" extensively as an effective rhetorical and political tool.[23]

Douglas recognized that Texas presented a unique set of circumstances. Indeed, that is why he devoted an entire book to the state; no other state received such singular treatment from him. One of the most distinctive features of Texas in environmental terms was, and is, its comparative lack of public federal lands. When Texas joined the United States in 1845, unlike the other western states, it kept its unappropriated lands. By the twentieth century, that meant that the federal presence in the form of Forest Service and National Park Service lands and their attendant wilderness and recreational programs was unusually small for a western state, since the influence of such lands dominates many western locales and their conservation politics. Consequently, Texas changes the typical account of wilderness preservation and Douglas's position there contrasted with his contemporaneous role with Cougar Lakes.

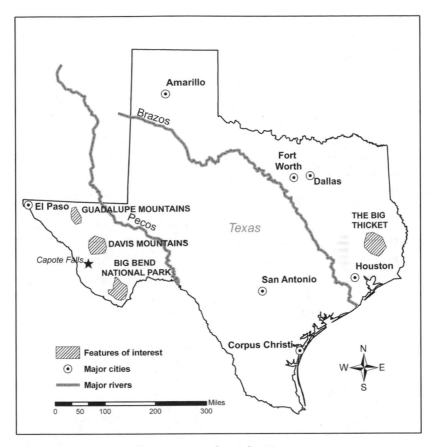

Areas of interest to William O. Douglas in his Texas conservation activities

Douglas centered much of his attention on the Big Thicket region in East Texas, near Beaumont.[24] His involvement on behalf of the Big Thicket revealed many of the political characteristics that could be expected of him. He wrote to powerful Washington, DC, politicians, including the president, the secretary of the interior, and members of Congress, as well as federal officials in the field in Texas. He also corresponded with local activists, encouraging the local involvement and grassroots democracy in which he placed so much of his faith. His research trips garnered media interest, which was something on which conservationists heavily depended. These combined actions created an effective amalgam of methods.

For the justice, the Big Thicket fight began in 1965 with a suggestion from Jim Bowmer, an attorney from Temple, Texas, and a strong voice for conservation in the state. Once, Bowmer and one of his law partners,

Bob Burleson, had invited prominent conservationists, including Justice Douglas, to a trip to Santa Helena Canyon in the Big Bend country. Douglas, a complete stranger to them, accepted the invitation. By the end of the trip, he considered them close friends. From that point, Bowmer served as an effective liaison between the justice and Texas environmental issues, the linchpin of another Committee of Correspondence. Without Bowmer, Douglas would not have had an inside view of Texas conservation problems, and his book would not have been as effective. Bowmer significantly shaped Douglas's efforts, travel plans, and book. Their friendship was one of Douglas's most important within conservation circles.[25]

Describing the Big Thicket as a "must" for Douglas's book, Bowmer portrayed the area as dwindling fast. It had comprised over a million forested acres, but in 1965, he claimed, it was down to about three hundred fifty thousand acres and losing fifty acres a day. A few years before, local conservationists had begun advocating for a park, which prompted timber interests to begin cutting at "twice the rate it was only a few years ago." At that pace, the region's unique ecology would rapidly decline and lose its distinctiveness. Bowmer's appeal worked. Douglas wrote him back two days later, agreeing to include a chapter on the Big Thicket in his book and arranging for a trip there after the first of the year.[26]

Douglas's subsequent research trip to the region made the local news and even the *Congressional Record*. Senator Ralph Yarborough of Texas developed a strong interest in this conservation cause and welcomed Douglas as an ally, for he understood the popular appeal and media attention Douglas drew to such situations. In the field, Douglas happily conversed with local botanists, made notations about flora and fauna in a notebook, and searched the woods for unique species. The press reported his visit faithfully and painted an effective portrait of the justice. One writer called him "as tough as a cowboy's boot," even at sixty-seven, a person who would "get his feet as muddy, his pants as scratched, and his nose as sunburned as any other man." Douglas relished the image.[27]

Furthermore, Douglas stirred things up by advocating a "Manhattan project approach" to conservation. He explained, "The need is for a crash program where red tape can be ignored and the job done. Trees such as these of the Big Thicket can be destroyed while endless arguments go on concerning the best way to save them." The poignant backdrop for this comment came in the form of a one-thousand-year-old magnolia tree that had been "assassinated" the previous year by vandals opposed to making the Big Thicket a national park. Local activists bemoaned the destroyed magnolia, arguing that it would have been preserved had it been included in a protected national park or wilderness area. The missed opportunity made this magnificent, ancient tree a casualty in the environmental battle. As dramatic as the backdrop was, the implications of Douglas's comments proved more significant. He argued that it was proper to "take what you need and debate about the price later"—a comment somewhat surprising for such a champion of democracy and due process. However, Douglas believed that extractive industries had long exploited the nation's natural resources without considering costs borne by later generations. Furthermore, he compared his proposed program to a national security measure, since such security actions often were paid for long after the fact. To him and many others, wilderness preservation constituted an equivalent national emergency and priority. For too long, Douglas implied, the nation's unique natural areas, like Texas's Big Thicket, had been unsupported by government and had thus been available for exploitation. He advocated massive expenditures to thrust the issue into the forefront of Texas conservation circles, and his contacts within the Johnson Administration suggested that action might commence finally.[28]

Douglas tried to interest Interior Secretary Stewart Udall and President Johnson in making the Big Thicket part of the national park system. The president, apparently, told Douglas that he would "give unlimited support to the Big Thicket if Udall takes the lead." And Udall promised "to get on the ball right away and see what can be done." Writing two weeks later, Udall informed Douglas that his department's efforts on behalf of the Big Thicket had begun as early as 1938 with the National Park Service recommending three decades before some type of preservation. More recently, the agency had surveyed the region and again recommended some type of federal protection, and Udall assured Douglas that a report was in the works proposing positive courses of action. The wheels of bureaucracy, though, rolled slowly and haltingly, and Texas timber interests certainly wished to keep preservationists at bay. That Douglas had the ears of President Johnson and Secretary Udall meant that the Big Thicket might receive a hearing at a high level, but this was no guarantee of action fast enough to forestall cutting, especially since the justice had in the past and would again in the future cross political swords with both Johnson and Udall. Still, for those interested in stopping the logging in the area and in uniting the islands of woods scattered throughout this region under some federal aegis, Douglas's public presence and behind-the-scenes lobbying were promising signs that supplemented the efforts by locals.[29]

After much field research, Douglas's book, *Farewell to Texas*, appeared in 1967. After opening with the parable of Ahab and Naboth, Douglas proceeded to the Big Thicket to show modern Ahabs at work in a unique ecological and historical region. He characterized the natural and historical features, highlighting the hardwoods running through the area not far from Houston. He described the "gargantuan" magnolia trees and "mammoth" gardenias. Turtles, alligators, water moccasins, catfish, and herons "thrive." The area's human inhabitants were "God-fearing," with larger-than-life characters like Judge Hightower, "a bear hunter by profession and a lawyer by avocation"—surely a figure after Justice Douglas's own heart. The Big Thicket area rested on a natural resource-based economy of sawmills and oil wells and was populated with characters typical of the mythic and real West.[30]

Fundamentally, Douglas wrote to convince readers and political leaders to act. To accomplish this conversion to conservation, Douglas chronicled collective results of loggers, oil drillers, real estate developers, and hunters. Once the forest had contained over three million acres, but by the 1960s, it had been "reduced to 300,000 acres due to oil drilling, pipe lines, highways, logging, and man's other 'development' programs." Besides the core area of three hundred thousand acres, only "scattered spots" and "isolated pockets" remained. Roads crossed the woods, ruining baygall habitat. Summer homes and subdivisions similarly ate up available land. Land prices had skyrocketed because of that development, making an acre that sold for $50 in 1960 sell for $300 six years later—a boon to developers but harmful to various wildlife species. Oil companies and their pipelines dissected and sacrificed the ecological integrity of the woods and ruined the land through flooding from wells. Lumber companies employed "ruthless cutting programs," consigning "the modern Naboth's Vineyard to an end that these wondrous pieces of God's creation do not deserve." In addition, the companies in some parts of the Big Thicket sprayed herbicides on hardwoods so that the faster-growing, and thus more profitable, pine could fill the acreage. This eliminated a rookery of hundreds of nesting birds, including herons, egrets, spoonbills, and anhingas. Finally, hunters poached wildlife to near-extinction. The collective results of this activity motivated conservationists to act. Because of entrenched local economic interests, Douglas and local conservationists viewed federal action as "their only hope."[31]

Historical, ecological, and contemporary circumstances made the simple reservation of land as protected park land or a wilderness area problematic in Texas. First, local tradition did not lend itself to strong support for federal preservation, and the restrictions on hunting, logging, or drilling such protection would imply would be particularly unwelcome. According to Douglas, the state government, "solidly controlled by The Establishment," undoubtedly would protect the interests of logging companies. Next, the Big

Thicket's ecological integrity, fractured so long ago, proved inconsistent with wilderness definitions in the Wilderness Act of 1964, since five thousand acres together did not always exist to satisfy statutory requirements. Furthermore, some local people simply opposed any park designation.[32]

Besides drawing media attention to and publicizing the efforts of a local conservationist organization, the Big Thicket Association, Douglas advocated his own program. He called for an education campaign to change local opponents' minds about nature. This typical Douglas plea—much like earlier efforts by Aldo Leopold—recognized that only through rethinking one's relationship with the natural world would change occur on the ground. Douglas acknowledged that the fragmented nature of the Big Thicket prevented its inclusion in the national park system on an equal level to other parks. Nevertheless, he and local conservationists viewed that federal action as necessary, since modern Ahabs aligned themselves with the state government, preventing an acceptable local solution. In 1966, Senator Yarborough introduced a bill in the Senate to make the Big Thicket into a national park, a bill Douglas supported.[33]

Douglas ended his chapter on the Big Thicket by framing the issue in a populist, pessimistic tone. "Time is on the side of the modern Ahabs," Douglas wrote, "not on the side of the people." He compared the quick pace of economic development with the slow pace of bureaucracy and democratic action. Additionally, he tapped a key strategy of the post-World War II wilderness movement and one he had used for Cougar Lakes: he nationalized the issue. To conservationists, certain natural areas deserved protection for national reasons, and those national imperatives often trumped local desires and economic needs. From Douglas's perspective, land protected as parks or wilderness was available to all Americans—a democratic resource—whereas land dedicated to economic development or resource extraction only benefited a few—a plutocratic resource. As he concluded: "[T]he Big Thicket is so unique and so lovely that it should belong to all the people," a development that eventually occurred albeit several years later.[34]

Beyond the Big Thicket, Douglas's research took him to many places throughout Texas. And at each stop, the justice sketched the place and people in generally similar ways. The local history and ecology differed, and the local conservation struggles may have varied. But the problems Douglas witnessed in Texas stemmed from some common circumstances—the uniquely Texan political, historical, and ecological conditions.

In the Big Bend region, Douglas highlighted the success of the unlikely partnership between small-town tourist advocates and local cattlemen who wished to sell to the federal government after they had overused the land, a not altogether uncommon story. The federal government acquired the overgrazed land. The formula adopted in Big Bend succeeded because land values had declined sharply because of overgrazing, and "government acquisition became attractive by entrepreneurial standards." With federal protection, the Big Bend National Park became a "regenerative force of nature." It was a somewhat paradoxical situation: normally independent-minded ranchers and local boosters turned to the federal government to acquire land, preventing a further economic sink. Douglas explained, "the philosophy of Adam Smith is so dominant in Texas that opposition to the establishment of national parks is fierce and unrelenting," except in the situation that arose in the Big Bend region whereby the land was "so worn out by owners" that they turned to the government to bail them out. Ironically, national park acquisition could occur only after environmental decimation. In the process, federal acquisition nationalized the landscape to subordinate local interests, even while serving the local tourist economy.[35]

In another part of the state, Douglas used the Davis Mountains to explain the importance of federal conservation in Texas. Douglas characterized them as this "wild tumble of mountains." The mountains, in West Texas, north of Big Bend National Park, were held in private hands, which impeded their federal environmental salvation. The beauty of such places as the Davis Mountains deserved to be protected for all Texans and Americans; it was "the inheritance of all the people," Douglas claimed, "a dividend of national citizenship." Here was the crux of Douglas's thought as he expressed it in Texas. Environmental resources belonged to all the people; they were, in fact, Americans' legitimate "inheritance." Wendell Berry, one of the American environmental tradition's leading thinkers, has located such a perspective rooted deeply in the Judeo-Christian heritage. According to Berry, God gave the Promised Land to the chosen people but placed conditions on the gift with the expectation that the land would be inherited, unharmed, for many successive generations. Douglas built on this religious perspective and also argued that such an inheritance depended on the public's ability to continue enjoying nature; continued extraction would preclude such pleasure. Just like Naboth's vineyard, Texas's wilderness had been inherited and should not be given away or sold. Texas had failed in its environmental mission, and without federal intervention the mountains would be "ruined." No matter Douglas's reservations about the record of some federal agencies, he believed the best political solution to the particular threats in Texas rested with the national government when state officials, and the "modern Ahabs" with whom they were aligned, did not act or acted destructively.[36]

Capote Falls offered another instructive tale. The falls flowed off a two-hundred-foot cliff in the middle of the West Texas desert. The description Douglas includes is one of sublime beauty with pastel colors brightening the surrounding rocks. The place, Douglas explained, "is a place for worship, not for a frolic. The beauty is so fragile, the solitude is so precious that the Canyon is only for those who walk reverently." Such a special place, the justice warned, deserved national park or monument protection, but it could not be open to the usual park crowds. This paradox underscored one of the conservation movement's greatest challenges that was emerging prominently at the time. Supporters like Douglas were forced to promote parklands for their protection from private economic ruin, but with such promotion came recreational development that often destroyed or jeopardized the very object of their affections. Although Douglas recognized the paradox, he, like most, did not or could not articulate an ideal solution.[37]

More troubling, the overgrazing at nearby ranches threatened Capote Falls. Douglas estimated that this place needed federal protection, like the Big Thicket and Davis Mountains. Indeed, according to Douglas's understanding, the only possible way for the land to be reserved was through use of the federal government's eminent domain power. Yet as most owners would, Texans resisted. Douglas harshly criticized the opposition: "Texas, still fighting the battle of socialism of the last century (a park is socialism, isn't it?), has not yet entered the present century when it comes to preserving large areas of its wonderland for outdoor recreation." Unleashing venom that was unusual even for him, Douglas soon took up the matter in the Washington, DC, corridors of resource administration but to little avail. [38]

In the final pages of his book, Douglas lambasted "modern Ahabs," who, Douglas wrote,

> *see a tree and think in terms of board feet.*
> *They see a cliff and think in terms of gravel.*
> *They see a river and think in terms of dams, because dams mean profitable contracts, don't they?*
> *They see a mountain and think in terms of minerals, roads, and excavations.*
> *They think of parks in terms of private enterprise—money-making schemes—not nature trails, but amusement centers.*

Providing places to recreate and for wilderness preservation was emerging then as an important national problem, the justice argued. In contrast to national trends, "Texas is mostly not concerned," Douglas charged. The hope for the state remained in a small number of Texans, like Jim Bowmer. Such conservationists were struggling against the modern Ahabs who, he claimed, "are more strongly entrenched in Texas than anywhere else."[39]

Researching *Farewell to Texas* had depressed the justice. His final paragraph revealed the depth of his cynicism about Texas conservation. The odds stacked against conservation seemed almost insurmountable. "That is why this is a melancholy book," Douglas wrote. "That is why when we think of conservation, nature trails, back-packing, camping, and outdoor recreation, we must say FAREWELL TO TEXAS—unless the dedicated minority receives an overwhelming mandate from the people." This ending effectively encapsulated his assessment, his fears, his hopes, and it directed a challenge to local conservationists to keep hope alive and to national conservationists and sympathetic politicians to work harder for Texas. It also demonstrated the central need conservationists faced in converting more to their cause.[40]

Reaction to the book varied. Once he changed the proposed title, *The Wilderness of Texas*, to *Farewell to Texas: A Vanishing Wilderness*, Douglas faced an angry First Lady. At a White House dinner, Douglas told Lady Bird Johnson of the change, and "She exploded. She did not like it at all. She said the title should have some hope in it." No permanent damage had been done to the relationship between these two, but even without reading the book, Lady Bird understood what Douglas had accomplished. He had taken a celebratory genre—nature writing—and made it a political tract and one less a celebration than a cautionary tale.[41]

Back in Texas, when the *Dallas Morning News* issued a critical editorial, Bowmer rushed to Douglas's defense in a letter to the editor. The Texas attorney recounted the pollution problems in the rivers, the invasion of exotic species on the rangeland, and the threats against mountains and canyons. Bowmer challenged the editor to take a trip around Texas with Bowmer, and the editor would see that Douglas's assessment withstood criticism. The editorial proved that Douglas helped place environmental concerns in the public discourse, furthering his role as a public intellectual for conservation.[42]

A debate over Texas's wilderness and recreational areas continued with the catalyst Douglas and others had furnished. Bowmer wrote to Douglas in March 1967 reporting the progress on various projects about which Douglas had inquired, including Guadalupe Mountain National Park ("I believe we can consider the Park a certainty"), the Big Thicket ("I believe we are making real progress in the Big Thicket program"), and Capote Falls ("[L]argely through your efforts, the National Parks [sic] Service and Bureau of Outdoor Recreation are conducting studies. ... [T]ime is growing short for the preservation of the Falls"). Bowmer concluded, "Don't give up on Texas yet!" And Douglas did not.[43]

In Congress, individuals invoked Douglas's name, perspective, and influence in hearings on Senator Yarborough's proposal for the Big Thicket National Park. In Texas, although generally overpowered by economic interests, local conservationists worked hard. For instance, the Texas Federation of Women's Clubs rallied around the Big Thicket park idea. Their newsletter, which Yarborough placed in the *Congressional Record*, urged their members to support Yarborough's bill and suggested that their members purchase Douglas's book. Douglas wrote the president of the federation with delight. He thanked her for the organization's support of the bill and wrote how important the Big Thicket's preservation was: "It must be saved for future generations to see and revere the marvelous beauties that once were America—before the smog, before the polluted streams, and before the asphalt and concrete that are possessing most of the land." Finally, the justice captured the essence: "The Big Thicket is America." It summarized Douglas's beliefs perfectly by aligning America's interest with environmental protection and by arguing that natural resources were fundamentally public resources. This short letter, also reprinted in the *Congressional Record*, appealed to one's sense of national pride. Douglas consistently equated environmental protection with patriotism, for the lands and waters of the United States provided a basis for the country's identity and future. Further, civic clubs like the Texas Federation of Women's Clubs were imbued with the grassroots democratic and patriotic spirit that would improve the state's and the nation's chances at environmental—even civic—salvation. For generations, such groups remained subordinated to economic imperatives; the new environmental era that Douglas was helping usher in brought these grassroots groups to stronger positions in conservation politics.[44]

Douglas did what he could with his contacts in Washington, DC, but after a fevered couple years in 1966 and 1967 his involvement declined. In 1974, Douglas reservedly celebrated a success for the Big Thicket. The area finally preserved as the Big Thicket National Reserve consisted originally of 84,450 acres in twelve separate units. Douglas found the achievement merely, "better than nothing."[45]

Douglas did much of the same in Texas as he did elsewhere for environmental causes, writing letters to Secretary of the Interior Udall, President and First Lady Johnson, and park superintendents. But he also worked with local, private citizens concerned about Texas's environment, like Bowmer and the Federation of Women's Clubs. These individuals and the communities they represented could put the promise of democracy to work by infusing debates with perspectives long overshadowed by economic priorities and powers. Douglas's celebrity helped them. In many ways, his presence became his greatest attribute, for it brought attention to his various causes. In the flurry of activity Douglas devoted to the state, the justice raised the political questions in Texas about the lack of environmental sensitivity, the proper role of government, the nature of property rights, and many other key questions germane to conservation.

In Texas, Douglas made his writing firmly political, more than he ever had before. The field research for the book and the final product merged, creating a celebration of landscape, a condemnation of "modern Ahabs," and a clear challenge to local and national environmental activists. With the biblical metaphor, Douglas, as he did so often as a public intellectual, put the debate into terms his audience composed of ordinary Americans could appreciate. Using it, he castigated Texas conservation politics at a number of levels. At one level, the metaphor referred to the lack of public lands; there were few national commons in the state, protected by a national government and its imperatives. At another, more important level, though, the "modern Ahabs" metaphor symbolized an illegal and illegitimate seizure of land. The state's "modern Ahabs" were challenged to account for their illicit abuse of Texas natural resources. Wilderness, Douglas explained, was "the inheritance of all the people," just like Naboth's vineyard was his legitimate inheritance. When Ahab took the vineyard on trumped-up charges of blasphemy that led to Naboth's stoning, he violated not only the land but also tradition. In Texas, "modern Ahabs" destroyed the environment and robbed the people of their heritage. In this place, Douglas envisioned nationally protected wildernesses and parklands to ensure future generations the opportunity to see and experience Texas' natural heritage—a heritage that could be protected, Douglas believed, only by federal strength.

A Wilderness in Their Backyard: Protecting the C&O Canal and Potomac Basin

But federal power could be a hindrance or insufficient, as Douglas's experience with the Potomac Basin revealed. If the Cougar Lakes campaign highlighted the problems of public management and the Texas efforts illuminated the struggle to assert federal authority in a place without it, Douglas's continued actions on behalf of the Chesapeake and Ohio Canal and larger Potomac Basin underscored the struggle to balance nature protection in places where population pressures were high. Moreover, and perhaps because it was so near the capital, Douglas faced a more complicated political situation that demanded vigilance and often resulted in frustrations. Consistent in all these efforts, though, was Douglas's conviction that conservation ought to protect the public interest, an interest government policy was failing to safeguard. Not only did he continuously call for public hearings, but to a greater degree than elsewhere he took the cause directly to the public through speeches, magazine articles, and organized hikes, all the while still wrangling with politicians behind the scenes.

Although best known for his C&O Canal work, Douglas invested energy in the entire Potomac River Basin. In the late 1950s and early 1960s, the Corps of Engineers, one of the organizations that Douglas most loathed and once called conservation's Public Enemy Number One, announced plans to dam and develop parts of the Potomac River.[46] These proposals brought the dire condition of the Potomac into the public's consciousness, but the Corps' solution raised Douglas's ire. The Potomac River was terribly polluted, and with anticipated population growth at 200 to 300 percent, finding a source of safe, healthy water became a high priority for the capital region. Pollution was "the foremost problem confronting all who live in the Washington, D.C., Metropolitan Area," Douglas wrote in *National Parks Magazine*. The Potomac, once a charming river, "is now a national disgrace." According to Douglas, thirty-one communities dumped sewage effluent into the river, creating a stench, a health hazard, and a conservation crisis. Infectious materials from the sewage flowed in the river and threatened capital-area residents' health with 40 percent higher bacteria count than the Public Health Service's standard. The water supply and its quality certainly demanded attention, but Douglas lambasted the Corps's proposals.[47]

Douglas thought the Corps of Engineers' solutions were unacceptable and unnecessary. Essentially, the Corps envisioned a dam to store water against the droughts that threatened the Potomac's water supply every dozen years or so. More importantly, it proposed sixteen major reservoirs that would be used as large flushing mechanisms. The primary function of the proposed high dam at River Bend, Douglas explained, "will be to supply water to wash the sewage down the river." Besides flushing sewage down the Potomac like a giant toilet, such a water release would help wash out the silt built up in the riverbed. In nearly identical speeches to the League of Women Voters of DC and the Daughters of the American Revolution (DAR), Douglas outlined these proposals, promptly criticized them, and countered with alternatives. Conservation practices on the farms upstream, including reforestation, reduced grazing, and contoured plowing, would vastly reduce the silt problem in the river. Next, because the Potomac River fluctuated significantly, any reservoir's water level would similarly rise and fall, exposing "ugly mud banks" and creating an "ugly lake." Douglas told the DAR that he could "think of no uglier mud hole that man could create." Moreover, "To create it out of land and sites so rich in history and so beautiful as the Potomac would be reckless and irresponsible," stated Douglas, appealing directly to the DAR's embrace of American heritage. The real solution, Douglas explained a number of times, included cleaning the water supply with sewage treatment plants. If the river's water were treated, raw sewage not dumped, and conservation measures taken, dams would be unnecessary. Then, relying on a cliché, Douglas claimed, "A nation that can conquer outer space and put a man on the moon certainly should be able to clean up its waterways." Of course, wresting the development plan away from the Corps of Engineers would be difficult. Douglas encouraged civic groups, like the DAR, to oppose the Corps. Local organizations had to lead the way, and Douglas encouraged and supported this action. By encouraging civic activism, Douglas promoted grassroots challenges to what seemed to be an unchecked federal agency, a favored tactic of his throughout the years.[48]

When a public hearing finally was scheduled, Douglas wrote to Colonel Warren R. Johnson of the Army Corps of Engineers to challenge the hearing's fairness because it would address only the Corps' plan, not any alternatives. To be sure, Douglas favored public hearings, for they were necessary to provide the public's input to critical environmental questions and to assure democratic responsiveness. But he doubted the Corps' hearing would fulfill such purposes. "It seems to me vitally important to get before the public not only the plans that the Army Engineers have, but all the alternative suggestions," Douglas wrote. He continued:

> I realize that at your hearing not everyone can speak. I also realize some government agencies will have spokesmen there. But there are other independent points of view that strong groups in the private sector have which I think should be heard. I realize of course that you will have a question period. But the question period is not adequate to present alternative plans. So my request comes down to two things, that Mr. Arthur Hanson, a Washington lawyer, and Dr. William Davies of the U. S. Geological Survey, each be given ten minutes to present their alternative proposals for meeting the water problem, as well as other aspects of the Potomac Valley development program.
>   ... I am sure they can in the ten minutes allotted to each of them, round out the phases of the problem which otherwise would be neglected.

Douglas wanted the hearing to be more representative and independent. Only that way could open democracy function and, he believed, environmental interests be served.[49]

Douglas moved to rally others around this democratic clarion call. "The Corps of Engineers has ridden roughshod over the people of the Basin in carrying the matter far as it has," Douglas wrote to Maryland Governor Millard Tawes, trying to convince the governor to assist the conservation cause. People throughout the Potomac Basin, Douglas asserted, were "overwhelmingly" opposed to the Corps' plans. Rather than debating minor alternatives within the technical solutions, which would be debated easily and endlessly by competing engineering experts, Douglas here concentrated on a political principle—open and honest public participation.[50]

The dam debate continued for several years showing the sometimes snail's pace of bureaucracy, but Douglas persisted with his argument. In 1965, he wrote to Russell Train, the first chair for the Council on Environmental Quality (1970-73) and the second Administrator of the Environmental Protection Agency (1973-77). At the time of Douglas's missive, Train was president of the Conservation Foundation, a private think tank founded by Fairfield Osborn, a noted conservationist. The Conservation Foundation planned to sponsor, along with other conservation organizations, Potomac Planning Workshops, in Train's words, to facilitate "comprehensive long-term planning ... accompanied by informed citizen participation." Douglas and the C&O Canal Association strongly opposed these workshops, a seemingly inconsistent position given Douglas's long desire to open such planning to the public. Douglas wrote to Train, a man Douglas had "long admired," to explain his opposition. The justice feared these public workshops would "in practical effect ... be used by the Corps to promote their program, which in the long run will despoil the Potomac Valley and 'develop' it for selfish commercial interests or for other narrow self-interested groups."[51] Train responded with a thoughtful letter explaining how the workshops operated and with much support for both citizen involvement and limited dam building. Still, Douglas was dissatisfied. To the justice, the planning sessions gave the Corps and the Public Health Service a "platform as principal speakers" and furnished no alternative views or state-of-the-art information about alternative technologies that might mitigate pollution better than the dam. Moreover, Douglas indicated there were "a large number of organizations with deep grass roots" involved in planning for the Potomac Basin already, organizations like the C&O Canal Association. In short, he felt the deck was stacked against grassroots conservation groups if only federal agencies occupied the formal platforms. Douglas had seen this strategy in the Northwest woods by the Forest Service, and he hoped Train would adjust in future workshops.[52]

Meanwhile, Douglas elaborated on his own alternatives for the Potomac Basin, proposals increasingly ensnared in larger Washington politics. He argued the most democratic development in the Potomac Basin would not be dams but trails. Douglas was adamant in making the case for recreational development as the number one priority for protecting the Potomac River Basin. The roots of his vision, of course, had begun in the early 1950s and his hike to stop highway development along the old canal. From the beginning of the controversy in 1959 over the Corps of Engineers' dam proposal, Douglas stressed the recreational potential that existed without unsightly reservoirs. In a speech that year, he argued that the canal's "best use," its "real value," would come under National Park Service management for "its recreational potentialities." Once the river was cleaned up of its pollution, Douglas was certain it would attract greater recreation activity. He encouraged "federal appropriations to get the canal locks repaired and restored" to get the entire canal in shape and opened as a canoeway, as well as providing freshwater and campsites for visitors. Virtually all of his writing about the C&O Canal—magazine articles, letters, and book chapters—delivered scathing attacks on large-scale industrial or residential development. Instead, he hoped to preserve the canal and larger Potomac Basin as a place for low-impact and non-mechanized recreation, such as hiking, canoeing, and bicycling in keeping with prevailing wilderness criteria. His vision, though, met head-on with grander dreams in the Johnson Administration. And Douglas and other C&O Canal advocates spent much of their energy trying to negotiate the political process to best support their idea of a protected canal with better recreational facilities.[53]

Douglas and others believed political circumstances in the early 1960s were opportune. He wrote Stewart Udall in December 1960 to congratulate him on his appointment as Secretary of the Interior. "I am sure it will mean many bold strokes to preserve our wilderness," Douglas hoped confidently. If Douglas's faith in Udall's promise was high, his opinion of Udall's actual performance had plummeted by the mid-1960s. Beginning in about 1965, the Johnson Administration with Udall as its point person tried to get congressional approval for a comprehensive bill to develop recreational opportunities throughout the Potomac Basin. Part of this omnibus bill included converting the C&O Canal from a national monument—a status it had received from an executive proclamation by President Dwight Eisenhower in the very last days of his administration—to a national park. Udall saw the canal as a centerpiece to this larger effort because "here is something we already have and own as a foundation on which we can build." However much they wanted the canal preserved as a national park, Douglas and the C&O Canal Committee intensely disliked the strategy of coupling the canal with other projects.[54]

Douglas and Udall disagreed on the omnibus proposal for a variety of reasons. To Udall, the bigger bill offered two important advantages: "1) We can … have a big bill to do the whole job that is *the President's* bill; 2) We will not fragment the support for saving the Potomac—and can achieve our maximum goals." Udall went on to explain that it was simply a question of tactics, and he preferred the "one-big-bill strategy." Of course as a political appointee, Udall was trying to find the best political situation for Johnson. Not having the same political loyalties to support, Douglas pushed for immediate action on the C&O Canal portion of the Potomac proposal. Writing to Representative Charles McC. Mathias, Jr. of Maryland, a supporter of a bill to grant the C&O Canal National Historical Park status, Douglas worried about the proposal getting "bogged down with a big massive bill which will have so many controversial features there will be no progress for years"—a prediction certainly consistent with the normal pace of congressional action. Douglas wrote to the Interior Secretary the same day, arguing that the omnibus bill "will meet with well-night [sic] 100% opposition from the conservation groups." The proposed bill supported some of the dreaded Corps of Engineers' proposals that were "wholly unnecessary and quite ruinous to the valley." More importantly, time was of the essence; with so many controversial aspects packed into the omnibus bill, Johnson and Udall would be long out of office before Congress could act. So, Douglas combined his personal desire for protection for his beloved canal and an appeal to political realities.[55]

Douglas tried also to reason with Udall that conservationists wanted action now, and that Udall's deliberate pace risked alienating his greatest constituency. "I don't want to make myself a nuisance, but I think I tell you the absolute truth when I say conservationist groups in the country will be allied against you," Douglas wrote Udall; "I don't think that is a healthy situation." Alternatively, though, Douglas suggested that Udall would obtain 100 percent support for a separate canal bill. The frustration mounted, and six months later in 1966 Douglas reported, "I sat in on a meeting of some conservationists recently and most of them seemed to be pretty much up in arms about the long delay in creating the C&O National Historical Park." Douglas pointed out that the park was consistent with Udall's grander vision for the greater Potomac project and would, in fact, complete one part of that project. "I am inclined to believe," Douglas pleaded, "it would be a pace-setter for all the rest of the project." Moreover, "We have waited already twelve years and in view of what I gather to be the mounting storms of opposition to the package program as, if, and when it is proposed, we may well wait another twelve years." Douglas's impatience showed, and he soon publicized his feelings in a *Parks and Recreation* article. Furthermore, he reminded Udall that the Senate had already passed the park bill twice. If Udall were more attuned to political realities, the justice implied, the secretary would rapidly lend support to this separate bill. But Udall did not. Douglas went so far as to write President Johnson telling him that the proposal for the Potomac Basin sent to him by his Secretary of the Interior would be "ruinous and disastrous" and urging Johnson to talk with Douglas for a few minutes "before you make up your mind." Ultimately, Douglas came to think that Udall "sabotaged" the plan for a C&O Canal National Historical Park during the Johnson Administration. That judgment, informed by years of simmering frustration against President Johnson and his administration, may have been harsh, but it captured Douglas's fervent hopes for ensuring the canal some greater measure of federal protection.[56]

Douglas continued to work for the park and praise efforts of allies. Ironically, in 1967, Udall's brother, Morris, a Representative from Arizona, co-sponsored a bill to create a C&O National Historic Park along with Henry Reuss of Wisconsin, Samuel S. Stratton of New York, and Charles McC. Mathias of Maryland. Such a congressional action would create "one of the great recreation spots in the East, offering camping, hiking, canoeing, fishing to hundreds of thousands of people." Douglas saw this action as promising. His aim, all along, was to preserve the canal for the people. Douglas and the others wanted an alternative to the city, so any child could be "introduced during the hot summer months to birds, to fish, to fox, raccoon, muskrats, and deer, to the mysteries of the woods, and to the joys of swimming and canoeing." Predictably, Douglas suggested, people responded favorably to this message; the canal could be a democratic meeting ground for all the people of the metropolitan area. For a decade, he had termed the canal "a wilderness at their back door" and by the late 1960s began dubbing it "the poor man's national park." In the 1930s, Bob Marshall had also envisioned wilderness parks being a democratic meeting ground, but often that ideal fell short of the reality. Still, the C&O Canal boasted two million annual visits in the late 1980s, suggesting at least a partial victory for widespread urban use. In the midst of further congressional wrangling over potential park bills, Douglas again emphasized the canal's "great convenience" to those in the metropolitan area. It could be a place for one "who has only an hour or so" or for those with more time to get closer to nature outside urban corridors. Douglas believed the park would preserve that access and improve the population's appreciation of nature, a goal deeply embedded in Douglas's wilderness and political vision.[57]

Not until late December 1970 could Douglas breathe a sigh of relief. Writing to the Senator from Washington State, Henry M. "Scoop" Jackson, Douglas thanked the politician for finally negotiating a park bill that satisfied both houses of Congress and would be signed in January 1971. The C&O Canal National Historical Park would become a reality on its own, not a part of an omnibus program. As Douglas had predicted, the park came after the Johnson Administration had left office. In Congress, a series of bipartisan sponsors had finally prevailed in getting the bill through the appropriate stages. Douglas was grateful for the end of a long process.[58]

Douglas took several lessons from this lengthy ordeal. He wrote an article for *National Parks and Conservation Magazine*, which he surely thought was long overdue, describing the successful preservation battle. "The moral of the story behind the creation of this park," Douglas taught, "relates not to politics, not to action by a federal agency, not to court orders, not to the mass media, not to public relations counsel, but to civic action." He was wrong. Undeniably, creating this park did have much to do with politics, the media, federal agencies, and public relations, and Douglas was always centrally involved in each of these. But for his audience, Douglas interpreted the lessons differently. His role and that of others in the original hike in 1954 had been catalytic only. True, they talked with the media and hiked past picketers and made news by hiking in the height of the automobile age. Yet, they merely captured the imagination of a city and prompted others to take up the mantle of reform.[59]

The long process between 1954 and 1970 showed the power of democratic, grassroots, civic action. After the 1954 hike, several interested individuals organized the C&O Canal Association, a group whose purpose was to promote the creation of a park and to protect the canal. They also included a committee called the Level Walkers, a watchdog group that divided the canal into small areas that local people helped to keep clean. These groups watched over the canal and kept the cause in the eye of the public. By 1970, the annual C&O hike attracted about a thousand hikers from children under seven to adults over seventy. People like Douglas, the justice modestly suggested, were only the stimulus. "The real work," he explained, "was done by hundreds of others up and down the valley who formed committees, petitioned Congress, encouraged their Congressional representative to back the park bill, got editorials in their local papers, and molded the opinion of people away from the cruel invaders of a freeway to a policy protective of the land and waters of this historic valley." Whether or not the modesty was false, Douglas did not include his own central role—giving speeches, writing articles, leading reunions hikes, instructing politicians. Always ready to praise American constitutional traditions, Douglas made clear the freedom of expression promised in the Bill of Rights enabled him and all other canal activists to hike and protest, to speak and lobby—in short, to be political actors. Although he also privately wrote politicians, much of Douglas's work centered on the public, explaining the issues, evangelizing the place, encouraging their vigilance and dedication.[60]

A month after Douglas's retirement from the Court in November 1975, Representative Richard Ottinger of New York introduced House Resolution 11226, "A bill to dedicate the Cheapeake [sic] and Ohio Canal National Historical Park to Justice William O. Douglas in grateful recognition of his contributions to the people of the United States." In his remarks, Ottinger called Douglas's efforts on behalf of the C&O Canal one of his "greatest conservation accomplishments and successes." Eighteen months later, a number of politicians drove to Georgetown to help unveil a commemorative bust of Douglas beside the canal in dedication to the former justice. Senator "Scoop" Jackson offered a fitting tribute: "Because Justice Douglas had a love for the earth and a willingness to fight for our natural heritage, we are all the richer. The evidence of his greatest success stretches out before us today from Washington to Cumberland. This should be—and it is—Bill Douglas' park." It was an appropriate compliment to a man in his last years, suffering the after-effects from a debilitating stroke, who committed much of his time to conservation causes. The ceremony, almost twenty-five years after Douglas had first rallied to the Canal's defense, was long overdue and a symbolic gesture to an individual whose conservation activism had crossed the continent.[61]

Conclusion

Cougar Lakes. The Big Thicket. The C&O Canal. None of these places resound in American environmental history like Hetch Hetchy, the Grand Canyon, or Echo Park. Yet there is ample reason to examine these places and Douglas as he worked to protect them. Different threats are revealed—scant legal protection, federal administrators with near-unchecked power, private landholdings jeopardizing preservation, population, pollution, and political pressures. Unique contexts shaped Douglas's specific strategies. In all these places, he used his public image and power to raise awareness of threats. The justice advocated for new laws to prevent abuses like those he saw with Forest Service personnel in the Cascades; when laws were changed, Douglas demanded compliance and stood ready to challenge any perceived shortcoming in an official's application. Douglas wanted federal protection for special Texas landscapes that were threatened by private industry or tourism; by doing so, he challenged local leadership and asserted a national primacy to protect such places for the future of *all* Americans. Finally, Douglas urged public involvement in land-use decisions and increased public use of natural recreation resources in the nation's capital; under the scrutiny of such a large population center, his work stood out in the context of that pressure and heightened political agendas. These examples span the continent and bridge various contexts to reveal that local places and histories and politics matter. Moreover, they confirm that the wilderness movement in this era was pragmatic and adaptive. Douglas and the wilderness movement at large encouraged use of wilderness for outdoor recreation, identified and supported local constituencies who favored wilderness designation, and promoted wilderness in areas that were smaller, not pristine, and near cities.[62]

Douglas and other conservationists had long argued for the need to permanently protect wilderness areas from encroachment by roads and destructive economic development. And Justice Douglas, especially, urged that resource management decisions be open to democratic processes to protect the public interest and minority rights. In an age with only weak legal protection for wilderness, the symbolic power of having an advocate from the nation's highest legal authority could not be overstated. Ultimately, the Wilderness Act and later the National Environmental Policy Act (1970) helped inscribe many of those ideals into an enduring place in the American political and natural landscape with significant ramifications. This transformation meant that wilderness management became much more beholden to democratic processes and the public, encouraging and allowing conservationists to shift their tactics from defense to offense.[63] With legal measures in hand, Douglas could potentially shape outcomes in the Court. Still, though, Douglas used his position on the Court in remarkably consistent ways, for even there, he saw a primary role in shaping the public's understanding of conservation.

CHAPTER FIVE

The Environmental Justice

Ecology has become the victim not only of oil companies and timber interests but of administrative agencies. And unless the role of government, operating through its agencies, becomes more ecologically conscious, our environment will continue to deteriorate.

William O. Douglas,
"Federal Policy and the Ecological Crisis," (1971)[1]

Somewhat paradoxically, the role that gave Douglas public standing, his position on the nation's highest court, was the most difficult position from which to engage the public on conservation concerns. Still, he found ways. This process began roughly but was made easier by a legal revolution in the 1960s and 1970s that found Congress passing a series of important laws, including the Wilderness Act and the Clean Water Act. And even before these measures improved the weapons in Douglas's arsenal, the justice located other ways to write about nature's value in his legal opinions. With new statutes, especially the National Environmental Policy Act (NEPA), more opportunities arrived at the Court and allowed Douglas to address conservation themes with greater frequency. His approach to judging did not root his writing only in law, so Douglas used opinions as simply one more avenue to express his conservation values and to educate the American public.

As most contemporary and subsequent observers have contended, Douglas was an unusual justice. For example, in the best-selling behind-the-scenes account of the first seven terms of the Burger Court, *The Brethren: Inside the Supreme Court*, authors Bob Woodward and Scott Armstrong characterized Douglas: "He was for the individual over government, government over big business, and the environment over all else."[2] One historian went so far as to characterize Douglas as an "anti-judge."[3] Such portraits, so pithily drawn, captured some of Douglas's essence, but as such catchy phrases are wont to do, they gloss over complexity and nuance.

Schooled in legal realism, Douglas saw law as serving important social and policy functions. Hence, sometimes legal realism is called functionalism. Consequently, realists contended that lawyers and judges must acknowledge and use extra-legal evidence in their reasoning. Indeed, they needed to recognize that law exists in social, political, and economic contexts. Douglas exemplified this approach as well as anyone, and he drew liberally on his own experiences beyond the law to inform his perspective on the law, a practice that certainly earned him ample criticism. And his opinions that reflect environmental themes demonstrate this method superbly, as he possessed such a well of experiences in conservation.

Because Douglas saw no strict lines between law and society, he enjoyed the freedom to pepper his opinions with all kinds of values—legal, scientific, social, personal, and ecological. Few cases reached the Court strictly concerning nature during Douglas's first two decades on the bench. When they did, beginning in 1960 and in rapid succession after 1970, Douglas used his platform to explore ideas and issues, to teach and preach, and to question and provoke. Consequently, Douglas enjoyed the unique forum of the Court to present his interpretations and even advocacy on environmental issues. The Court offered him an opportunity not afforded to any other conservationist before or since, furnishing him with yet another public forum in which to publicize and advance his environmental ideas. Although the law and the Court certainly provided the canvas on which Douglas painted these opinions, they did not fully frame or contain his writing and thinking. To understand these opinions, then, is necessarily to look beyond the law and to see the ways Douglas once again reached the public to teach about conservation.

Legal Realism and Douglas's Perspectives

When he arrived at Columbia Law School in 1922, Douglas entered a program in the midst of an intellectual movement known as legal realism. Later as faculty both at Columbia and Yale Law School and as a member and chair of the Securities and Exchange Commission, Douglas participated in and furthered the training and practice of legal realism. Although this school's influence never dominated legal training and certainly ebbed institutionally after World War II, its approach to legal problems and to judging profoundly shaped Douglas throughout his lengthy career on the Court. Indeed, legal realism likely freed him to maintain an active life off the Court, and it no doubt invigorated him so that his restless intellectual energy could roam where it led him. And while this practice may have made him a less effective justice than both his critics and defenders wanted, it made him a more experienced judge and more valuable conservationist.

Legal realists reacted against the notion that judges simply find law by logically examining doctrine and general legal principles that exist somehow autonomously. As early as the 1880s, Oliver Wendell Holmes had expressed skepticism that judges dispassionately applied legal axioms to reach decisions. Instead, they decided the outcome of the case for reasons external to the law, such as political, economic, or moral interests, and then applied legal reasoning retroactively. Judicial tradition, of course, meant judges typically couched their opinions in the language of legal doctrine, but that was mere subterfuge. Holmes's ideas exposed the very human and fallible nature of legal practice and inspired the schools of sociological jurisprudence and then legal realism.[4]

By the 1920s, legal realism was challenging legal education's prevailing mode—the case method. Associated with legal formalism, the case method approach asked law students to study judges' opinions, identify the legal principles applied, and evaluate whether they used the proper legal maxims and employed them faithfully. Formalism purported to be a scientific method, applying formal doctrinal analysis to identify predictable results based not on fleeting legislation but on purportedly timeless legal truths. Legal realists eschewed this emphasis on doctrine and argued that doctrine obscured rather than illuminated. Realists were far more interested in law's *function* in society than in abstract, formal legal rules. At Columbia, Douglas fell under the influence of the prominent scholar Underhill Moore, who personified the realist spirit of conducting social scientific research into how a law actually functioned in practice rather than in theory. Douglas served as Moore's research assistant and began publishing articles and then case books that utilized a functional approach that recognized how economics, society, and public policy all necessarily interacted with the law and judges' interpretations of the law. This messy process was not an unfortunate flaw, according to realists, but something to analyze and embrace through careful analysis drawn from various disciplinary perspectives.[5]

Not only was the law to be interpreted this way by law students, but lawyers and judges might practice law more deliberately in this vein. Accordingly, realist judges did not necessarily write opinions only for legal scholars but also for other audiences, including an informed public. Such opinions, thus, might be considered expansive essays explaining the realist judge's values and the expected effects of law in society, not doctrinal analyses. Douglas usually approached his opinions in this manner, and according to him, that made "the law more relevant to life." The approach allowed practitioners to embed legal decisions within personal, political, and contemporary circumstances, as well as legal canons. Moreover, as some scholars have observed, realism allowed practitioners to challenge prevailing legal assumptions at the same time that many cultural and economic assumptions were rapidly changing in the 1920s and 1930s. Douglas imbibed the realist message as a student, taught it as faculty,

*Portrait of Justice
William O. Douglas
shortly after his
appointment to the U.S.
Supreme Court*

practiced it as member and later chair of the Securities and Exchange Commission, and embodied it as Supreme Court justice. A realist easily fit into the public intellectual role.[6]

Many have faulted Douglas as a justice. Critics begin with what might be seen as personal or collegial failings. One scholar called Douglas a "lonely colleague" who "was not interested in converting his colleagues to his views," a practice necessary to build coalitions that would produce majority opinions and legal precedents, and it was a practice that Douglas neglected to pursue. As a "loner," Douglas had few, if any, friends on the Court and was, according to another scholar, nearly "puritanical" in his work ethic. He placed a premium on getting the work done, so that he wrote his decisions and quickly moved on. This perspective left little time to discuss and debate the merits of various legal opinions and may well have marginalized Douglas's influence. Indeed, some have argued that his opinions were done in a "slapdash manner" and that this was evidence of intellectual laziness, a charge that bears some truth but may also overstate the case. Collectively, these criticisms paint Douglas as a quick-working and independent justice, jealous of his personal time and demanding that others not waste it. Such a style may well have made him a more effective administrator than member of the nine-body Supreme Court.[7]

More persistent were criticisms that realism and Douglas's application of the philosophy too thoroughly eschewed doctrine and judging standards. Douglas was unwilling to write strictly doctrinal analyses while on the bench. In an interview, he once proclaimed, "I'd rather create a precedent than find one." He certainly had the intellectual talent for it, but his personal impatience, occasional disinterest, and realist training convinced him there was no need to laboriously construct arguments based on received legal wisdom. In this practice, Douglas elided the duties of a judge by not explaining his legal reasoning, a serious shortcoming in a Supreme Court justice. Indeed, an important alternative that challenged legal realism was process jurisprudence. This school stressed the methods, or process, by which judges decided their cases, imploring them to be constrained and to follow comparatively strict rules. This was decidedly not Douglas's way, and critics have faulted him deeply. Instead, Douglas's opinions have been described as "persuasive essays written in support of certain important social values." As such, they illustrate the relationship between Douglas's ideas, society, and law, and he used those opinions didactically. He once explained that he saw his role on the Court much like that of a professor: "I'd like to educate them [the public] on what judges are, what judges should be, what civic affairs should be." This perspective, of course, precisely encapsulates how Douglas used his judicial prominence for conservation.[8]

Hidden Harbingers

It took some time for modern conservation and the Court to meet. Before 1960, when Douglas published his first opinion that clearly and fully articulated an environmental perspective, opportunities to voice his values concerning nature were few and far between. When they did appear, they were found in surprising places. These harbingers foreshadowed the judicial course on which Douglas had set, reflecting his approach to judging in which personal values profoundly influenced the crafting of the opinion and in which the audience appears to be broader than the legal community.

In *Edwards v. California* (1941), Douglas produced a concurring opinion in which he wrote passionately on behalf of the poor and the right to travel. At stake was the constitutionality of a California law that prevented indigent people from migrating to the state, the so-called "Okie law." First, Douglas argued vociferously against the class bias in the legislation. Such a law, in Douglas's opinion, would

> *introduce a caste system utterly incompatible with the spirit of our system of government. It would permit those who were stigmatized by a State as indigents, paupers, or vagabonds to be relegated to an inferior*

class of citizenship. It would prevent a citizen because he was poor from seeking new horizons in other States. It might thus withhold from large segments of our people that mobility which is basic to any guarantee of freedom of opportunity. The result would be a substantial dilution of the rights of national citizenship, a serious impairment of the principles of equality.

Echoes of Douglas's youthful resentment toward those who treated him as a second-class citizen because of his socioeconomic class permeated this opinion. Indeed, much later, Douglas's widow, Cathleen Heffernan Douglas, wrote that his concurring opinion here "was based upon his experience with migrant workers on the wheat and fruit farms of eastern Washington," explicitly acknowledging how the personal had become political. At the time, Richard Neuberger, a fellow Pacific Northwestern liberal with an interest in underrepresented groups and the environment, wrote Douglas to thank him for the opinion.[9]

Rather than simply railing against class discrimination. Douglas took the opinion further. His concurrence rested largely on the right to travel. "I am of the opinion," Douglas explained, "that the right of persons to move freely from State to State occupies a more protected position in our constitutional system than does the movement of cattle, fruit, steel and coal across state lines. While the opinion of the Court expresses no view on that issue, the right involved is so fundamental that I deem it appropriate to indicate the reach of the constitutional question which is present." Douglas later acknowledged that although the right to travel "is not specifically granted by the Constitution," several precedents indicate it was an implied right. The *Edwards* opinion illustrated how Douglas drew from his experience and mapped it onto a larger philosophy of movement. Furthermore, to him, freedom to move definitely included the ability to move through untrammeled nature.[10]

From this opinion, Douglas began to construct a legal philosophy concerning the right to travel, the freedom of movement, or even the right to wander that he later articulated more fully in *Kent v. Dulles* (1958), *Aptheker v. Secretary of State* (1964), and *Papachristou v. City of Jacksonville* (1972). The first two of these decisions concerned travel restrictions on suspected subversives, while the third focused on a city vagrancy law. Their connection to environmental matters, then, is tangential at best. However, in *Papachristou*, Douglas opined in a unanimous decision that wandering or strolling historically furnished "our people the feeling of independence and self-confidence, the feeling of creativity. These amenities have dignified the right of dissent and have honored the right to be nonconformists and the right to defy submissiveness. They have encouraged lives of high spirits rather than hushed, suffocating silence." Douglas, then, extolled arguably America's greatest wanderer, Henry David Thoreau, as well as pointing out the place of wanderers in the literature of Walt Whitman. He identified freedom of movement as a constitutional right in part because wandering, or one might even say hiking, played a significant role in American culture. His own life offered ample testimony to this.[11]

Another peripheral case, this one about the state's police power in urban zoning and slum clearance, allowed Douglas the opportunity to declare environmental values. In *Berman v. Parker* (1954), he argued for a unanimous Court that "[m]iserable and disreputable housing conditions may do more than spread disease and crime and immorality. They may also suffocate the spirit by reducing the people who live there to the status of cattle. ... They may also be an ugly sore, a blight on the community which robs it of charm, which makes it a place from which men turn. The misery of housing may despoil a community as an open sewer may ruin a river." He continued to the crux of the constitutional issue (i.e., state's police power), while interweaving his broader aesthetic argument; public welfare values "are spiritual as well as physical, aesthetic as well as monetary. It is within the power of the legislature to determine that the community should be beautiful as well as healthy, spacious as well as clean." His statements employed environmental comparisons, incorporated aesthetic reasoning, and preferred openness. Many of these predilections were extraneous to the simple constitutional issues, demonstrating Douglas's strategy.[12]

Berman v. Parker revealed Douglas at work fashioning unlikely places for commentary about natural values. However, the decision contains surprising significance. Some scholars have located in *Berman* the "foundation which sustains the constitutionality of most environmental legislation" in that it extends the boundaries of the public welfare concept to include healthy, spacious living. Others have argued Douglas's exclusionary zoning decisions like *Berman* and more especially *Village of Belle Terre v. Boraas* (1974) contributed to his effort to institutionalize a wilderness ethic by ensuring that citizens might create zones of peace and quiet "where yards are wide, people few, and motor vehicles restricted" within bustling population centers. Finally, *Berman* was significant for identifying environmental values and encouraging their preservation in urban areas, something often lacking among most environmental thinkers in 1954, who often concentrated on wilderness areas far from population centers. By crafting his argument so expansively, Douglas spoke beyond narrow legal terms to broader social values.[13]

Douglas did the same by including scientific evidence in 1960, when he first commented on an unequivocally environmental case, *Murphy v. Butler*. In 1957, Long Island residents initiated a lawsuit to stop the U.S. Department of Agriculture's program of applying DDT, a dangerous pesticide, in Long Island's neighborhoods to eradicate Dutch elm disease and reduce the mosquito population. Making its way through the courts, the suit reached the Supreme Court in 1960. Cases brought to the Court require four votes to grant hearing to the petition, called a writ of certiorari. Lacking sufficient interest, the Court denied the writ, so the pesticide-spraying program would continue. Douglas, however, thought the issue too important to pass without notice. So in a move somewhat rare, he published a dissent to the denial of certiorari. "In my view the issues involved in this case are of such great public importance that I record my dissent to the denial of certiorari," Douglas explained. He noted how scientific experts questioned the efficacy of the spraying campaign and indicated that overapplication constituted a serious problem. Foreshadowing the arguments soon to be made famous by Rachel Carson, Douglas explained the many negative consequences of DDT. Cattle that fed on sprayed pastures produced contaminated milk containing DDT residues; fish died; spiders and other pests increased because predatory insects had been eliminated; and "children coughed from the spraying and their eyes watered." He acknowledged that expert witnesses equivocated, but the justice maintained "the questions tendered are extremely significant and justify review by this Court." Carson later quoted from Douglas's dissent in her classic book, *Silent Spring*, which largely inspired the popular environmental movement. In addition, Douglas heard supportive words from a self-professed housewife interested in "wholesome foods," and the *Saturday Review* reprinted the dissent as "Dissent in Favor of Man," suggesting broader interest from the public than on the Court. That he felt compelled to comment at all rather than just let the case die a quiet death demonstrated Douglas's concern and commitment to the cause if not to a particular legal position. Indeed, some have argued this dissent amounted simply to an editorial and marked his "first blatantly policyled [sic] opinion, demonstrating that by 1960 he had consciously decided to politick from the bench, and had decided that such activism was elemental to the role of judiciary." Besides a reflection of Douglas's increasing politicization, the experience of this case also indicates the difficulty in simply gaining hearings of issues with environmental components, especially before the legislative changes that lay in store in the 1960s and 1970s.[14]

In defining the right to wander or in expanding the notion of public welfare to include spacious and quiet yards or in urging the Court to just listen to competing scientific claims, Douglas moved where he felt compelled. He spoke in non-traditional, and sometimes hidden, ways, ways somewhat mystifying from legal precepts but fully understandable when considered from his personal experience and his desire to engage and inform the public.

Complexity in Environmental Decisions

Douglas faced other challenges, too. If few opportunities presented themselves before 1960, the issues the Court faced over natural resources later typically involved complex situations. The cases highlighted here demonstrate the competing demands Douglas tried to balance. The legal issues with which he wrestled reflected the growing intricacy of considering nature when public and private development plans competed, when interest groups challenged each other over access to scarce resources, and when legislation offered ambiguous advice. Moreover, several conflicts in the Pacific Northwest centered on various issues important to Douglas, including dam development and fishing rights. Because of his familiarity with the issues and region, Douglas predictably relied on personal experience and beliefs, as well as legal terms. The Court recognized his expertise in these cases, evidenced by his writing the majority opinions. For Douglas, at the center of each case were salmon and the effect of various activities on the species' ability to survive pressures of modern life and government's and industry's practices. He rendered somewhat unique readings of the legal and social circumstances that allowed him to promote his ultimate goal: conservation of salmon. That typical willingness to stretch limits marks these opinions as illustrative.

The first case built on a long-standing political and environmental struggle concerned with tapping the Snake River's hydroelectric power potential. In the 1940s and 1950s, the federal government wanted to build a high dam at Hells Canyon on the border between Oregon and Idaho. Instead, after much maneuvering and reconsidering, three private dams were built for Idaho Power Company. This remarkable story in which Northwesterners reversed course in their support of big dams and public power is but a backdrop to Douglas's appearance on the Snake River stage.[15] In 1960, the federal government renewed its interest in building a hydroelectric dam, this time at a place called High Mountain Sheep. Simultaneously, a consortium of four private companies also applied to build at the same location. For either the public or private venture to gain a license required the Federal Power Commission to weigh in, which it did, favoring private development. Later, Secretary of Interior Stewart Udall asked both the private and public companies to address how they planned to incorporate fish protection, and ultimately, encouraged a postponement until fishery management could be more adequately addressed. A series of hearings, rehearings, and appeals first to the FPC and then to various courts prevented dam construction from going forward. In spring of 1967, the issue went to the Supreme Court.[16]

In *Udall v. Federal Power Commission* (1967), Douglas did the unthinkable. He suggested the FPC rethink whether to build any dam at all. He acknowledged a key issue was whether the dam should generate power for a public or private company—indeed, this was the *only* issue that most observers saw. But Douglas quickly pushed further and questioned "whether *any* dam should be constructed." Secretary Udall's concern that another dam on the Columbia-Snake river system might "seriously impair" spawning grounds put the case in a different light for Douglas. Such laws as the Federal Power Act (1920), Fish and Wildlife Coordination Act (1958), and the Anadromous Fish Act (1965) all required recreation or wildlife and fish conservation be considered before authorizing hydroelectric power development. This legislative authority might have been enough, but in this 6-2 decision Douglas presented other ideas. "The ecology of a river is different from the ecology of a reservoir built behind a dam," Douglas argued, using the "ecology" for the first time in Supreme Court history and showing that scientific perspectives ought to be considered. In fact, FPC reports had acknowledged that dams and reservoirs harmed fish and wildlife. Douglas significantly elevated this observation from an unfortunate consequence to the paramount question. In addition, he predicted that hydroelectric power needs would be decreasing in the future with the imminent arrival of nuclear energy, rendering the proposed dam redundant. All of these concerns coalesced to build Douglas's case against further dams.[17]

Finally, and most importantly, Douglas turned to the question of public interest. The justice wrote at length:

> *The issues of whether deferral of construction would be more in the public interest than immediate construction and whether preservation of the reaches of the river affected would be more desirable and in the public interest than the proposed development are largely unexplored in this record. ...*
>
> *The question whether the proponents of a project "will be able to use" the power supplied is relevant to the issue of the public interest. So too is the regional need for the additional power. But the inquiry should not stop there. ... The grant of authority to the Commission to alienate federal water resources does not, of course, turn simply on whether the*

project will be beneficial to the licensee. Nor is the test solely whether the region will be able to use the additional power. The test is whether the project will be in the public interest. And that determination can be made only after an exploration of all issues relevant to the "public interest," including future power demand and supply, alternate sources of power, the public interest in preserving reaches of wild rivers and wilderness areas, the preservation of anadromous fish for commercial and recreational purposes, and the protection of wildlife.

The need to destroy the river as a waterway, the desirability of its demise, the choices available to satisfy future demands for energy—these are all relevant to a decisions ... but they were largely untouched by the Commission.

Douglas emphasized the public interest powerfully, arguing the concept must be inclusive and broadly conceived. Asking *which type* of dam to build, instead of *whether* a dam should be built, would no longer suffice. Free-flowing rivers and salmon and elk mattered, Douglas insisted, drawing on statutory requirements, contemporary data, and personal experience. In the end, the decision should not be surprising from someone who wrote several years before: "Man and his great dams have frequently done more harm than good."[18]

The impacts of Douglas's opinion in *Udall* were myriad. Technically, the Court's opinion remanded the case to the FPC to reconsider the license while focusing not on the priority of whether a private or public project should proceed but on the broader question of public interest. After nearly a decade of wrangling about the issue, however, the practical effect was to end the possibility of a dam at High Mountain Sheep. It was the first time the Court had rejected a license for a dam since the Federal Water Power Act (1920) gave the FPC that power. Furthermore, the decision marked a turning point when federal courts began asserting their interpretation of the public interest and stopped deferring to federal agencies. As such, it was, according to western legal expert Charles F. Wilkinson, "trailblazing" and "stood as a bright model of vigilant judicial review in complex natural resources litigation." Locally, too, the decision counted. As Douglas had done for other locales through other means, his opinion saved a stretch of river from being changed; for local conservationists, that was an achievement beyond their expectations. Douglas received a handwritten note from Udall, who praised the opinion as a "conservation landmark," but perhaps Douglas was more gratified by a letter from two wildlife management students from who praised him for "giving public interest in wild rivers, wilderness and wildlife a chance. We wish to say 'thank-you' and 'keep up the good work!!' "[19]

Justice William O. Douglas at work in his office at the U.S. Supreme Court

Dams were not the only threats to fish, however. If anything, the next set of cases introduced more delicate issues, as they contained elements of social justice along with salmon conservation. In the Treaty of Medicine Creek (1854) between the United States and several tribes in western Washington, including the Puyallups and Nisquallys, tribal groups retained the "right of taking fish, at all usual and accustomed grounds and stations … in common with all citizens of the Territory." In the past, the Court had routinely confirmed Indians' right to fish. Because the ecological changes since 1854 had sharply diminished anadromous fish runs, states had instituted conservation measures to limit fishing. In particular, they restricted the gear used to harvest fish, banning certain fixed gear and types of nets. Concerned with salmon conservation a century later, the State of Washington enacted conservation measures, such as prohibiting set nets at river mouths off Indian reservations. These constraints curbed Indians' subsistence and commercial fishing activities under the guise of "reasonable and necessary" conservation.[20]

Puyallup Tribe v. Department of Game of Washington (1968), or *Puyallup I*, became one of Douglas's most difficult cases because it pitched against each other two causes for which he cared. Over the course of his tenure, Douglas generally supported Indian self-determination and treaty rights. But as he construed the legal question here, treaty rights and conservation of salmon clashed. So Douglas set out to balance fishing rights with conservation. The justice conceded that Indians possessed the right to fish. Searching for a way to promote conservation, however, Douglas distinguished the right to fish and the method of fishing. "[T]he manner in which the fishing may be done and its purpose ... are not mentioned in the Treaty," Douglas interpreted. "We would have quite a different case if the Treaty had preserved the right to fish at the 'usual and accustomed places' in the 'usual and accustomed' manner." The State may regulate fishing, Douglas explained, if it were concerned with the manner of fishing and if the regulations applied to Indians and non-Indians alike; however, the State could not restrict the right to fish per se. Douglas drew a fine line, but one that allowed Washington to restrict Indian fishing and in theory save salmon runs.[21]

Although the Court certainly diminished Indian sovereignty with this unanimous opinion, Douglas feared a potential extinction of anadromous fish in the Puyallup and Nisqually rivers. Given the long-standing support the Supreme Court had given to treaty rights, the tribes earlier in the suit had stipulated that Indian fishers

> had fished contrary to state fishing conservation laws and regulations since 1960; that "[i]f permitted to continue, the [tribe's] commercial fishery would virtually exterminate the salmon and steelhead fish runs of the Nisqually River"; and that "it is necessary for proper conservation of the salmon and steelhead fish runs of the Nisqually River ... that the [state agencies] enforce state fishery conservation laws and regulations to the fishing activities of the defendants at their usual and accustomed grounds.

Douglas could not abide a future in which there might not be any salmon or steelhead runs. And although he despaired about denying Indians their fishing rights, he believed the end of salmon and steelhead would harm them as much as anyone. Douglas felt he had to attempt this precarious social, environmental, and legal balancing act.[22]

The opinion in *Puyallup I* sparked subsequent debates and lawsuits. When *Washington Game Department v. Puyallup Tribe,* or *Puyallup II,* reached the Court in 1973, the question centered on whether the state's prohibition on net fishing for steelhead was a necessary conservation measure. This practice closed the Puyallup River to commercial fishing by Indians but opened it to sport anglers almost all of whom were not Indians. Again writing the Court's decision, Douglas identified the discriminatory effect of Washington's policies. He demanded the state institute policies that "fairly apportioned" the steelhead catch "between Indian net fishing and non-Indian sports fishing." The decision thus made Indians partners in the river fishery again with the treaty rights somewhat restored. As Douglas explained, "The aim is to accommodate the rights of Indians under the

Treaty and the rights of other people." However, he was quick to add that such rights were not absolute:

> We do not imply that these fishing rights persist down to the very last steelhead in the river. Rights can be controlled by the need to conserve a species; and the time may come when the life of a steelhead is so precarious in a particular stream that all fishing should be banned until the species regains assurance of survival. The police power of the State is adequate to prevent the steelhead from following the fate of the passenger pigeon; and the Treaty does not give the Indians a federal right to pursue the last living steelhead until it enters their nets.

This statement read like a typical Douglas opinion, balancing complexity and values—legal and personal. He salvaged some rights for Indian fishers but kept the conservation of a species as his overriding priority. He no doubt saw protecting species for future generations of Indians and non-Indians as the more pressing priority.[23]

Puyallup I and *II* and the *Udall* case show Douglas wrestling with a multitude of competing issues—public versus private power, social justice versus species viability, legal precedence versus exploring new ground. The type of review he gave these issues stemmed fundamentally, though, from his personal experience on western rivers and with salmon and steelhead. Indeed, it is difficult to imagine any of his brethren on the Court being able to fashion such opinions. They may have analyzed the legal precedents with equal skill and reached similar conclusions, but they would not have expressed the opinion as Douglas did. Having floated and fished Northwestern rivers, Douglas valued free-flowing rivers teeming with fish. His fears—of more dams and of the possibility of extinction by overfishing—guided his writing. By the late 1960s and early 1970s, as these opinions intimate, Douglas had greater opportunities to draw on that personal experience.

National Environmental Policy Act Dissents

Environmentalists celebrated the zenith of their popular and legislative success in 1970 when President Richard Nixon signed the National Environmental Policy Act (NEPA) on January 1, and later the first Earth Day was celebrated. NEPA codified important environmental values and required significantly more attention to environmental conditions in federal projects. The act's purpose was laudable and broad: "To declare a national policy which will encourage productive and enjoyable harmony between man and his environment; to promote efforts which will prevent or eliminate damage to the environment and biosphere and stimulate the health and welfare of man; to enrich the understanding of the ecological systems and natural resources important to the Nation; and to establish a Council on Environmental Quality." Such a wide-ranging and potentially revolutionary law suggests the extent to which environmental values like those Douglas had long promoted finally permeated American society and politics. For instance, the law required that during the decision-making process federal agencies must consider "environmental amenities and values," enumerate ecological impacts of the proposed actions, develop alternative plans, and open planning to public hearings. NEPA reflected a growing consensus in the United States and among politicians that legal means were necessary to remedy environmental problems. Adroit politicians like President Richard Nixon played to this consensus in an effort to attract moderate and younger voters. Arguably, Nixon and other supporters of NEPA failed to anticipate fully how fully the law would change the political and natural landscape.[24]

Douglas, however, recognized NEPA's power immediately.[25] After all, he had spent a considerable part of the 1960s outlining legislative reforms such as those that NEPA embodied. Most notably, to advance environmental protection and challenge various development projects, advocates used the portion of NEPA that required "a detailed statement" on the environmental impact of proposed federal projects. Environmental impact statements (EIS) compelled federal agencies to assess "adverse environmental effects" and propose less deleterious alternatives. Since NEPA compelled agencies to disclose the EIS to the public for a period of comment and discussion, it represented to Douglas a victory for democracy and open decision making. Ideally, the EIS and public comment period would reveal ecologically damaging proposals and challenge agencies' status quo, consequences Douglas favored, even though the law did not mandate that federal agencies follow the alternative with the minimum environmental impact.[26] These documents became part of the public record to be read, debated, and challenged by citizens especially in the form of lawsuits. Thus, the requirement brought the public, especially environmental organizations, into the decision-making process to a degree never before seen. Douglas, of course, had called for such hearings for years. Now that such measures enjoyed legal mandate, only a matter of time remained until NEPA would reach the Supreme Court. More than any of the brethren, Douglas recognized NEPA's importance and enormous potential, and it provided him a chance in his final Court years to plead his conservationism with new federal authority in his legal arsenal.

The first possible test appeared at the Court in late 1970, but there were insufficient votes to grant a hearing. As in *Murphy v. Butler*, Douglas recorded his dissent to the denial of certiorari in *San Antonio Conservation Society v. Texas Highway Department* (1970), a dissent joined by Justices Hugo Black and William Brennan. Under the Federal Highway Act, the Texas Highway Department was preparing to build ten miles of highway through a park in the Brackenridge Basin-Olmos Basin at the headwaters of the San Antonio River. No one produced an impact statement for this project for which the federal government provided 50 percent of the funds. NEPA insisted on an EIS for such a project, and Douglas complained, "The Court does not tell us why none be made." Such noncompliance boded poorly for the environment and the future of NEPA.[27]

Douglas readily grasped this case's importance for precedence, declaring he did not "think we will have a more important case this Term." Moreover, citing the legislative history of NEPA extensively, Douglas demonstrated a sharp sense of NEPA's power less than a year after the president had signed it. Rather than remaining focused on spectacular wilderness areas, NEPA incorporated broader environmental concerns, including the more mundane urban parks—"the breathing space of urban centers," as Douglas characterized them. Additionally, in the congressional debates, Douglas pointed out, members of Congress had specifically cited highways as causing erosion and pollution. Through NEPA, Douglas claimed, "Congress has resolved that it will not allow federal agencies nor federal funds to be used in a predatory manner so far as the environment is concerned. ... Congress has said that *ecology has become paramount* and that nothing must be done by federal agencies which does ecological harm when there are alternative, albeit more expensive, ways of achieving the result." In fact, Congress had not elevated ecological standards quite as high as Douglas suggested; NEPA did not compel projects to follow the least harmful path. Yet, NEPA did force the consideration of environmental factors, something clearly ignored in this instance. Douglas openly vented his frustration that he now had access to forceful environmental legislation but could not convince the Court to test its power and enforce its provisions.[28]

Even when appropriate federal agencies compiled an EIS, though, Douglas could object. In 1971, the Atomic Energy Commission (AEC) prepared for an underground nuclear test explosion, called Project Cannikin, on Amchitka, an island in Alaska's Aleutian chain. The Committee for Nuclear Responsibility sought an injunction to prevent the nuclear test, but the Court denied it. Douglas predictably dissented, concerned about "some apparently obvious defects in AEC's Impact Statement." Douglas accused the AEC of deliberately distorting or ignoring opposing views of the possible danger of Project Cannikin inducing an earthquake, tsunami, or longer-term ecological effects from radioactive water. In a lengthy appendix to his dissent, Douglas repeatedly quoted Russell Train, head of the Council on Environmental Quality, who cast some doubt on the safety of this proposed nuclear test, including the possibility that "radioactive water of concentrations perhaps 100,000 times permitted maximums will reach the sea near Amchitka" within a decade of the detonation. Douglas favored the CEQ as a more disinterested executive agency than the AEC. Indeed, he had long argued in favor of an executive power to coordinate environmental policies within the federal government and offer sound ecological advice to the president, precisely the function NEPA had designed for the CEQ. Here was a prime example why such a disinterested council was necessary: to combat a disingenuous, faulty EIS prepared by the AEC. The AEC knew of the scientific objections raised by the CEQ but "simply ignored" or deliberately distorted those opposing views.[29]

Douglas heard from the public on this case before and after his opinion, suggesting its importance to a broad constituency. A lieutenant colonel in the Air Force sent Douglas a telegram urging him to stop this nuclear test as unconstitutional and as likely to produce earthquakes, one of the ecological concerns raised by the CEQ and the U.S. Geological Survey that Douglas focused on in his dissent. After his dissent, Douglas read another telegram that probably gratified him while reflecting the increasingly pessimistic times to some: "IN AN AGE OF DECREASING RESPONSIVENESS AND MORAL RESPONSIBILITY BY GOVERNMENT THANK YOU FOR TRYING." Of course, not all correspondents supported Douglas's positions and their messages symbolized the frustration many conservatives felt toward the justice. One castigated Douglas for misunderstanding the AEC and complained that his decisions were routinely "jackpot, political, and spiteful." Moreover, the writer argued, "This incident should be sufficient to request a [sic] impeachment by Congress on the grounds of inefficiency in aiding the defence [sic] of our nation. And there are many more incidents of equal importance that could be included, in other cases. Lyndon Johnson and Earl Warren are no longer around, so you can be free in throwing your weight around in various ways." That Douglas elicited such emotional responses exposed the chords—positive and negative—he struck with a public facing important environmental and social questions. And it demonstrated that his opinion did reach the public. However, following nearly two years on the books, the Court had failed to rigorously enforce NEPA according to Douglas's expectations and desires.[30]

Reaching the full promise of NEPA proved elusive, and Douglas feared the Court's inaction was gutting the act. A series of cases consolidated in *Scenic Hudson Preservation Conference v. Federal Power Commission*

(1972) found Douglas more pessimistic. The Federal Power Commission had granted Consolidated Edison Company a license to construct a storage power project at Storm King Mountain on New York's Hudson River. Local and national conservation groups had opposed this project for nearly a decade through a series of legal maneuvers. Yet again in a dissent to the denial of certiorari and yet again concerning whether a federal agency had satisfied NEPA's impact statement requirement, Douglas excoriated the FPC for accepting Con Ed's license despite a limited environmental assessment. Besides considering the EIS "too imprecise," the justice objected to the FPC's contention that environmental groups bore the burden of proof of establishing a project's ecological harm. The Commission argued that NEPA only required an EIS when citizens brought environmental conditions to an agency's attention. Such an interpretation clearly contradicted NEPA's statutory requirements. In Douglas's view, the FPC's approach betrayed a fundamental and perhaps calculated misunderstanding of the law.[31]

Moreover, neither Con Ed nor the FPC considered alternatives. The Commission merely affirmed that the proposal to build the storage power project constituted the only practical option. For Douglas, such a conclusion simply confirmed the bureaucracy's preference without considering less ecologically injurious options, including no project at all—a suggestion made by a Court of Appeals judge. Determining alternatives, after all, was one of NEPA's touchstones. To Douglas, NEPA ought to lay bare for Congress, the CEQ, and the public the various alternatives along with the reasons the federal agency had chosen the option it preferred. So NEPA's purpose "is not served where all that is basically told is that the preferred alternative is cheaper and more reliable, though involving adverse implications for the surrounding ecology." With anemic environmental disclosures like this one, Douglas pointed out, NEPA will utterly fail: "If this kind of impact statement is tolerated, then the mandate of NEPA becomes only a ritual and like the peppercorn a mere symbol that has no vital meaning. The decision below is, in other words, the beginning of the demise of the mandate of NEPA." Douglas feared NEPA had already become merely symbolic, just thirty months after President Nixon had signed the law. He was losing hope that in NEPA lay some legislative salvation to ecological problems through democratic means. Accordingly, he escalated his dire rhetoric. If the Court would not compel compliance, who would?[32]

Unfortunately, things got worse. During the following term, Douglas presented his most telling commentary on NEPA thus far and revealed in most personal terms what he believed was at stake. The Federal Aviation Agency, the State of Hawaii, and Ralph M. Parsons Company were jointly constructing the Reef Runway Project at Honolulu International Airport. The Parsons Company, which helped prepare the EIS, stood to gain millions of dollars as a consultant to the project if it was approved. The Court allowed the project to go forward following an injunction Douglas granted. In *Life of the Land v. Brinegar* (1973), Douglas dissented from his colleagues' action. He believed that such a financial reward jeopardized the objectivity of the EIS: "It seems to me a total frustration of the entire purpose of NEPA to entrust evaluation of the environmental factors to a firm with a multimillion dollar stake in the approval of this project. NEPA embodies the belated national recognition that we have been 'brought to the brink' by myopic pursuit of technological progress and by a decision-making mechanism resting largely on the advice of vested interest groups." Sounding his standard argument against the Establishment, Douglas implied that "those with enough money" could elude governmental regulations, evidenced by the inadvisable oil drilling near Santa Barbara, the NEPA-exempted trans-Alaska pipeline, and Detroit's assault on the atmosphere—all very recent public environmental controversies. Douglas indicted the "manufacturing-industrial complex" that had destroyed so many American environmental resources and created "technological sewers." He even reproached commercial recreational interests that overdeveloped wilderness areas. The economic assault on nature had simply gone too far.[33]

Douglas's language was not that of a dispassionate observer or legal scholar searching for proper precedents. Indeed, his dissent became as impassioned as anything he had ever written when he connected his biggest love (i.e., nature) to his biggest hate (i.e., the Establishment) to his preferred solution (i.e., the open democratic process):

NEPA was designed to correct in part the information void underlying our national decision-making mechanism. Congress knew what happens when we heed the counsel only of those who measure national advancement by GNP and the Dow Jones industrial average. Congress knew that we can trust them to supply us with voluminous economic data, but it also knew that we cannot trust them to supply us with an improved quality of life. They are not advocates of the interests of mountains, forest, streams, rivers, oceans, and coral beds, or of the wildlife that inhabit them or the people who enjoy them. They are not useful when it comes to appraising the values of an unspoiled meadow or glacier or reef, for they think only in terms of dollars. They lack the sensitivity to be entrusted with evaluating what effect dredging will have on our estuaries. These estuaries are essential in part of the life cycle of two-thirds of the marine life. Dredging makes these estuaries biological deserts for years to come. Congress knew that the final say on these environmental matters should not be under the direct or indirect control of those who plan to make millions out of their destruction.

The people have long heard and too long heeded the advice of those with a monetary stake.

A more eloquent statement of NEPA's purpose is difficult to find. This plea could have been made on behalf of any number of places Douglas knew or controversies about which he cared. It represented a near-total capitulation of legal principles. Douglas simply had tired of corporations, bureaucracies, and courts disregarding ecology, and he lashed out. He relied on general principles consistent with his worldview and punctuated his statement with raw emotion. Although he never was strict in following the niceties of drafting legal opinions, by this time—nearly three years after NEPA's passage—he seemed to surrender all pretense. Moreover, his audience clearly went beyond his Court colleagues and the principals involved in the case; Douglas's voice sounded an alarm for all. As such, *Life of the Land v. Brinegar* perhaps best symbolized his values, frustrations, and dashed hopes.[34]

None of these dissents matter greatly to the canons of environmental or constitutional law. They are revealing nevertheless. They say much about Douglas's personality and the politics of the day. These dissents reveal some of Douglas's most developed environmental sensibilities and reflect his deep experience with environmental issues. His dissents read and should be considered as personal testimonies to various environmental threats, including roads, pollution, and garbage. Such personal perspectives are unusual in Supreme Court opinions. According to one legal scholar, Douglas used "legal opinions as sounding boards for his personal beliefs, rather than using his opinions to shape the law incrementally." Douglas's approach, then, failed the usual tests for the worth of an opinion and perhaps is evidence of his increasing impatience with the legal and political systems. His writings about NEPA evince this tendency well, since many of these dissents represent cases the full Court never heard. Moreover, the scholar maintained that Douglas viewed the judiciary as a necessary agent in the administrative state to balance competing interests and to represent the public interest. Douglas recognized NEPA's promise, focusing as much on its "inspirational goals" as its "action-forcing provision[s]."[35] In this sense, Douglas's NEPA dissents reveal his environmental values and his belief that law could be used to protect such ideals through the proper and faithful use of legal means. Perhaps nowhere is this sympathy to the public interest and the environment as clear as in *Life of the Land v. Brinegar*. And nowhere is his dismay at the Court's inaction so palpable.

In the midst of these NEPA decisions Douglas published *The Three Hundred Year War: A Chronicle of Ecological Disaster*, a largely pessimistic compendium of worldwide environmental problems. In it, he castigated federal agencies like the Tennessee Valley Authority and the Soil Conservation Service for their routine resistance and downright dishonesty. Some administrators, he claimed, withheld relevant scientific documents that showed harmful effects of projects. Furthermore, Douglas charged agencies with playing "hide-and-seek with these NEPA requirements so that there will be a better chance of having their own way." Lamentably, economic cost-benefit analyses superseded almost all else in agencies' decision making. Douglas acknowledged that economic considerations mattered, but "the web of life that is jeopardized in most schemes requires vastly different considerations." Remarkably, despite repeated frustrations on the bench and an increasingly cynical attitude, Douglas managed to grasp some hope and maintain slight faith in NEPA. Even though agencies might have been trying to circumvent NEPA with poorly executed EIS, Douglas hoped "the long-suppressed naturalist or biologist in the bureau ... [would] at last be allowed to educate his superiors, his Congressman and Senator, and the public at large," just as Douglas had been attempting. Just maybe, NEPA could surmount the resistance federal bureaucracies embodied.[36]

At the end of his judicial career, NEPA had seemingly offered Douglas a way to fully enshrine environmental protection into legal precedent. Although the Court failed to meet Douglas's best hopes, he was not done. Douglas had one final approach to transform American law into a tool to protect nature, one last lesson to teach the public.

Sierra Club v. Morton and Nature's Rights

Undoubtedly, Douglas's most famous environmental opinion came in *Sierra Club v. Morton* (1972). Unlike his writing in the NEPA decisions, Douglas was not particularly pessimistic in *Sierra Club*. Still, he was consistent, with his penchant for drawing deeply on his own experience and eschewing formal legal conventions. He wrote a dissent that proposed pushing environmental law in new directions. *Sierra Club* marked Douglas's furthest extension of environmental rights. And although as a dissent it did not constitute legal precedence, the opinion galvanized conservationists and has stood ever since as a testament to Douglas's ability and willingness to tap into changing ideas and times and present his opinion in a public form.

This case presented a number of important environmental issues and became a test case for the Sierra Club. In 1965, the Forest Service solicited the bids for recreation development plans in the Mineral King Valley of the Sequoia National Forest. In 1969, the agency accepted Walt Disney Enterprise's $35 million plan that included hotels, pools, ski trails and lifts, parking lots, and other amenities to serve fourteen thousand daily visitors. In a cooperative spirit, the State of California agreed to build a twenty-mile-long highway through the Sequoia National Park to reach the resort site and install the necessary high-voltage power lines. Clearly, this was a significant venture. The Sierra Club protested the initial call for development but was refused a public hearing. When the club filed suit in 1969, it touched off a long legal debate focusing on the issue of standing. Traditionally, litigants must prove they have suffered some injury in fact to be able to sue. And the Sierra Club itself had suffered no injury. Some in the organization *felt* injured because they found the potential development harmed their environmental and aesthetic sensibilities. The real injury, the Sierra Club believed, and hoped the courts would agree, was felt by the valley itself. Would the Supreme Court agree? Would it find the Sierra Club possessed standing to sue? Would it find Mineral King Valley had the standing to sue through human guardians?[37]

The Court, predictably, was divided. A plurality determined that the Sierra Club did not suffer any injury because it had not explained how individual club members had been harmed. The opinion signaled that although aesthetic, recreation, or environmental harms were legitimate injuries, individuals still must feel that harm in a demonstrable way. (Subsequently, the Sierra Club drafted a new complaint alleging individual harm and successfully sued.)[38]

Justices Harry Blackmun, William Brennan, and Douglas all filed separate dissents. Blackmun wrote quite an impassioned dissent. "The Court's opinion is a practical one espousing and adhering to traditional notions of standing," he began. "If this were an ordinary case, I would join the opinion and the Court's judgment and be quite content." However, Blackmun pointed out that *Sierra Club v. Morton* was something extraordinary, raising questions that were becoming increasingly important. He asked rhetorically, "Must our law be so rigid and our procedural concepts so inflexible that we render ourselves helpless when the existing methods and the traditional concepts do not quite fit and do not prove to be entirely adequate for new issues?" Blackmun presented two alternatives. He wanted the Sierra Club to slightly amend its suit to meet the Court's standing threshold. (It did.) Or Blackmun suggested an expansive reading of standing that recognized that the Sierra Club's legitimate history of conservation granted them standing. In any event, the result from the Court's decision was undesirable, Blackmun asserted. Sounding like Douglas, he explained that the decision meant the construction of an overpriced and overbudgeted resort complex and the defacement of Mineral King Valley.[39]

Douglas agreed, although he went further in a wide-ranging dissent. Typically, justices do not recommend new legislation, but Douglas began by arguing that a federal rule ought to exist allowing "environmental issues to be litigated before federal agencies or federal courts in the name of the inanimate object about to be despoiled, defaced, or invaded by roads and bulldozers and where injury is the subject of public outrage." The case then, he explained, would properly be *Mineral King v. Morton*. Giving inanimate objects rights was surely not so revolutionary. After all, as Douglas pointed out, ships and corporations had legal personalities in the eyes of the law. "So it should be as respects valleys, alpine meadows, rivers, lakes, estuaries, beaches, ridges, groves of trees, swampland, or even air that feels the destructive pressures of modern technology and modern life," Douglas contended.[40]

But how would that work? There certainly were logistical questions about allowing valleys, rivers, and other natural objects standing, but Douglas dismissed these issues as easily surmountable. People who know and have "a meaningful relation" to the natural system, "[t]hose who hike it, fish it, hunt it, camp in it, frequent it, or visit it merely to sit in solitude are legitimate spokesmen for it, whether they may be few or many," he wrote. "Those who have that intimate relation with the inanimate object about to be injured, polluted, or otherwise despoiled are its legitimate spokesmen." If such advocates were empowered, "[t]he voice of the inanimate object ... should not be stilled." We must allow this "before these priceless bits of Americana (such as a valley, an alpine meadow, a river, or a lake) are forever lost or are so transformed as to be reduced to the eventual rubble of our urban environment, the voice of the existing beneficiaries of these environmental wonders should be heard." Cognizant of environmental carpet-bagging, Douglas thought it important that only those with strong connection to places serve as the legal representatives. But putting the suit in the natural system's own name would work best:

> *Then there will be assurances that all of the forms of life which it [the natural system] represents will stand before the court—the pileated woodpecker as well as the coyote and bear, the lemmings as well as the trout in the streams. Those inarticulate members of the ecological group cannot speak. But those people who have so frequented the place as to know its values and wonders will be able to speak for the entire ecological community.*

By framing the issue this way, Douglas moved the discussion further than his colleagues and put nature firmly at the center, something the other justices were either unwilling to do or unable to do as effectively with Douglas's moral authority.[41]

Douglas had help in formulating this idea. He clearly was building on Aldo Leopold's notion of the land ethic, articulated a quarter-century earlier. More recently, Christopher D. Stone, a law professor at the University of Southern California with a background in philosophy, published an article the same spring in the *Southern California Law Review*, entitled "Should Trees Have Standing?: Toward Legal Rights for Natural Objects." In this influential article, Stone, who once clerked at the Supreme Court, reminded readers that children, African Americans, and many others had been historically granted no rights of standing by society only to have that position remedied later. Now seemed the perfect time to extend rights to nature.[42]

Indeed, Douglas cited Stone's article in his opening paragraph and proceeded to draw on a variety of other sources for inspiration, marking this opinion as a particularly strong example of his realist approach. He cited the typical relevant case law, federal statutes, and law review articles. However, he also included articles from *Harper's* and the *New York Times Magazine*, Ralph Nader Study Group reports, books on conservation history, and forestry and environmental journals. These footnotes, in fact, offered a pointed critique of federal land management with the Forest Service receiving particular scorn for shirking its true multiple-use mandate for balanced management in favor of a policy of clear-cutting that favored lumber businesses. Douglas drew from such a wide array of contemporary and interdisciplinary sources much more readily than his colleagues, marking him still a realist long after the movement had lost its vigor. On the other hand, had he been truly interested in only the *function* of the law, as realists were apt to be, Douglas would have likely have agreed with Blackmun's second alternative, to grant the Sierra Club de facto standing and been done with it. That he did not illustrated his desire to push the law into philosophically new directions, his need to express what he believed was at stake, and his commitment to presenting ideas to the public. Matching the passion of his anti-Establishment fervor in *Life of the Land v. Brinegar*, Douglas waxed poetic about nature in *Sierra Club v. Morton*: "The river … is the living symbol of all the life it sustains or nourishes—fish, aquatic insects, water ouzels, otter, fisher, deer, elk, bear, and all other animals, including man, who are dependent on it or who enjoy it for its sight, its sound, or its life. The river as plaintiff speaks for the ecological unit of life that is part of it." No other justice could have written this.[43]

Douglas's dissent made waves on and off the Court, when he delivered it and since. The dissent inspired Blackmun. In his own dissent, Blackmun called Douglas's an "eloquent opinion," and he requested Douglas read it from the bench. Furthermore, although he substantially agreed with Douglas, Blackmun wrote his own dissenting opinion in part because he thought Douglas's eloquent statement was too personal for him to join. Off the Court, the Wilderness Society published the dissent in its magazine, *Living Wilderness*, calling it a "stirring dissent … [that] we regard as important judicial history." *The North American Review* also published it under the title "Nature's Constitutional Rights" with introductory remarks that claimed Douglas's dissent constituted "a major advance in American jurisprudence and perhaps a turning point in our inherited traditions of man-nature relationships." Not all rejoiced, though, as a worried attorney critiqued in caustic verse:

> *If Justice Douglas has his way—*
> *O come not that dreadful day—*
> *We'll be sued by lakes and hills*
> *Seeking a redress of ills.*
> *Great mountain peaks of name prestigious*
> *Will suddenly become litigious.*
> *Our brooks will babble in the courts,*
> *Seeking damages for torts.*
> *…*
> *If secretaries fail to heed*
> *Demands of clubs asserting need*
> *To save the world from degradation,*
> *Let there be no deprivation*
> *We'll grant the right to litigate*
> *To objects quite inanimate.*
> *The stones against them will cry out*
> *And get a judgment without doubt.*
> *If courts below should tend to tarry*
> *We'll slap them down on certiorari*
> *'Til the day when every towering peak*
> *Gets its First Amendment right to speak,*
> *And secretaries dare not move*
> *Lest some boulder disapprove.*
> *Let Nature hold unfetterd [sic] sway*
> *O'er mere Man who's made of clay.*

"Yours is the Earth," the poet says,
"and everything that's in't."
But if you get a use permit,
Bill Douglas will dissent.

Despite such acerbic responses at the time, scholars since have weighed in and found Douglas's dissent worthy. One scholar has rightfully called it "more famous than the majority opinion" and argued that the nation came "tantalizingly close" to reaching a cooperative land ethic based on Aldo Leopold's ideas, a moral position with which Douglas concluded his dissent. Another argued that Douglas's dissent, along with Stone's article, "located the conceptual door to the rights of nature." For his own part, Stone stated that with his dissent in *Sierra Club v. Morton*, Douglas "instated himself as the leading judicial champion of the environment."[44] Undoubtedly, he is correct.

Conclusion

That such accolades could be given to a dissent producing virtually no value as precedent reveals the ambiguity of judging Douglas as an environmental justice. He could write powerful statements about nature's rights or lambaste the shoddy fulfillment of EIS requirements or educate the public about the dangers of DDT. But rarely did he transform the law or convince a majority of his colleagues to take sufficient heed when nature was at stake. A more collegial justice may well have been able to persuade the Court more often, but the courage of his convictions regarding nature was too strong to compromise. And although it is easy to judge him harshly as a justice for not fashioning more erudite opinions of long-lasting effect, to do so is to misunderstand Douglas's way of thinking and writing about the law. Like a good legal realist, Douglas drew from a wide body of scholarship and experiences. Aldo Leopold found his way into Supreme Court opinions, and Henry David Thoreau's rambling ways made an appearance. Such were not the typical supporting evidence for most justices. Moreover, when *The Living Wilderness* and *The North American Review* reprinted his *Sierra Club* dissent, they demonstrated what Douglas had long believed—that his role, even as a cloistered justice, was to engage the public, educate them about the law's function, and inspire them to think broadly about social changes. In this, Douglas succeeded.

CONCLUSION

Transitions and Legacies

Many people assume that a Supreme Court Justice should be remote and aloof from life and should play no part even in community affairs. But if Justices are to enjoy First Amendment rights, they should not be relegated to the promotion of innocuous ideas.

William O. Douglas, *Go East, Young Man: The Early Years: The Autobiography of William O. Douglas,* (1974)[1]

As Justice William O. Douglas's public career wound down, he became more outspoken. His *Sierra Club* dissent showed as much. His publications also evidenced his increased radicalism peppered with his mounting impatience. Douglas reflected important changes in the conservation movement. By 1970, important legislation had been passed and perhaps twenty million Americans participated in the first Earth Day. These achievements suggested the widespread acceptance and popularity of many environmental values. This period was a critical transition point, though, as the movement—now known more as environmentalism than conservation—grew and diversified its ideas and interests. Inevitably, the movement appeared less consensual and divisions appeared with some focusing more on wilderness or urban issues, population or technology problems, local or global scales, social or biological emphases, and radical or mainstream solutions. Douglas stood in the midst of this swirling ferment.[2]

After publishing some portions of the manuscript in *Playboy,* Douglas produced a radical statement in his 1970 *Points of Rebellion.* The slim tract was meant to describe—indeed, to celebrate—dissent and explain why the nation had experienced so much of it over the previous few years. Passages seemed to suggest a revolution, potentially violent, was coming against the Establishment. A harsh indictment of American society, *Points of Rebellion* emphasized a variety of environmental themes. Indeed, Douglas saw environmental activism as another symptom of broad disaffection against Establishment values akin to civil rights protests and campus challenges over free speech. He listed ecological catastrophes: "Everyone knows—including the youthful dissenters—that Lake Erie is now only a tub filled with stinking sewage and wastes." And, "Pesticides have killed millions of birds, putting some of them in line for extinction." Still again, "Hundreds of trout streams have been destroyed by highway engineers and their faulty plans." Such problems naturally led to protest, Douglas explained: "Youthful dissenters are not experts in these matters. But when they see all the wonders of nature being ruined they ask, 'What natural law gives the Establishment the right to ruin the rivers, the lakes, the ocean, the beaches, and even the air?'" His seeming understanding of youthful protest made him, as one scholar noted, the only person over thirty the protesters trusted. Although similar to earlier Douglas comments, these held a sharper edge.[3]

Points of Rebellion built on a strong foundation and went in somewhat new directions. Douglas pointed out that the poor often suffered the most. He referred to West Virginia coal-mining communities as colonies of the Establishment, colonies that devastated workers' health and the landscape. He also pointed to the "technology revolution in agriculture" that displaced rural residents into urban slums. The justice furnished examples of highways being relocated through African-American neighborhoods where protests would not be heard. "The values at stake," Douglas asserted, "are both aesthetic and spiritual, social and economic; and they bear heavily on human dignity and responsibility." Like the movement as a whole, Douglas pushed toward a greater recognition of social inequities tied up with environmental problems. Such were many of the newer and angrier concerns as the 1970s developed.[4]

Two years after he published *Points of Rebellion*, Douglas produced his last environmental book. *The Three Hundred Year War: A Chronicle of Ecological Disaster* presented a compendium of natural catastrophes. Various chapters on radiation, pesticides, garbage, water, and more included a wide array of statistics all pointing to a devastated natural world and corrupted economic and political system. Again, Douglas underscored the class- and race-based correlation of living in polluted environments. Reflecting on this growing problem, he wrote, "When we speak of the survival of man and his habitat, we must think not only about wilderness areas, pure air and water, free-flowing rivers, abundant wildlife, and the like but also of ghettos, poverty, unemployment and the large bloc of people who suffer from pollution and its related ills and who are not beneficiaries of the affluence that produced it." This broadening of concerns represented a belated recognition of what came to be known as environmental racism, an issue increasingly prevalent among the host of problems environmentalism addressed in the next two decades. A great deal of Douglas's early writing and activism focused on wildland protection, but moving into the 1970s, he was gradually more sensitive to factors that anticipated the growth of the environmental justice movement. His references to the C&O Canal as the "Poor People's Park" were an earlier manifestation of this vision.[5]

For Douglas, the connection between social and ecological ills stemmed from a failure to act against divisive and destructive Establishment forces. Thus, he urged action. On the one hand, Douglas focused on government programs. For instance, he urged the Environmental Protection Agency and the Department of Labor to create jobs and retrain workers to help mitigate layoffs related to pollution-control measures. On the other hand, he encouraged public activism. "Civic action by ecologists and workers alike," he claimed, "can sort out the bugaboos from the serious threats" to jobs. Indeed, how to control pollution and create healthy work and living environments "is the stuff out of which great public debates will be generated." By stressing *public* debate, Douglas remained consistent with so much of his activism and political philosophy, and he acknowledged his implicit faith that Americans would choose less deleterious options regarding the environment.[6]

This faith was strong. In *The Three Hundred Year War*, the justice explained, "I have a deep faith that our people will not want to destroy the great American outdoors—an important segment of our spiritual heritage and the greatest bit of outdoors in the whole wide world." The American public would decide in nature's favor, Douglas believed, if they were "informed ... [and] freed from the powerful influence of the present public relations approach to conservation." Douglas had spent two decades trying to ensure an informed public did understand the real issues of conservation. Whether he recognized it or not, the role of public intellectual for conservation was becoming harder. However admirable his faith, the *public* nature of the debate threatened to take the message into diffused directions. As the movement transitioned to more diverse constituencies and issues, environmentalism's public widened. Speaking coherently to that public became more difficult, as the public itself and its interest in the environment became more varied.[7]

Ultimately, this new trend indicated a difficulty in focusing on the public, as Douglas did, and a question about democracy. Along with others, Douglas placed tremendous trust in Americans' willingness to challenge environmental ills, provided they possessed the necessary information.[8] If the public knew about threats to wilderness, consequences of pollution, or failures of environmental agencies, then surely they would protest and demand change. This confidence in the public was often well placed, as Americans often stood up to polluters and ecological irresponsibility. However, at other times, a majority favored an action that conservationists might deem hazardous or simply immoral. So, while Douglas might urge public hearings, those hearings might reveal that the public wanted the snail darter exterminated, a timber sale held, or a wild area opened to mining. Such a scenario, then, required figures like Douglas to educate the public about conservation and to persuade them that environmental values provided a better alternative than extinction, clear-cutting, and open-pit mining. At times, one side prevailed; next time, the other side did. Such is the nature of democracies, and while that process may not have yielded the results Douglas always wanted, the alternative without public input clearly represented a failure of democracy.

Another challenge for public intellectuals, then, has been matching their ideas and actions to the public. At times, intellectuals of all types outpace the public's readiness for ideas. Douglas and other conservationists found ready audiences when they advocated pollution control or asserted that public hearings would promote more democratic management of natural resources, because the public generally understood the negative health consequences of pollution and valued democratic participation. However, when Douglas posited the need for "a wilderness bill of rights" or the rights of nature to have standing to sue, he exceeded much of the public's willingness to go along. The public, along with jurists at the time and since, have been unwilling to accept such ideas. And in fact, the use of the rights argument has been more effectively appropriated by property rights activists, opponents of the very sort of environmental reform that Douglas favored.[9] Thus, Douglas expressed relatively new ideas that extended environmental and legal thinking, but his inability to persuade others clearly limited the larger impact of those ideas. Nonetheless, as is often the case with judicial dissents, the future may well find the public more receptive.[10]

This also raises the question of Douglas's efficacy as a public intellectual. Although public intellectuals serve vital roles, such as coordinating various ideas and actions and reporting them to a broad public, those activities often do not enact change by themselves. So, Douglas might write popular books that crystallized the ideas of Henry David Thoreau, John Muir, Aldo Leopold, and Rachel Carson for a broad audience, but that was no guarantee that readers would accept the ideas and act on them (although they often did). He might lead a hike but the more substantive organizing and lobbying might be taken up by others like Howard Zahniser or Polly Dyer. He might sound off in a judicial dissent in ways that pleased conservationists but made no impact on the law or management of resources. Or, he might anticipate transitions in the movement and push for environmental justice in ways many mainstream politicians and activists were at the time unwilling to support. Thus, on the one hand, it might be easy to dismiss Douglas as a mere figurehead who accomplished little on his own and left the more persistent and important tasks to others. But this misses the importance of Douglas's role, a role that proved significant in both symbolic and tangible ways. Importantly, the *public* clearly associated Douglas with foresight in getting environmental ideas in the public sphere and specific changes enacted.

Douglas's accomplishments mattered. On the C&O Canal towpath, in the pages of *Ladies' Home Journal*, in judicial dissents, and in countless private letters, Douglas invited public participation in the critical questions of the day. That so many read his books and articles, joined him on hikes, wrote and spoke on their own behalf, and otherwise engaged these questions was a tribute to Douglas and his conservation work.[11] More substantively, the C&O Canal National Historical Park, dedicated to Douglas, enjoys its protected status thanks in large part to his work on its behalf for two decades. Although others certainly contributed, Douglas's work for the central Cascade Mountains undoubtedly made the William O. Douglas Wilderness Area aptly named. That no dam blocks the Snake River at High Mountain Sheep can be attributed to the justice. Other legacies are less tangible, to be sure. The wilderness bill of rights and the proposed right of nature to sue are ideas Douglas more than anyone introduced into the American environmental tradition. Perhaps most significant at the time was the simple fact that an important public figure devoted abundant time and energy to environmental issues in ways visible to a large American public. No one of Douglas's stature in public life had engaged in such concerns as early or as long, leading one observer to call him the "most prominent conservationist in public life" in the three decades after World War II.[12] Douglas helped lead the way, helped transition the movement from an obscure to a prominent issue in American life.

On New Year's Eve 1974, Douglas and his wife, Cathleen Heffernan Douglas, traveled to Nassau, Bahamas. Not long after arriving, the justice collapsed, the victim of a stroke. Although he hoped for a full recovery and returned to the Court on March 24, 1975, his "once robust body was thin and lifeless." He continued serving, but his new disabilities proved too difficult to surmount. Several awkward public appearances, including a speech to the Sierra Club and a hearing in a Yakima court, demonstrated Douglas's physical weakness and his intellectual decline. Finally and grudgingly, he resigned on November 12, 1975. His public life over, Douglas gradually disappeared into the background. He died January 19, 1980.[13]

The end of Douglas's career prompted serious reflection from others in American public life. His legacy was substantial, if one believed Congress and the media. Congress compiled and published numerous tributes by politicians, journalists, and others on the occasion of Douglas's retirement. As an individualist, a defender of the disadvantaged, and a tireless champion of the Bill of Rights, Douglas received accolades. However, to a significant degree, comments focused on his environmental record.

Among those tributes, many noted Douglas's roots and personality. The justice's own Congressional representative, Mike McCormack, explained, "Douglas grew up in the shadow of the Cascades and spent countless days hiking and climbing in them, sometimes risking his life in daring feats of rock climbing, sometimes covering incredible distances with a heavy pack, sometimes proving that he could live off the land in any weather, but in all cases, expressing his love for it."[14] At the same time, Representative Robert F. Drinan of Massachusetts noted Douglas's personal need to act: "The multifaceted nature of Justice Douglas' life illustrates his strong belief that principles of conduct ought to be implemented through concrete action. It was not enough for him to be a writer on conservation matters: William Douglas annually led a hardy band of hikers along the C. & O. Canal to demonstrate the need to preserve this historic waterway."[15] The *Washington Post* recognized that Douglas embodied a particularly strong personality associated with the country. "Justice Douglas is always so insistently himself—so intensely individualistic—that he has attracted violent detractors as well as ardent admirers in his long career," the *Post* wrote. "Physically rugged, an outdoorsman by inclination, gifted intellectually, temperamentally lonely and independent, he is as indigenously American as Uncle Sam. He loves his country passionately—its mountains and rivers and wild places if not its crowded cities—as he loves its great traditions and its ideals of personal freedom and opportunity."[16]

While those comments focused on Douglas's personality, others simply praised his general environmental work. New York Representative Benjamin S. Rosenthal claimed, "Bill Douglas ranks also as one of our foremost conservationists. His dedication to the preservation of our national heritage of pure waters and air and unspoiled vistas is matched only by his devotion to the precepts of liberty and equality."[17] According to Representative Gilbert Gude of Maryland, "The people were also the beneficiaries of Justice Douglas' love and appreciation for the environment. ... He has sought, over the years, to protect these irreplaceable resources from exploitation, so that they can be enjoyed by all people of the nation."[18] No stranger to environmental politics, Senator Edmund S. Muskie of Maine, proclaimed of Douglas, "Throughout his life, he has displayed a fervent commitment to the preservation of our environment, a commitment which reflects his own sense of oneness between man and nature."[19] Meanwhile, Representative Herman Badillo of New York saw freedom working in Douglas's many actions: "Justice Douglas has always ardently supported every attempt to preserve our free environment in its natural state. ... His judicial opinions frequently sought to protect this uniquely American treasure, to the joy and satisfaction of all succeeding generations."[20]

Badillo's comment hinted at the important ways Douglas linked his political and environmental philosophies. New York's Representative Charles B. Rangel was more explicit, stating, "His opinions and dissents written for the Court give testimony to his philosophy of individual rights—whether the rights in question belonged to blacks, women, the accused, or—in the case of environmental decisions—even to the air we breathe and the rivers that run through our land."[21] Meanwhile, the *Washington Post,* the paper in whose pages Douglas began his public conservation career, offered a strong tribute to this conjunction of interests:

> In the many tributes to Douglas after he retired from the Court this month, environmentalists have cited his crusades for the canal and other parks about as often as civil libertarians have quoted his impassioned defense of free speech. But Douglas' love for the land should not be put in separate chapters or paragraphs. The two are actually inseparable. The unifying concept is the necessity for space, a cause that Douglas has championed with equal fervor on the trail and on the Bench. ...
>
> In Douglas' view, the expanses of nature are as precious as the liberties protected by the first amendment. Therefore the claims of nature should be equally recognized in court. This reasoning seemed to lie behind Douglas' famous dissent in Sierra Club v. Morton, *also known as the Mineral King case—an opinion which many lawyers regard as quixotic, and which many environmentalists have memorized.* ...
>
> In reviewing this record, it is easy to fall back on the obvious metaphors and praise Douglas for his judicial pioneering, pathfinding, and trailblazing. The images are accurate to some extent, for Douglas has served most happily and effectively as a scout, restlessly exploring the terrain ahead of other men. Yet it is crucial to recognize that when Douglas has invited people to join him on a march, it has really been an invitation not just to visit a place, but to enter into a process—the

process of discovery and testing and affirmation that is available to free people in a spacious land.[22]

Among the most important comments, perhaps, were those that praised Douglas's prescience. Representative Don Edwards of California asserted that "[d]ecades ago his concern for the Earth and all living creatures was the forerunner of our national awareness of environmental concerns."[23] Representative Henry S. Reuss of Wisconsin stated, "Justice Douglas was also a precursor of the present concern about our environment. A rugged outdoorsman, he knew and loved the mountains of the American West. … He warned of the danger of pollution of our lakes and streams."[24] And family friend Senator Edward M. Kennedy of Massachusetts observed, "Long before it was popular and fashionable, he was a champion of the environment in his eloquent books and writings and decisions. … As much as anyone in public life, he personifies the rugged individuality that symbolized the spirit and promise of America."[25] Such comments indicated the extent to which prominent politicians viewed Douglas as a leading and early voice for the environment.

A final area of praise was directed toward specific causes and achievements Douglas's actions had facilitated. Representative Morris K. Udall of Arizona explained Douglas's role on two occasions:

> *[H]is tireless efforts have given major impetus to two of our most significant efforts to share this natural heritage with our fellow citizens and our posterity.*
>
> *As a sponsor of the Wilderness Act, I know the crucial role played by Mr. Justice Douglas in awakening the Nation to this vanishing resource. His books … helped call attention to the need for a national wilderness preservation system.*
>
> *And, within a few miles of this Chamber, there is another reminder of the energy and dedication of William O. Douglas—the Chesapeake & Ohio Canal National Historic [sic] Park. Those who recall the long battle to save this important national treasure know the pivotal importance of his untiring efforts.*[26]

Similarly, Washington's Representative Lloyd Meeds found Douglas's work closer to home important, stating, "I personally wish to thank him for the many times he aided important causes in the State, including the development of the North Cascades National Park. I am sure Justice Douglas appreciates the efforts among Washington State residents and representatives to establish another beautiful recreation area in the Cascade Range—the

A thoughtful William O. Douglas, gazing across rugged terrain in the Cascade Range

Alpine Lakes Wilderness Area."[27] Finally, Texas Representative Bob Eckhardt perfectly captured Douglas's key role in Committees of Correspondence: "Justice Douglas willingly gave effective and sage advice to the East Texas conservationists finding their way through the labyrinth of Washington, D.C., in search of Federal aid. He continues to serve in his capacity as an honorary member of the advisory board of the Big Thicket—but he is an honorary member who has voluntarily paid dues."[28] These were but some of the ways Douglas was remembered. Collectively, this public outpouring and others like it strongly indicate that Douglas's work as a public intellectual for conservation was effective. His dedication to the environment had become a principal way the public remembered and celebrated him.

🔿

As he retired, Douglas wrote a poignant letter to his colleagues on the Court. It read in part:

I am reminded of many canoe trips I have taken in my lifetime. Those who start down a water course may be strangers at the beginning but almost invariably are close friends at the end. There were strong headwinds to overcome and there were rainy as well as sun-drenched days to travel. The portages were long and many and some were very strenuous. But there were always a pleasant camp in a stand of white bark birch and inevitably there came the last campfire, the last breakfast cooked over last night's fire, and the parting was always sad.

And yet, in fact, there was no parting because each happy memory of the choice parts of the journey—and of the whole journey—was of a harmonious united effort filled with fulfilling and beautiful hours as well as dull and dreary ones. The greatest such journey I've made has been with you, my Brethren, who were strangers at the start but warm and fast friends at the end.[29]

The environment had become Douglas's way of ordering his world. His collegial good-bye, a metaphoric journey from strangeness and uncertainty to familiarity and friendship, appropriately captured his story. More than just journey through America's natural landscape, William O. Douglas helped transform it.

Notes

Introduction

1. William O. Douglas, "America's Vanishing Wilderness," *Ladies' Home Journal* 81 (July 1964), 77.
2. Douglas, "America's Vanishing Wilderness," 37-41, 77. Women's magazines and clubs had long participated in conservation, but a review of the contents of *Ladies' Home Journal* in 1964 shows that Supreme Court justices did not write articles and environmental issues did not typically appear. Kimberly A. Jarvis, "Gender and Wilderness Conservation," in *American Wilderness: A New History*, ed. Michael Lewis (New York: Oxford University Press, 2007): 149-65 offers a fine overview. The classic statement is Carolyn Merchant, "Women of the Progressive Era Conservation Movement, 1900-1916," *Environmental Review* 8 (Spring 1984): 57-85.
3. Douglas, "America's Vanishing Wilderness," 39.
4. Ibid., 40.
5. Mark Harvey, *Wilderness Forever: Howard Zahniser and the Path to the Wilderness Act* (Seattle: University of Washington Press, 2005) is the best source for the Wilderness Act. Also see Harvey, "Loving the Wild in Postwar America," in *American Wilderness*, ed. Michael Lewis, 187-203; James Morton Turner, "The Politics of Modern Wilderness," in *American Wilderness*, ed. Michael Lewis, 243-61; Michael Frome, *Battle for the Wilderness*, revised ed. (Salt Lake City: University of Utah Press, 1997); Roderick Nash, *Wilderness and the American Mind*, third ed. (New Haven, CT: Yale University Press, 1982); and Craig W. Allin, *The Politics of Wilderness Preservation* (Westport, CT: Greenwood Press, 1982). For the interwar roots of wilderness activism, see Paul S. Sutter, *Driven Wild: How the Fight Against Automobiles Launched the Modern Wilderness Movement* (Seattle: University of Washington Press, 2002).
6. A note on terminology is necessary. For the most part, I will use conservation or conservationist, not environmentalism or environmentalist, to describe Douglas's work, because most activists in Douglas's circles and of his generation still called themselves conservationists until the mid-1970s or so. While not a perfect characterization, Samuel P. Hays's distinction between conservation and environmentalism is useful. He saw conservation as primarily focused on efficient management of resources by experts, while environmentalism emphasized amenities for a better quality of life. Many of Douglas's concerns bridged this divide. See Hays, in collaboration with Barbara D. Hays, *Beauty, Health, and Permanence: Environmental Politics in the United States, 1955-1985* (New York: Cambridge University Press, 1987), 21-22.
7. Douglas, "America's Vanishing Wilderness," 77. Kevin Marsh shows local and national coordination well in *Drawing Lines in the Forest: Creating Wilderness in the Pacific Northwest* (Seattle: University of Washington Press, 2007). See also Hays, *Beauty, Health, and Permanence*; and Turner, "Politics of Modern Wilderness," for this strategy.
8. Douglas, "America's Vanishing Wilderness," 77. The best assessment of Douglas's judicial career, including his stance on minority rights is Howard Ball and Phillip J. Cooper, *Of Power and Right: Hugo Black, William O. Douglas, and America's*

Constitutional Revolution (New York: Oxford University Press, 1992); see also the essays in Stephen L. Wasby, ed., *"He Shall Not Pass This Way Again": The Legacy of Justice William O. Douglas* (Pittsburgh: University of Pittsburgh Press for the William O. Douglas Institute, 1990); and the letters in Melvin I. Urofsky, with the assistance of Philip E. Urofsky, ed., *The Douglas Letters: Selections from the Private Papers of Justice William O. Douglas* (Bethesda: Adler and Adler, 1987), esp. 148-62.

9. Stephen Fox included him with five other "free-lancers," amateurs whose careers were outside conservation but who used their prominence to expose Americans to various elements of conservation politics. Besides Douglas, Fox includes John D. Rockefeller, Bernard DeVoto, Joseph Wood Krutch, Charles Lindbergh, and Aldo Leopold. Considering Leopold an amateur in conservation makes little sense, given his decades of formal work in the Forest Service and as a professor. As the only figure within this group with a government appointment, Douglas gained a level of public standing with somewhat greater salience than the others to speak and act on these issues. Fox, *The American Conservation Movement: John Muir and His Legacy* (Madison: University of Wisconsin Press, 1981), 218-49.

10. Edward Shils, *The Intellectuals and the Powers and Other Essays* (Chicago: University of Chicago Press), 3-22; Edward W. Said, *Representations of the Intellectual: The 1993 Reith Lectures* (New York: Vintage Books, 1994), 3-23, 85-102, quotation from 11; Richard A. Posner, *Public Intellectuals: A Study of Decline* (Cambridge, MA: Harvard University Press, 2001), esp. 1-40, quotation from 35. I thank Sean Quinlan for assistance with these ideas. "Public philosopher" is Charles Reich's term, quoted in Stephen L. Wasby, "Introduction," in *"He Shall Not Pass This Way Again"*, xvi; "national teacher" is James F. Simon's from *Independent Journey: The Life of William O. Douglas* (New York: Harper and Row, 1980), ch. 25.

11. Similarly, educating the public was a key role that scientists Rachel Carson and Barry Commoner played in contemporaneous times. Rachel Carson, *Silent Spring* (Boston: Houghton Mifflin, 1962, reprint: Boston: Houghton Mifflin, 2002); Linda Lear, *Rachel Carson: Witness for Nature* (New York: Henry Holt and Company, 1997); Mark Hamilton Lytle, *The Gentle Subversive: Rachel Carson, Silent Spring, and the Rise of the Environmental Movement* (New York: Oxford University Press, 2007); and Michael Egan, *Barry Commoner and the Science of Survival: The Remaking of American Environmentalism* (Cambridge, MA: The MIT Press, 2007).

12. Political scientists have explored the opening up of the political process and greater regulation in William M. Lunch, "Science, Civil Rights and Environmental Policy: A Political Mystery in Three Acts," a paper presented to the Western Political Science Association (March 2004), copy in author's possession; Lunch, *The Nationalization of American Politics* (Berkeley: University of California Press, 1987); and George Hoberg, *Pluralism by Design: Environmental Policy and the American Regulatory State* (New York: Praeger, 1992). This emphasis on the public is not to deny Douglas's work away from the public eye, for in several of the struggles described in this book, Douglas lobbied privately with politicians and federal administrators.

13. Simon, *Independent Journey*; G. Edward White, "The Anti-Judge: William O. Douglas and the Ambiguities of Individuality," in *The American Judicial Tradition: Profiles of Leading American Judges*, expanded edition (New York: Oxford

University Press, 1988): 369-420; and Bruce Allen Murphy, *Wild Bill: The Legend and Life of William O. Douglas* (New York: Random House, 2003) all do a nice job disentangling the truths and untruths in Douglas's autobiographical writings. By far, Murphy delves most deeply into Douglas's personal shortcomings, filling *Wild Bill* with salacious details. For Douglas and his staff and colleagues, see Melvin I. Urofsky, "Getting the Job Done: William O. Douglas and Collegiality in the Supreme Court," in *"He Shall Not Pass This Way Again,"* ed. Stephen L. Wasby, 33-49; Melvin I. Urofsky, "William O. Douglas and Felix Frankfurter: Ideology and Personality on the Supreme Court," *The History Teacher* 24 (November 1990): 7-18; William O. Douglas, *The Court Years, 1939-1975: The Autobiography of William O. Douglas* (New York: Random House, 1980); and Joseph P. Lash, ed., *From the Diaries of Felix Frankfurter* (New York: W. W. Norton, 1975), esp. 309-38. Lash's chapter title for the diaries from 1947 is "Wrath against Douglas." For judicial activism, see L. A. Powe, Jr., "Justice Douglas, the First Amendment, and the Protection of Rights," in *"He Shall Not Pass This Way Again,"* ed. Stephen L. Wasby, 85-86; Dorothy J. Glancy, "Douglas's Right of Privacy: A Response to His Critics," in *"He Shall Not Pass This Way Again,"* ed. Stephen L. Wasby, 164-65; and Charles F. Wilkinson, "Justice Douglas and the Public Lands," in *"He Shall Not Pass This Way Again,"*, ed. Stephen L. Wasby, 244 .

14. Urofsky, "Douglas and Frankfurter," 17; Charles A. Reich, *The Greening of a Nation* (New York: Bantam Books, 1970); Wasby, "Introduction," xvi; and Michael Frome, *Chronicling the West: Thirty Years of Environmental Writing* (Seattle: The Mountaineers, 1996), 12. Frome dedicated his book to Douglas's memory.

15. The two main biographies of Douglas account for nearly a thousand pages of text, of which fewer than two dozen are dedicated to conservation. See Simon, *Independent Journey*; and Murphy, *Wild Bill*. The only major exception to this trend is Diana Rachel Hyman, "Defenses of Solitude: Justice Douglas, the Right to Privacy, and the Preservation of the American Wilderness," (Ph.D. Dissertation, Harvard University, 2003).

16. Criticisms of wilderness activism abound. Robert Gottlieb's redefinition of the movement is a good introduction, as well as the critical chapters in the two collections, *The Great New Wilderness Debate* and *Uncommon Ground*. See Gottlieb, *Forcing the Spring: The Transformation of the American Environmental Movement*, revised and updated (Washington, DC: Island Press, 2005); J. Baird Callicott and Michael P. Nelson, eds., *The Great New Wilderness Debate: An Expansive Collection of Writings Defining Wilderness from John Muir to Gary Snyder* (Athens: University of Georgia Press, 1998), esp. parts two (Third and Fourth World Views of the Wilderness Idea) and three (The Wilderness Idea Roundly Criticized and Defended); and William Cronon, ed., *Uncommon Ground: Toward Reinventing Nature* (New York: W. W. Norton, 1995). Also, Benjamin Johnson, "Wilderness Parks and Their Discontents," in *American Wilderness*, ed. Michael Lewis, 113-30; and Christopher Conte, "Creating Wild Places from Domesticated Landscapes: The Internationalization of the American Wilderness Concept," in *American Wilderness*, ed. Michael Lewis, 223-41. Mark Harvey nicely summarizes and responds to the charges against wilderness in *Wilderness Forever*, 248-49.

17. NIMBY stands for Not In My Back Yard.

18. Place-based approaches include Marsh, *Drawing Lines*; and Roger Kaye, *Last Great Wilderness: The Campaign to Establish the Arctic National Wildlife Refuge* (Fairbanks: University of Alaska Press, 2006). Cultural and ideological approaches include William Cronon, "The Trouble with Wilderness; or, Getting Back to the Wrong Nature," in *Uncommon Ground*, ed. William Cronon, 69-90; Nash, *Wilderness Mind*; and Sutter, *Driven Wild*. Political approaches include Allin, *Politics of Wilderness*; and Hays, *Beauty, Health, and Permanence*.

19. Douglas, "America's Vanishing Wilderness," 41.

Chapter One

1. William O. Douglas, *Of Men and Mountains* (New York: Harper and Brothers, 1950; San Francisco: Chronicle Books, 1990), xi.

2. Ibid., xiii; and William O. Douglas, *Go East, Young Man: The Early Years: The Autobiography of William O. Douglas* (New York: Random House, 1974), 198, 199. The University of Washington Library's Special Collections contains Pacific Northwest Biographical Pamphlet files within its Pacific Northwest Collection that include several newspaper clippings about the horseback-riding accident. Unfortunately, incomplete bibliographic information is available; I include all that is there: "13 Ribs Smashed, Lung Pierced; Not Critical" ; "Justice Douglas Crushed Under Horse on Mountain" (October 3, 1949), 1; and "Justice Douglas, Seriously Hurt, Is Resting Well" (October 3, 1949).

3. James F. Simon, G. Edward White, and Bruce Allen Murphy are all scholars who have debunked portions of Douglas's autobiographical writings. Murphy's work most extensively pulls apart Douglas's image, seeing it as simply a ploy in Douglas's never-ending pursuit of the presidency, a narrow interpretation. Simon, *Independent Journey: The Life of William O. Douglas* (New York: Harper & Row, 1980); White, "The Anti-Judge: William O. Douglas and the Ambiguities of Individuality," in *The American Judicial Tradition: Profiles of Leading American Judges*, expanded edition (New York: Oxford University Press, 1988): 369-420; and Murphy, *Wild Bill: The Legend and Life of William O. Douglas* (New York: Random House, 2003).

4. William O. Douglas, Speech before the Minnesota Historical Society, St. Paul, MN, May 26, 1962, transcript in the Yakima Valley Museum, Yakima, WA [hereafter YVM]; and Douglas, *Go East, Young Man*, 7. Reliable biographical information concerning Douglas's early years is found several biographies. Unless otherwise noted, I have used Simon, *Independent Journey*, 17-65; Howard Ball and Phillip J. Cooper, *Of Power and Right: Hugo Black, William O. Douglas, and America's Constitutional Revolution* (New York: Oxford University Press, 1992), 33-40; and Murphy, *Wild Bill*, 3-42. These accounts help balance Douglas's own inaccurate memoirs.

5. Douglas, *Men and Mountains*, 21.

6. Ibid., 22, 28-29.

7. Douglas, *Go East, Young Man*, 12.

8. Canadian nature writer Don Gayton calls the deeply affecting childhood landscape the "primal landscape." Gayton, *Landscapes of the Interior: Re-Explorations of Nature and the Human Spirit* (Gabriola Island, B.C.: New Society Publishers, 1996), 71-77. See also, Elliott West, *Growing Up with the Country: Childhood and the Far Western Frontier* (Albuquerque: University of New Mexico Press, 1989). Douglas, *Men and Mountains*, 36,

9. Murphy strongly claims that Douglas manufactured his case of polio to give *Of Men and Mountains* some dramatic flair. He relies on interviews with many acquaintances and second-hand accounts. (*Wild Bill*, 282-86, 620-22.) Others have criticized Murphy's conclusions and argued that, if not with polio, Douglas certainly was critically ill as a toddler. (Melvin I. Urofsky, "Review of Bruce Allen Murphy, *Wild Bill: The Legend and Life of William O. Douglas*," H-Law, H-Net Reviews [June, 2003], URL: http://www.h-net.org/reviews/showrev. cgi?path=284821059374840. Accessed July 9, 2007.) Given incomplete records and the passage of time, it is unlikely that a certain conclusion can be reached. For the present purposes, the importance is not in whether Douglas contracted infantile paralysis but in how Douglas presented his recovery to the public.
10. Douglas, *Men and Mountains*, 32, 33.
11. Ibid., 33-34.
12. Douglas, *Go East, Young Man*, 115-16; Jeffrey P. Hantover, "The Boy Scouts and the Validation of Masculinity," in *The American Man*, Elizabeth H. Pleck and Joseph H. Pleck, eds. (Englewood Cliffs, NJ: Prentice-Hall, 1980): 285-301; Peter J. Schmitt, *Back to Nature: The Arcadian Myth in Urban America* (New York: Oxford University Press, 1969; reprint, Baltimore: The Johns Hopkins University Press, 1990); T. J. Jackson Lears, *No Place of Grace: Antimodernism and the Transformation of American Culture, 1880-1920* (New York: Pantheon Books, 1981); and Louis S. Warren, *Buffalo Bill's America: William Cody and the Wild West Show* (New York: Vintage, 2005).
13. Theodore Roosevelt, *Theodore Roosevelt: An Autobiography* (New York: Macmillan, 1913; reprint, New York: Charles Scribner's Sons, 1922), 1-53, quotations from 27, 50. For Roosevelt, the strenuous life, frontier, and masculinity, see Theodore Roosevelt, "The Strenuous Life," in *The Works of Theodore Roosevelt: Volume XIII* (New York: Charles Scribner's Sons, 1926); and *Winning of the West* four volumes (New York: G. P. Putnam's Sons, 1889-1896); Roderick Nash, *Wilderness and the American Mind*, third ed. (New Haven: Yale University Press, 1982), 150; Gail Bederman, *Manliness and Civilization: A Cultural History of Gender and Race in the United States, 1880-1917* (Chicago: University of Chicago Press, 1995), 170-215; Richard Slotkin, *Gunfighter Nation: The Myth of the Frontier in Twentieth-Century America* (Norman: University of Oklahoma Press, 1998); Arnaldo Testi, "The Gender of Reform Politics: Theodore Roosevelt and the Culture of Masculinity," *Journal of American History* 81 (March 1995): 1509-33; John F. Kasson, *Houdini, Tarzan, and the Perfect Man: The White Male Body and the Challenge of Modernity in America* (New York: Hill and Wang, 2001); Aaron Sachs, *The Humboldt Current: Nineteenth-Century Exploration and the Roots of American Environmentalism* (New York: Viking, 2006); and Michael L. Johnson, *Hunger for the Wild: America's Obsession with the Untamed West* (Lawrence: University Press of Kansas, 2007). Douglas's concern about physicality does not seem to have had the overtly racist tones described by Gail Bederman and others. Bederman, *Manliness and Civilization*; Sylvia D. Hoffert, *A History of Gender in America: Essays, Documents, and Articles* (Upper Saddle River, NJ: Prentice Hall, 2003), 283-90; Robyn Muncy, "Trustbusting and White Manhood in America, 1898-1914," *American Studies* 38 (Fall 1997): 21-37; Joe L. Dubbert, "Progressivism and the Masculinity Crisis," in *The American Man*, eds. Elizabeth H. Pleck and Joseph H. Pleck (Englewood Cliffs, NJ: Prentice-Hall, 1980): 303-

20; John Higham, "The Problem of Assimilation in the United States," in *Major Problems in American Immigration and Ethnic History*, ed. Jon Gjerde (Boston: Houghton Mifflin, 1998): 16-22; and Hantover, "The Boy Scouts and Masculinity." Douglas mentions Roosevelt sporadically in *Go East Young Man*.

14. Douglas, *Men and Mountains*, x, 35.

15. Ibid., 63-99, quotation from 69. Marjorie Hope Nicholson, *Mountain Gloom and Mountain Glory: The Development of the Aesthetics of the Infinite* (Ithaca: Cornell University Press, 1963, reprint; Seattle: University of Washington Press, 1997); Mark Stoll, "Religion 'Irradiates' the Wilderness," in *American Wilderness: A New History*, ed. Michael Lewis (New York: Oxford University Press, 2007), 35-53; and Adam M. Sowards, "Spiritual Egalitarianism: John Muir's Religious Environmentalism," in *John Muir in Historical Perspective*, ed. Sally M. Miller (New York: Peter Lang, 1999), 123-36.

16. Douglas, *Men and Mountains*, 76, 82, 84.

17. Ibid., 85-99, quotations from 88, 89-90, 90. Frederick Jackson Turner, "The Significance of the Frontier in American History," in *The Turner Thesis concerning the Role of the Frontier in American History*, revised ed., ed. George Rogers Taylor (Boston: Heath, 1956), 1-18; Roosevelt, *Winning of the West* (four volumes); Warren, *Buffalo Bill's America*; and Aldo Leopold, *A Sand County Almanac with Essays on Conservation from Round River* (New York: Ballantine Books, 1966), 237-64. I am grateful to Michael P. Nelson who helped me clarify the various strands of thought in Douglas's comment. See his "An Amalgamation of Wilderness Preservation Arguments," in *The Great New Wilderness Debate: An Expansive Collection of Writings Defining Wilderness from John Muir to Gary Snyder*, eds. J. Baird Callicott and Michael P. Nelson (Athens: University of Georgia Press, 1998), 154-98.

18. Douglas, *Men and Mountains*, 95-99, quotations from 98, 99. Susan R. Schrepfer, *Nature's Altars: Mountains, Gender, and American Environmentalism* (Lawrence: University Press of Kansas, 2005); Sachs, *The Humboldt Current*; and Paul S. Sutter, *Driven Wild: How the Fight Against Automobiles Launched the Modern Wilderness Movement* (Seattle: University of Washington Press, 2002), 194.

19. Walter Nugent, *Into the West: The Story of Its Peoples* (New York: Alfred A. Knopf, 1999).

20. Turner, "The Significance of the Frontier;" and Roosevelt, *Winning of the West* (four volumes).

21. Richard White and Louis Warren make this point about the use of Turner's and Buffalo Bill's myth clear in "Frederick Jackson Turner and Buffalo Bill," in *The Frontier in American Culture*, ed. James R. Grossman (Berkeley: University of California Press, 1994); and *Buffalo Bill's America*. See also Slotkin, *Gunfighter Nation*; and Johnson, *Hunger for the Wild*.

22. Douglas, *Men and Mountains*, 35. Roosevelt, *Autobiography*; and John Muir, *A Thousand-Mile Walk to the Gulf* (Boston: Houghton Mifflin, 1916; reprint, Boston: Houghton Mifflin, 1981).

23. Douglas, *Men and Mountains*, 90.

24. Douglas, *Go East, Young Man*, 94-108.

25. Ibid., 124-130 and *Men and Mountains*, 15, 5. Simon, *Independent Journey*, 63-65; and White, "The Anti-Judge," 373-74. According to Murphy, Douglas may have arrived with more than six cents, but he had to borrow tuition money from a

friend; Murphy, *Wild Bill*, 42. A useful study of the paradigmatic Horatio Alger success story is Jeffrey Louis Decker, *Made in America: Self-Styled Success from Horatio Alger to Oprah Winfrey* (Minneapolis: University of Minnesota Press, 1997).

26. Douglas, *Go East, Young Man*, 153, original emphasis. More about Douglas's legal career and ideas can be found in chapter five. The careerism evident in his professorial life is well known but mostly irrelevant here. See Simon, *Independent Journey*, 92-113; and Murphy, *Wild Bill*, 72-105.

27. Douglas, *Go East, Young Man*, 254-93.

28. "Douglas, Jurist: Appointment to Supreme Court Puts Hard Hitter on the Bench," *Newsweek* (March 27, 1939), 13; and "Douglas Nominated to Supreme Court: Approval of SEC Chairman Held Imminent," *Seattle Post-Intelligencer* (March 21, 1939), n.p. During the New Deal, the Supreme Court declared several of Roosevelt's reforms unconstitutional. To counter the seeming obstinacy of the Court, the president proposed granting his office the power to add federal judges once sitting judges turned seventy. The proposition was a thinly veiled power play designed to force conservative judges off the bench, and it would be Roosevelt's most serious political blunder of his presidency.

29. Simon, *Independent Journey*, 191-94; Douglas, *Go East, Young Man*, 456-63; Congress, Senate, 76th Cong., 1st sess. *Congressional Record* 84, pt. 4 (April 3, 1939): 3706-13; and Congress, Senate, 76th Cong., 1st sess. *Congressional Record* 84, pt. 4 (April 4, 1939): 3773-88.

30. Dean of Yale's Law School, Robert Hutchins, praised Douglas's professorial abilities; see Simon, *Independent Journey*, 109. "Horatio Alger" comes from "Douglas Nominated." Richard Neuberger, *They Never Go Back to Pocatello: The Selected Essays of Richard Neuberger*, edited and introduced by Steve Neal, foreword by Maurine Neuberger (Portland: Oregon Historical Society Press, 1988), 108-25, quotations from 111, 112, 116, 125. Murphy debunks Douglas's supposed poverty but notes that the Douglas family finances bounced up and down and created constant financial insecurity, an insecurity Douglas's mother fed to her children in heavy helpings; Murphy, *Wild Bill*, 20-24.

31. In the twentieth century, Sandra Day O'Connor's own western childhood on a ranch is the closest analog, but Yakima and the Lazy B Ranch were really worlds apart in geography and class. Sandra Day O'Connor and H. Alan Day, *Lazy B: Growing Up on a Cattle Ranch in the American Southwest* (New York: Random House, 2002).

32. Neuberger, *They Never Go Back*, 115-16.

33. Ibid., 109; "Douglas for the Cabinet," *Coos Bay [OR] Times*, May 9, 1942, 2. Emphasis added. "When Will Douglas Enter War Effort," *Oregon Labor Press* (Portland), n.d., 2. Both articles found in Box 16, File Folder 29, "William O. Douglas (Folder 2), 1941-1959," in Edwin Palmer Hoyt Papers, WH1226, Western History Collection, Denver Public Library [hereafter EPHP]. For Douglas's western roots, see also Haig Bosmajian, "The Imprint of the Cascade Country on William O. Douglas," *Journal of the West* 32 (July 1993): 80-86; Edwin R. Bingham, "American Wests through Autobiography and Memoir," *Pacific Historical Review* 56 (February 1987): 13-18; and Adam M. Sowards, "William O. Douglas: The Environmental Justice," in *The Human Tradition in the American West*, ed. Benson Tong and Regan Lutz (Wilmington, DE: Scholarly Resources, Inc., 2002), 155-70.

34. Fred Rodell, "Bill Douglas, American," *American Mercury* 61 (December 1945): 657, 665. Several years later, Rodell was still at it. In 1952, he wrote an article in the *Nation*, expressing his frustration that Douglas was not a presidential contender, for in Rodell's opinion, he ought to be the next president. Rodell, "I'd Prefer Bill Douglas," *Nation* 174 (April 26, 1952): 400-402. An article in 1956 called Douglas a "headline hunter," suggesting this characteristic was long-lasting and annoying to some. See Politicus, "Justice Douglas—Headline Hunter," *The American Mercury* 83 (August 1956): 121-26.

35. Hugh Russell Fraser, Letter to "The Open Forum," *The American Mercury* 62 (February 1946): 251.

36. "Justice Douglas, Seriously Hurt, Is Resting Well," *Seattle Times* (October 3, 1949), n.p.; and William O. Douglas, Yakima, WA, to E. Palmer Hoyt, Denver, CO, October 27, [1949], in Box 16, File Folder 28: William O. Douglas (Folder 1), 1948-1956, EPHP.

37. "Douglas Writes Book about N.W.," *Seattle Times* (September 1, 1948), n.p.; Douglas to Cass Canfield, December 24, 1947; Douglas to John Fisher, March 29, 1949, in *The Douglas Letters: Letters: Selections from the Private Papers of Justice William O. Douglas*, edited and introduced by Melvin I. Urofsky, with the assistance of Philip E. Urofsky (Bethesda, MD: Adler and Adler, 1987), 310, 312-13; and Simon, *Independent Journey*, 283-84. Murphy found *Of Men and Mountains* so mythical, he called his chapter focused on it, "Of Men and Myths"; Murphy, *Wild Bill*, 281-86.

38. James C. Duram, *Justice William O. Douglas* (Boston: Twayne Publishers, 1981), 57-61. Positive contemporary reviews are George R. Stewart, "The Magic Mountains," *New York Times* (April 9, 1950), sec. VII, 3; and Orville Prescott, "Books of the Times," *New York Times* (April 10, 1950), 17. For the popularity of the frontier in the 1950s, see Slotkin, *Gunfighter Nation*, 347-488; and Gerald D. Nash, *Creating the West: Historical Interpretations, 1890-1990* (Albuquerque: University of New Mexico Press, 1991), esp. 49-70. Also, Decker, *Made in America*.

39. Douglas, *Go East, Young Man*, 53; and Douglas, *Men and Mountains*, 36.

40. Douglas, *Men and Mountains*, 41. As an example of his nonconformity, Douglas along with Justice Hugo Black routinely supported the First Amendment rights of accused communists—a decidedly unpopular position in Cold War America. Black and Cooper, *Of Power and Right*, 136-57. Douglas powerfully presented his ideas about the problems of anticommunism in "The Black Silence of Fear," *New York Times Magazine* (January 13, 1952): 7, 37-38.

41. Douglas, *Men and Mountains*, 48.

42. Ibid., 49; Duram, *Justice Douglas*, 58.

43. Douglas, *Men and Mountains*, 1, 3.

44. Douglas, *Men and Mountains*, 7, 5. Elon Gilbert quoted in Bingham, "American Wests," 16. A prominent example of Douglas leaving Washington, DC, before Court business concluded concerned a last-minute stay he issued of the Rosenberg execution. See Simon, *Independent Journey*, 298-313; Murphy, *Wild Bill*, 315-27; and Michael E. Parrish, "Cold War Justice: The Supreme Court and the Rosenbergs," *American Historical Review* 82 (October 1977): 805-42.

45. Douglas, *Men and Mountains*, 315, 322, and 324; and Schrepfer, *Nature's Altars*, 39-41.

46. Douglas, *Men and Mountains*, 328.

47. For nature as a leveler, see Douglas, *Men and Mountains*, 56-57, 90; and Duram, *Justice Douglas*, 60.

48. Urosfky, ed., *The Douglas Letters*, 240.

Chapter Two

1. William O. Douglas, *My Wilderness: The Pacific West* (Garden City, NY: Doubleday and Company, 1960), 199.

2. Paul S. Sutter has persuasively argued that the fight against roads and automobiles launched the wilderness movement in the 1920s and 1930s; *Driven Wild: How the Fight Against Automobiles Launched the Modern Wilderness Movement* (Seattle: University of Washington Press, 2002).

3. Samuel P. Hays, *Conservation and the Gospel of Efficiency: The Progressive Conservation Movement, 1890-1920* (Cambridge, MA: Harvard University Press, 1959; reprint, New York: Atheneum, 1975); Char Miller, *Gifford Pinchot and the Making of Modern Environmentalism* (Washington, DC: Island Books, 2001); and Robert Gottlieb, *Forcing the Spring: The Transformation of the American Environmental Movement*, revised and updated edition (Washington, DC: Island Press, 2005), 52-60. Hays' new preface in the reprint edition is particularly effective at explaining his structural argument. Alan Brinkley characterizes the shifting perspectives of liberalism in *The End of Reform: New Deal Liberalism in Recession and War* (New York: Knopf, 1995), 9.

4. The Hetch Hetchy fight is chronicled in many sources. Recently, Robert W. Righter has contributed an excellent revisionist account that reveals the nuances to this struggle and thus rescues it from the caricature it had become. See Righter, *The Battle over Hetch Hetchy: America's Most Controversial Dam and the Birth of Modern Environmentalism* (New York: Oxford University Press, 2005). See also, Miller, *Gifford Pinchot*, 136-44, 169-73. Less nuanced treatments include Stephen Fox, *The American Conservation Movement: John Muir and His Legacy* (Madison: University of Wisconsin Press, 1981), 103-47; and Roderick Nash, *Wilderness and the American Mind*, third ed. (New Haven: Yale University Press, 1982), 161-81.

5. Righter, *Battle over Hetch Hetchy*.

6. Sutter, *Driven Wild*.

7. Neil M. Maher, *Nature's New Deal: The Civilian Conservation Corps and the Roots of the American Environmental Movement* (New York: Oxford University Press, 2008); Bryant Simon, "'New Men in Body and Soul': The Civilian Conservation Corps and the Transformation of Male Bodies and the Body Politic," in *Seeing Nature through Gender*, ed. Virginia J. Scharff (Lawrence: University Press of Kansas, 2003): 80-102; and Sutter, *Driven Wild*.

8. Maher, *Nature's New Deal*; Sutter, *Driven Wild*; and Brinkley, *End of Reform*.

9. Samuel P. Hays in collaroration with Barbara D. Hays, *Beauty, Health, and Permanence: Environmental Politics in the United States, 1955-1985* (New York: Cambridge University Press, 1987).

10. William O. Douglas, *My Wilderness: East to Katahdin* (Garden City, NY: Doubleday and Company, 1961), 189-90.

11. Barry Mackintosh, *C&O Canal: The Making of a Park* (Washington, DC: History Division, National Park Service, Department of the Interior, 1991), 1-59; Franklin D. Roosevelt, Washington, DC, to Harold L. Ickes, Washington, DC, May 11,

1934; Harold L. Ickes, Washington, DC, to Franklin D. Roosevelt, Washington, DC, May 28, 1934; Frederic A. Delano, Washington, DC, to Harold L. Ickes, Washington, DC, May 16, 1934; and Franklin D. Roosevelt, Washington, DC, to Harold L. Ickes, Washington, DC, May 29, 1934, all in Edgar B. Nixon, ed., *Franklin D. Roosevelt and Conservation, 1911-1945*, Volume One, 1911-1937 (Hyde Park, NY: General Services Administration, National Archives and Records Service, Franklin D. Roosevelt Library, 1957), 275, 281-83.

12. Mackintosh, *C&O Canal*, 57-59, quotation from 57-58. Also, Barry Mackintosh, "Shootout on the Old C.&O. Canal: The Great Parkway Controversy, 1950-1960," *Maryland Historical Magazine* 90 (Summer 1995): 141-63. On automobiles in national parks see, David Louter, *Windshield Wilderness: Cars, Roads, and Nature in Washington's National Parks* (Seattle: University of Washington Press, 2006).

13. The State of Maryland and the federal government were to be unequal partners in the road project because of property rights-of-way. Mackintosh, *C&O Canal*, 60-66.

14. Ibid., quotations from 65. Neill Phillips, February 20, 1953, Box 7:129, Folder: States/DC: C&O Canal, 1950s, in Wilderness Society Records, CONS130, Conservation Collection, The Denver Public Library [hereafter WSR]. The Wilderness Society Records have been reorganized since I researched them. Accordingly, box numbers and folder names may have changed.

15. "Potomac Parkway," *Washington Post* (January 3, 1954), 4B; and Mackintosh, *C&O Canal*, 67-69. Sutter explores the elitism charge in *Driven Wild*.

16. William O. Douglas, Washington, DC, to the Editor, Washington, DC, January 15, 1954, Environment, Box 543, C&O Canal, Committee and Hiking Group A-L (1954-1956), in William O. Douglas Papers, Library of Congress, Washington, DC [hereafter WODP], punctuation follows this version. The letter also is found in *The Douglas Letters: Selections from the Private Papers of Justice William O. Douglas*, edited and introduced by Melvin I. Urofsky with the assistance of Philip E. Urofsky (Bethesda, MD: Adler & Adler, 1987), 236-38; and "Potomac Sanctuary," *Washington Post* (January 19, 1954), 14. Mark Harvey indicates that Stewart Brandborg of the Wilderness Society recalled that Howard Zahniser drafted the letter to the *Post*; I have located no evidence in Douglas's papers to confirm this claim. See Harvey, *Wilderness Forever: Howard Zahniser and the Path to the Wilderness Act* (Seattle: University of Washington Press, 2005), 277, n. 9.

17. Douglas to Editor. Harvey points out the importance of first-hand experience in generating enthusiasm for wilderness in "Loving the Wild in Postwar America, in *American Wilderness: A New History*, ed. Michael Lewis (New York: Oxford University Press, 2007), 190-91.

18. Douglas to Editor.

19. "We Accept," *Washington Post* (January 21, 1953), 10; and Mackintosh, *C&O Canal*, 68-69. In his study of wilderness activism, Michael Frome captures well the tension of recreational access in two successive chapters, entitled "Recreation for Everyone ..." and "... But Not Everyone at Once"; Frome, *Battle for the Wilderness*, revised edition (Salt Lake City: University of Utah Press, 1997), 77-102. Critical to understanding the interwar roots of this issue are Sutter, *Driven Wild*; and Maher, *Nature's New Deal*, 151-80. Daniel J. Boorstin criticized the tendency at this time to create such newsworthy events, or "pseudo-events," as he calls them in *The Image, or What Happened to the American Dream* (New York: Atheneum, 1962), 3-44.

20. "Justice Douglas, Journalists Debate C&O Canal Plans on 189-Mile Hike," *American Forests* 60 (April 1954), 42; "Nature's Show, *Washington Post* (January 26, 1954), 14; "The C and O Walkathon," *American Forests* 60 (May 1954): 18-19, 54; and "Potomac Wilderness," *Washington Post* (February 17, 1954), copy in Box 7:129: Folder: States/DC: C&O Canal, 1950s, WSR. Not all letters to the *Post* were positive. One writer found Douglas's letter full of "baffling statements" and assured the editors they would not see a badger, a muskrat, or a fox. "Nature's Lore," *Washington Post* (January 29, 1954), 24. For Marshall and minority rights, see Sutter, *Driven Wild*, 208-9, where he discusses Marshall's important article, "The Wilderness as Minority Right," published in 1928.

21. Howard Zahniser, Washington, DC, to William O. Douglas, Washington, DC, February 11, 1954, in Box 7:130; Folder: States/DC: C&O Canal, 1954-1961, WSR. Zahniser sent several almost identical letters on the same day to Paul Schaefer, Schenectady, NY; Sigurd F. Olson, Ely, MN; Richard M. Leonard, San Francisco, CA; and Harvey Broome, Knoxville, TN, February 12, 1954, in ibid.; and Harvey, *Wilderness Forever*, 172-76.

22. "Solitary Dissent," *Time* (February 1, 1954), 15; Douglas to Frederick W. Luehring, June 9, 1966, in *Douglas Letters*, 237-38; and Mackintosh, *C&O Canal*, 69. On the Olympic Beach hike four years later women were not only allowed, but they accounted for nearly one-quarter of the hikers.

23. "The Challenger Arrives," *Washington Post* (March 20, 1954), 1; "Beef, Oratory Rare at Pre-Canal Hike Banquet," *Washington Post and Times-Herald* (March 20, 1954), 13; "Douglas Party Goes 22 Miles to Paw Paw," *Washington Post and Times-Herald* (March 21, 1954), 17M; and Aubrey Graves, "Frustrated Doughfoot Foiled Again by Recall to Desk from Canal Trail," *Washington Post and Times-Herald* (March 21, 1954), 2B.

24. William O. Douglas, *Go East, Young Man: The Early Years: The Autobiography of William O. Douglas* (New York: Random House, 1974), 210-11; Harvey Broome, Knoxville, TN, to Howard Zahniser, Washington, DC, April 7, 1954; Harvey Broome, "Impressions," all in Box 7:130; Folder: States/DC: C&O Canal, 1954-1961, WSR; Sigurd F. Olson, Ely, MN, to Howard Zahniser, Washington, DC, 6 April 1954, in Box 7:129; Folder: States/DC: C&O Canal, 1950s, WSR; and "Canal Hike," *Washington Post* (March 22, 1954), 8.

25. Broome to Zahniser, April 7, 1954; Sigurd F. Olson, Ely, MN, to William O. Douglas, Washington, DC, April 6, 1954, in Box 7:129; Folder: States/DC: C&O Canal, 1950s, WSR; Merlo J. Pusey, Washington, DC, to William O. Douglas, Washington, DC, March 30, 1954, Environment, Box 543, C&O Canal Committee and Hiking Group P-Z (1954-1956), in WODP; "The Woods Walkers," *Time* (March 29, 1954), 20; "School Band Greets C&O Canal Hikers," *Washington Post and Times-Herald* (March 24, 1954), 18; "Newsboy Tells of Hiking 33 Miles in Day," *Washington Post and Times-Herald* (March 23, 1954), 3; and "10 Canal Hikers Remain in Running," *Washington Post and Times-Herald* (March 25, 1954), 14. Two years after the hike, an article in *The American Mercury* called Douglas a "headline hunter" and dubbed the C&O Canal hike a "publicity stunt" and "outdoor exhibitionism." Politicus, "Justice Douglas—Headline Hunter," *The American Mercury* 83 (August 1956), 121.

26. Sig Olson and Others, "The C&O Canal Song of the Justice Douglas-Washington Post Expedition," March 20-27, 1954, in Box 7:130; Folder: States/DC: C&O

Canal, 1954-1961, WSR, 1-3; Mackintosh, *C&O Canal*, 71; and David Backes, *A Wilderness Within: The Life of Sigurd F. Olson* (Minneapolis: University of Minnesota Press, 1997), 226, quotation from 227.

27. "9 Bona Fide Hikers Left in Canal Trek," *Washington Post and Times-Herald* (March 25, 1954), 14A; Aubrey Graves, "Canal Hikers Just 18 Miles from (Sigh!) Washington," *Washington Post and Times-Herald* (March 27, 1954), 1; and Aubrey Graves, "9 Stalwarts Stick Out Canal Hike," *Washington Post and Times-Herald* (March 28, 1954), 1. The Immortal Nine were Douglas, Harvey Broome, Olaus Murie, Constant Southworth, Grant Conway, Albert E. Farwell, George F. Miller, Jack Permain, and Colin Ritter.

28. William O. Douglas, Washington, DC, to Howard Zahniser, Washington, DC, March 28, 1954; Howard Zahniser, Washington, DC, to William O. Douglas, Washington, DC, March 31, 1954; Sigurd F. Olson, Ely, MN, to William O. Douglas, Washington, DC, April 6, 1954, all in Box 7:129: Folder: States/ DC: C&O Canal, 1950s, WSR; and John H. Cover, to William O. Douglas, Washington, DC, March 30, 1954, in Box 7:130; Folder: States/DC: C&O Canal, 1954-1961, WSR.

29. "C&O Canal: A Report," *Washington Post* (March 31, 1954), 12; and "C and O Walkathon," 18.

30. William O. Douglas to Douglas McKay, April 22, 1954, in *The Douglas Letters*, 238-40; "C and O Walkathon," 54; "C&O Canal: A Report"; Hays, *Beauty, Health, and Permanence*, 120; and James Morton Turner, "The Politics of Modern Wilderness," in *American Wilderness: A New History*, ed. Michael Lewis (New York: Oxford University Press, 2007), 247.

31. Harvey, *Wilderness Forever*, 175-76.

32. William O. Douglas, Washington, DC, to Douglas McKay, Washington, DC, March 6, 1956, in Box 7:129: Folder: States/DC: C&O Canal, 1950s, WSR; McKay to Douglas, March 13, 1956, in ibid.; William O. Douglas, Washington, DC, to Howard Zahniser, Washington, DC, April 4, 1956, in Box 7:130; Folder: States/ DC: C&O Canal, 1954-1961, WSR; Douglas to Merlo John Pusey, April 4, 1956, in *The Douglas Letters*, 241; Douglas to Harvey Broome, April 4, 1956, quoted in T. H. Watkins, "Commentary: Justice Douglas Takes a Hike," in *"He Shall Not Pass This Way Again": The Legacy of Justice William O. Douglas*, ed. Stephen L. Wasby (Pittsburgh: University of Pittsburgh Press for the William O. Douglas Institute, 1990), 251; and Fox, *American Conservation Movement*, 242.

33. "Justice Douglas, Journalists Debate," 42; Hays, *Beauty, Health, and Permanence*, 1-39; Richard West Sellars, *Preserving Nature in the National Parks: A History* (New Haven, CT: Yale University Press, 1997), 180-91; and Mark W. T. Harvey, *A Symbol of Wilderness: Echo Park and the American Conservation Movement* (Albuquerque: University of New Mexico Press, 1994; reprint, Seattle: University of Washington Press, 2000).

34. Byron Fish, "Olympic Wilderness Hikers Hope to Chill Coast-Road Plan," *Seattle Times* (August 19, 1958), 30; Carsten Lien, *Olympic Battleground: The Power Politics of Timber Preservation* (San Francisco: Sierra Club Books, 1991), 299-320; Louter, *Windshield Wilderness*, 96; Sellars, *Preserving Nature*, 173-95; and Richard White, "'Are You an Environmentalist or Do You Work for a Living?': Work and Nature," in *Uncommon Ground: Toward Reinventing Nature*, ed. William Cronon (New York: W. W. Norton, 1995): 171-85.

35. William O. Douglas to Preston Macy, January 10, 1952; Macy to William O. Douglas, January 18, 1952; William O. Douglas to Macy, February 9, 1952, Box 3, Folder 5: General Correspondence, 1951-1952, all in Preston P. Macy Papers, University of Washington Manuscripts and University Archives, Seattle, WA [hereafter PMP]; and William O. Douglas, "My Favorite Vacation Land," *The American Magazine* 154 (July 1952): 38-41, 94-99, quotation from 41.

36. William O. Douglas to Dr. Lorin W. Roberts, Decatur, GA, September 28, 1956; in WODP, Environment, Box 559, Olympic National Park, 1949-1969; William O. Douglas to Conrad L. Wirth, March 9, 1957, in *The Douglas Letters*, 241-42; "Justice Douglas, 70 Hikers to Begin Wilderness Trip," *Seattle Times* (August 18, 1958), 10; Louis R. Huber, Invitation and Press Release, August 4, 1958; Press Release, August 9, 1958, folder 9, box 5, John Osseward Papers, University of Washington Manuscripts and University Archives [hereafter JOP]; Sally Warren Soest, ed., *Voice of the Wild Olympics* (Seattle: Olympic Park Associates, 1998), 36; and William O. Douglas to Dr. Conrad Wirth, April 3, 1958, Environment, Box 559, Olympic National Park, 1949-1969, WODP. Language in the press release is found earlier in David R. Brower to William O. Douglas, April 1, 1957, Environment, Box 559, Olympic Beach, WA (1957-1962), WODP. Dyer's recollection places the invitation to Douglas in 1956. The first reference to the beach hike in the Douglas Papers, however, is in 1957 from Douglas asking Zahniser if a field trip would be feasible. Polly T. Dyer, e-mail message to author, September 27, 2004; and William O. Douglas to Howard Zahniser, October 3, 1957 in Howard Zahniser (misc. correspondence) folder, box 383, WODP.

37. "Justice Douglas, 70 Hikers;" Douglas, *Pacific West*, 40; and Louter, *Windshield Wilderness*, 68-104, quotation from 104. Hal K. Rothman discusses the notion of parkland as sacred space in *The Greening of a Nation?: Environmentalism in the United States since 1945* (Fort Worth, TX: Harcourt Brace, 1998), 46. Such a notion proved a powerful rallying point, even if it blurred the more complex mission of the park to both preserve natural features and to promote tourism.

38. Fish, "Olympic Wilderness Hikers," 30; and August Slathar, Letter to the Editor, *Port Angeles (Washington) Evening News* (November 29, 1958), 2.

39. Louis R. Huber, Press Release, August 21, 1958, folder 9, box 5, JOP, 4, emphasis in original; Clayton Fox, "68 Footsore Hikers Wind Up Beach Trek near LaPush," *Olympic (Port Angeles) Tribune* (August 22, 1958), 1; Press Release, August 9, 1958; William O. Douglas to Wirth, April 3, 1958; and Soest, *Voice of the Wild Olympics*, 36. For communities turning to tourism for economic salvation, see Hal K. Rothman, *Devil's Bargains: Tourism in the Twentieth-Century American West* (Lawrence: University Press, of Kansas, 1998).

40. "Beach Hikers Getting Late Start on Three-Day Trek to LaPush Area," *Olympic Tribune* (August 29, 1958), 3; Fish, "Olympic Wilderness Hikers," 30; Hays, *Beauty, Health, and Permanence*; Rothman, *Greening of a Nation?*, 46; and Turner, "Politics of Wilderness."

41. Clayton Fox, "First Day of Beach Hike Easy, Only One Point to Climb Over," *Olympic Tribune* (September 19, 1958), 3.

42. Unfortunately, the source does not list Morse's first name. "Justice Douglas, Party, Finish Protest Hike," *Seattle Times* (August 22, 1958), 12; and Harvey Broome, *Faces of the Wilderness* (Missoula, MT: Mountain Press Publishing Company, 1972), 128, 137, 126. For science in early wilderness campaigns, see Harvey,

Symbol of Wilderness, 155-56; Roger Kaye, *Last Great Wilderness: The Campaign to Establish the Arctic National Wildlife Refuge* (Fairbanks: University of Alaska Press, 2006); and Maher, *Nature's New Deal*, 151-80.

43. Clayton Fox, "Last Night of Hike Happy Affair, Speeches around the Campfire," *Olympic Tribune* (September 19, 1958), 3; and Broome, *Faces of the Wilderness*, 126-37. Broome's comments were a common idea associated with wilderness; see Harvey, "Loving the Wild," 192. For importance of local leaders, see Hays, *Beauty, Health, and Permanence*, 120.

44. Fox, "68 Footsore Hikers"; and "Hikers Glad to Reach Cedar Creek after Rugged Day on Rocks," *Olympic Tribune* (September 19, 1958), 3. The question of minority rights is taken up in the next chapter.

45. Lien, *Olympic Battleground*, 303; "Justice Douglas, Party, Finish Protest Hike," *Seattle Times* (August 22, 1958), 12; Fox, "Last Night of Hike Happy Affair"; Fox, "68 Footsore Hikers"; and Soest, *Voice of the Olympics*, 36-37, emphasis in original.

46. L. V. Venable, Letter to the Editor, *Port Angeles Evening News* (January 28, 1959), 2; William Cronon, "The Trouble with Wilderness; or, Getting Back to the Wrong Nature," in *Uncommon Ground: Toward Reinventing Nature*, ed. William Cronon (New York: W. W. Norton, 1995), 69-90; Harvey, *Symbol of Wilderness*; and Turner, "Modern Wilderness Politics."

47. The late T. H. Watkins, former editor of *Wilderness* magazine and vice president of the Wilderness Society, afforded Douglas a great deal of the credit for stopping the road "and for a good part of most of the depressingly few conservation victories we have enjoyed since World War II." Watkins, "Commentary," 252; and Soest, *Voice of the Olympics*, 38.

48. Sigurd F. Olson, Ely, MN, to Daniel B. Beard, Port Angeles, WA, December 3, 1958, Sigurd F. Olson Papers, Minnesota Historical Society, Box 80, emphasis added. For the need for public exposure, see Harvey, *Symbol of Wilderness*; and Roderick Nash, *Wilderness and the American Mind*, 3rd edition (New Haven: Yale University Press, 1982), 213. Criticism of pseudo-events is found in Boorstin, *The Image*, 7-76.

49. Mark Harvey has written the authoritative history of the Echo Park controversy, while other historians also place it as a centerpiece in the transformation of the conservation movement. See Harvey, *Symbol of Wilderness*; and "Battle for Dinosaur: Echo Park Dam and the Birth of the Modern Wilderness Movement," *Montana: the Magazine of Western History* 45 (Winter 1995): 32-45. Also, Nash, *Wilderness*, 209-19; and Rothman, *The Greening of a Nation?*, 34-48.

Chapter Three

1. William O. Douglas, *A Wilderness Bill of Rights* (Boston: Little, Brown and Company, 1965), 87.

2. William O. Douglas, *Strange Lands and Friendly People* (New York: Harper and Brothers, 1951); *Beyond the High Himalayas* (Garden City, NY: Doubleday & Company, 1952); *North from Malaya: Adventure on Five Fronts* (Garden City, NY: Doubleday & Company, 1953); *Russian Journey* (Garden City, NY: Doubleday & Company, 1956); and *West of the Indus* (Garden City, NY: Doubleday & Company, 1958).

3. William O. Douglas, *My Wilderness: The Pacific West* (Garden City, NY: Doubleday and Company, 1960), front matter; *A Wilderness Bill of Rights* (Boston: Little, Brown and Company, 1965), front matter, emphasis added. Hal K. Rothman, Mark Harvey, and Samuel P. Hays have shown the widespread popularity of many environmental reforms at this time in Rothman, *The Greening of a Nation?: Environmentalism in the United States since 1945* (Fort Worth: Harcourt Brace, 1998); Harvey, "Loving the Wild in Postwar America," in *American Wilderness: A New History*, ed. Michael Lewis (New York: Oxford University Press, 2007): 187-203; and Hays, in collaboration with Barbara D. Hays, *Beauty, Health, and Permanence: Environmental Politics in the United States, 1955-1985* (New York: Cambridge University Press, 1987). For Douglas's national prominence, see Stephen Fox, *The American Conservation Movement: John Muir and His Legacy* (Madison: University of Wisconsin Press, 1981), 239.

4. For wilderness and environmentalism in the 1960s, see Mark Harvey, *Wilderness Forever: Howard Zahniser and the Path to the Wilderness Act* (Seattle: University of Washington Press, 2005); Adam Rome, "'Give Earth a Chance': The Environmental Movement and the Sixties," *Journal of American History* 90 (September 2003), 527-34; and Rothman, *Greening of a Nation*. For good introductions to the 1960s, see Mark Hamilton Lytle, *America's Uncivil Wars: The Sixties Era from Elvis to the Fall of Richard Nixon* (New York: Oxford University Press, 2006); and Terry H. Anderson, *The Movement and the Sixties: Protest in America from Greensboro to Wounded Knee* (New York: Oxford University Press, 1995). For Carson, see Rachel Carson, *Silent Spring* (Boston: Houghton Mifflin, 1962, reprint: Boston: Houghton Mifflin, 2002); Linda Lear, *Rachel Carson: Witness for Nature* (New York: Henry Holt and Company, 1997); and Mark Hamilton Lytle, *The Gentle Subversive: Rachel Carson, Silent Spring, and the Rise of the Environmental Movement* (New York: Oxford University Press, 2007).

5. Craig W. Allin, *The Politics of Wilderness Preservation* (Westport, CT: Greenwood Press, 1982), 60-95; and Hays, *Beauty, Health, and Permanence*, 99-135, especially 121.

6. Mark W. T. Harvey, *A Symbol of Wilderness: Echo Park and the American Conservation Movement* (Albuquerque: University of New Mexico Press, 1994; reprint, Seattle: University of Washington Press, 2000); Harvey, *Wilderness Forever: Howard Zahniser and the Path to the Wilderness Act* (Seattle: University of Washington Press, 2005); Harvey, "Loving the Wild," 187-203; Kevin Marsh, *Drawing Lines in the Forest: Creating Wilderness in the Pacific Northwest* (Seattle: University of Washington Press, 2007); James Morton Turner, "The Politics of Modern Wilderness," in *American Wilderness: A New History*, ed. Michael Lewis (New York: Oxford University Press, 2007): 243-61; and Hays, *Beauty, Health, and Permanence*. For examples of Douglas's strategy, see William O. Douglas, "America's Vanishing Wilderness," *Ladies' Home Journal* 81 (July 1964): 37-41, 77; and Douglas, *Wilderness Bill of Rights*.

7. Douglas, *Pacific West*, 9, 57. Margaret E. Murie, *Two in the Far North* (New York: Knopf, 1957; reprint, Anchorage: Alaska Northwest Books, 1997), 333-39; and Roger Kaye, *Last Great Wilderness: The Campaign to Establish the Arctic National Wildlife Refuge* (Fairbanks: University of Alaska Press, 2006), 97-99. Harvey identifies these and the following values as common in the postwar wilderness movement; see Harvey, "Loving the Wild," 187-93.

8. Douglas, *Pacific West*, 92, 93, 94-95. Emphasis added. The irony of Douglas's own use of a jeep apparently was lost on him.

9. Ibid., 156, 104. See chapter one for more on individualism and nature.

10. Douglas, *East to Katahdin*, 76.

11. Ibid., 217-18. In Maine, Douglas found similar experiences at Mount Katahdin and lamented: "Man, though soft, flabby, and unfit for adventure, now can go anywhere" (288).

12. Robert L. Griswold, "The 'Flabby American,' the Body, and the Cold War," in *A Shared Experience: Men, Women, and the History of Gender*, eds. Laura McCall and Donald Yacovone (New York: New York University Press, 1998): 323-39; Richard Slotkin, *Gunfighter Nation: The Myth of the Frontier in Twentieth-Century America* (New York: Atheneum, 1992; reprint, Norman: University of Oklahoma Press, 1998), 489-504; and Susan Schrepfer, *Nature's Altars: Mountains, Gender, and American Environmentalism* (Lawrence: University Press of Kansas, 2005). For various postwar assaults on nature, see Adam Rome, *The Bulldozer in the Countryside: Suburban Sprawl and the Rise of American Environmentalism* (New York: Cambridge University Press, 2001); Paul W. Hirt, *A Conspiracy of Optimism: Management of the National Forests since World War Two* (Lincoln: University of Nebraska Press, 1994); and Donald Worster, *Rivers of Empire: Water, Aridity, and the Growth of the American West* (New York: Oxford University Press, 1985).

13. Douglas, *Pacific West*, 17 (first quotation), 107 (second quotation), 40 (fourth and fifth quotations); Douglas, *Of Men and Mountains* (New York: Harper and Brothers, 1950, reprint; San Francisco: Chronicle Books, 1990), x (third quotation). On Muir's religious approach see Donald Worster, "John Muir and the Roots of American Environmentalism," in *The Wealth of Nature: Environmental History and the Ecological Imagination* (New York: Oxford University Press, 1993): 184-202; and Adam M. Sowards, "Spiritual Egalitarianism: John Muir's Religious Environmentalism," in *John Muir in Historical Perspective*, ed. Sally M. Miller (New York: Peter Lang, 1999): 123-36. Mark Harvey has demonstrated the important role Zahniser's religion had in shaping his environmental worldview; see *Wilderness Forever*, passim. "Caring for creation" is philosopher Max Oelschlaeger's term from *Caring for Creation: An Ecumenical Approach to the Environmental Crisis* (New Haven: Yale University Press, 1994).

14. Douglas, *Pacific West*, 90, 159; and Douglas, *East to Katahdin*, 261.

15. Carson *Silent Spring*; Lear, *Rachel Carson*; and Maril Hazlett, "Voices from the Spring: *Silent Spring* and the Ecological Turn in American Health," in *Seeing Nature through Gender*, ed. Virginia J. Scharff (Lawrence: University Press of Kansas, 2003): 103-28.

16. Douglas, *Pacific West*, 11, 24, 25. Murie, *Two in the North*, 333-39.

17. Douglas, *Pacific West*, 30. President Jimmy Carter dedicated the area to Douglas as the William O. Douglas Arctic Wildlife Range, a designation that lasted less than a year when Congress passed a comprehensive change in name and management. For more on Arctic conservation, including Douglas's role in it and the priority of preserving ecological processes in the range, see Kaye, *Last Great Wilderness*.

18. Douglas, *East to Katahdin*, 127 (first quotation), 134, 138 (second quotation). Climate scientists were discovering in fits and starts how vulnerable even the global climate system was at this time; see Spencer Weart, *The Discovery of Global Warming* (Cambridge, MA: Harvard University Press, 2003).

19. Historical context and criticism for the balance of nature concept can be found in Donald Worster, *Nature's Economy: A History of Ecological Ideas*, second edition (New York: Cambridge University Press, 1994); Worster, "The Ecology of Order and Chaos," in *The Wealth of Nature: Environmental History and the Ecological Imagination* (New York: Oxford University Press, 1993): 156-70; Stephen Budiansky, *Nature's Keepers: The New Science of Nature Management* (New York: Free Press, 1995); Michael G. Barbour, "Ecological Fragmentation in the Fifties," in *Uncommon Ground: Toward Reinventing Nature*, ed. William Cronon (New York: W. W. Norton, 1995): 223-55; Daniel B. Botkin, *Discordant Harmonies: A New Ecology for the Twenty-First Century* (New York: Oxford University Press, 1990); and Michael Lewis, "Wilderness and Conservation Science," in *American Wilderness: A New History*, ed. Michael Lewis (New York: Oxford University Press, 2007): 205-21.

20. Douglas, *Pacific West*, 66-68, quotations on 66 and 68.

21. Paul S. Sutter, *Driven Wild: How the Fight Against Automobiles Launched the Modern Wilderness Movement* (Seattle: University of Washington Press, 2002), 60-73, 84-89, 252-54; Marsh, *Drawing Lines*; Harold K. Steen, *The U.S. Forest Service: A History*, Centennial Edition (Durham, NC, and Seattle: Forest History Society in association with University of Washington Press, 2004), 152-62, 209-213; C. Frank Brockman, *Recreational Use of Wild Lands* (New York: McGraw-Hill, 1959), 166-68; and Allin, *Politics of Wilderness Preservation*, 60-95.

22. Hirt, *Conspiracy of Optimism*, 171-92; Steen, *Forest Service*, 278-307; Charles F. Wilkinson, *Crossing the Next Meridian: Land, Water, and the Future of the West* (Washington, DC: Island Press, 1992), 127-28; and Marsh, *Drawing Lines*.

23. Douglas, *East to Katahdin*, 31-33, quotation 31. In his Foreword to Bernard Frank's *Our National Forests*, Douglas hinted at the activities the Forest Service was engaged in to improve erosion. See Douglas, "Foreword," in Bernard Frank, *Our National Forests* (Norman: University of Oklahoma Press, 1955), vii-viii. Such positive assessments became rarer over time.

24. Douglas, *East to Katahdin*, 53-54, 234.

25. Ibid., 236.

26. Douglas, *Pacific West*, 196-201, quotations from 199.

27. Ibid., 200, 201. Douglas was even more forceful in his private correspondence. A series of letters to regional politicians, administrators, and conservationists reveals Douglas's deep understanding and his dissatisfaction with Forest Service management in this area he knew well. Over several years, Douglas wrote to Senators Wayne Morse and Richard Neuberger, Secretary of Agriculture Orville Freeman, and such conservationists as Howard Zahniser, David Brower, and John Osseward. See letters in Correspondence, Box 360, Richard Neuberger (1947-1973); Correspondence, Box 383, Howard Zahniser (miscellaneous correspondence); Correspondence, Box 358, Wayne Morse (1941-1972); Environment, Box 559, Olympic National Park, 1949-1969, all in William O. Douglas Papers, Library of Congress, Washington, DC [hereafter WODP]; Box 1, Folder 1, Double K Mountain Ranch Papers, Manuscripts, Special Collections, University Archives, University of Washington, Seattle, WA; and Container 10, Folders 30-31, David R. Brower Papers in Sierra Club Members Papers, Bancroft Library, University of California, Berkeley. The best account of the politics of boundary making is Marsh, *Drawing Lines*. For the larger wilderness movement,

Harvey, *Wilderness Forever*; Harvey, "Loving the Wild;" Hays, *Beauty, Health, and Permanence*, 99-136; and Roderick Nash, *Wilderness and the American Mind*, third edition (New Haven: Yale University Press, 1982), 200-237.

28. For costs of suburban development, see Rome, *Bulldozer in the Countryside*; Ted Steinberg, *Down to Earth: Nature's Role in American History* (New York: Oxford University Press, 2002), 206-25; and Hirt, *Conspiracy of Optimism*, 50-53. For Mission 66, see Richard West Sellars, *Preserving Nature in the National Parks: A History* (New Haven: Yale University Press, 1997), 173-214. For chemical issues, see Carson, *Silent Spring*; and Richard A. Walker, *The Conquest of Bread: 150 Years of Agribusiness in California* (New York: The New Press, 2004).

29. A useful overview of the postwar era is found in James T. Patterson, *Grand Expectations: The United States, 1945-1974* (New York: Oxford University Press, 1996). For the civil rights movement, see Harvard Sitkoff, *The Struggle for Black Equality, 1954-1992*, revised ed. (New York: Hill and Wang, 1993). For environmentalist strategies, see Hays, *Beauty, Health, and Permanence*, esp. 458-90.

30. Hays, *Beauty, Health, and Permanence*; Patterson, *Grand Expectations*, 565; Rome, "'Give Earth a Chance,'" 527-34; Alan Brinkley, *The End of Reform: New Deal Liberalism in Recession and War* (New York: Knopf, 1995), 9-10; and James Morton Turner, " 'The Specter of Environmentalism': Wilderness, Environmental Politics, and the Evolution of the New Right," *Journal of American History*, forthcoming, copy in author's possession. Robert Gottlieb redefined the environmental movement to include many quality of life issues and dated them from the turn of the twentieth century and *Forcing the Spring: The Transformation of the American Environmental Movement*, revised and updated edition (Washington, DC: Island Press, 2005). Sutter, *Driven Wild* also identifies consumer issues as animating wilderness advocates in the 1920s and 1930s.

31. Civil rights movements diversified throughout the 1960s to also focus on the plights of American Indians, Mexican Americans, Asian Americans, all manner of women, and homosexuals. At the time when environmentalism was responding to political shifts, though, the black civil rights movement was dominant.

32. Brinkley, *End of Reform*, 10; Patterson, *Grand Expectations*, 524-92; and Turner, "Specter of Environmentalism." A useful excerpt of *The Port Huron Statement* is found in "The Port Huron Statement," in " 'Takin' it to the Streets': A Sixties Reader*, second ed., eds. Alexander Bloom and Wini Breines (New York: Oxford University Press, 2003), 50-61.

33. Carson, *Silent Spring*; Michael Egan, *Barry Commoner and the Science of Survival: The Remaking of American Environmentalism* (Cambridge, MA: The MIT Press, 2007); Lytle, *America's Uncivil Wars*, 60; Lytle, *Gentle Subversive*; and "Port Huron," 51.

34. William O. Douglas, "The Wilderness and the New Frontier," a speech delivered at the 7th Biennual Wilderness Conference, San Francisco, CA, April 7, 1961, transcript at Yakima Valley Museum, Yakima, Washington (hereafter YVM), quotations from 1-2, 20; original emphasis and capitalizations. References come from this version. The conference proceedings were collected and published in David Brower, ed., *Wilderness: America's Living Heritage* (San Francisco: Sierra Club, 1961), where the title to Douglas's speech was changed to "Wilderness and Human Rights." Douglas's speech was included in a subsequent collection of

wilderness writings; see William Schwartz, ed., *Voices for the Wilderness* (New York: Ballantine Books, 1969): 109-21.

35. Douglas, "Wilderness and New Frontier," 8, 9. Bryant Simon, "'New Men in Body and Soul': The Civilian Conservation Corps and the Transformation of Male Bodies and the Body Politic," in *Seeing Nature through Gender*, ed. Virginia J. Scharff (Lawrence: University Press of Kansas, 2003): 80-102; and Neil M. Maher, *Nature's New Deal: The Civilian Conservation Corps and the Roots of the American Environmental Movement* (New York: Oxford University Press, 2008), 77-113.

36. Douglas, "Wilderness and New Frontier," 8, 20-21. A useful history of environmental ethics and rights is Roderick Frazier Nash, *The Rights of Nature: A History of Environmental Ethics* (Madison: University of Wisconsin Press, 1989).

37. William O. Douglas, "A Wilderness Bill of Rights," in Environment, Box 566, Wilderness Bill of Rights (1962-1966), WODP, 1-2. His oral presentation of the Wilderness Bill of Rights appeared in the proceedings, "From the Discussion," in Brower, ed., *Wilderness*, 169-71.

38. Douglas, "Wilderness Bill of Rights," 1, 2, and passim. Context for these changes in governance is found in William M. Lunch, "Science, Civil Rights and Environmental Policy: A Political Mystery in Three Acts," a paper presented to the Western Political Science Association (March 2004), copy in author's possession; Lunch, *The Nationalization of American Politics* (Berkeley: University of California Press, 1987); and George Hoberg, *Pluralism by Design: Environmental Policy and the American Regulatory State* (New York: Praeger, 1992). Douglas wished his conflict of interest clause to be extended to all government agencies.

39. William O. Douglas to Edmond Nathaniel Cahn, January 10, 1962; 151; and William O. Douglas to Young Lawyers Section of the Washington State Bar Association, September 10, 1976, in *The Douglas Letters: Selections from the Private Papers of Justice William O. Douglas*, edited and introduced by Melvin I. Urofsky with the assistance of Philip E. Urofsky (Bethesda, MD: Adler & Adler, 1987), 151, 162. See also, William O. Douglas, *A Living Bill of Rights* (Garden City, NY: Doubleday and Company, 1961); and Howard Ball and Phillip J. Cooper, *Of Power and Right: Hugo Black, William O. Douglas, and America's Constitutional Revolution* (New York: Oxford University Press, 1992), 320.

40. Douglas, *Wilderness Bill of Rights*, 87, 26, 86. Also see Ball and Cooper, *Of Power and Right*; and Patterson, *Grand Expectations*, 562-92.

41. Douglas, *Wilderness Bill*, 109-10. Mark Harvey has shown that Zahniser struggled with negotiating his lobbying and the tax-exempt status of the Wilderness Society. The Sierra Club's Executive Director, Michael McCloskey, has also written about this challenge. See Harvey, *Wilderness Forever*; and Michael McCloskey, *In the Thick of It: My Life in the Sierra Club* (Washington, DC: Island Press, 2005), 272-77.

42. Douglas, *Wilderness Bill*; Marsh, *Drawing Lines*; Harvey, *Wilderness Forever*; and Nash, *Wilderness Mind*.

43. Maryland's proposed Conservation Bill of Rights was attached to William O. Douglas, Washington, DC, to Jim Bowmer, Temple, Texas, October 16, 1967 in Correspondence, Box 311, Jim Bowmer (1967), WODP. William O. Douglas, Speech before the Adirondack Mountain Club, Keene Valley, NY, June 18, 1962, YVM. Jim Bowmer also worked on fashioning a Wilderness Bill of Rights for Texas's state constitution; Jim D. Bowmer, Temple, TX, to William O. Douglas,

Washington, DC, March 10, 1967, in Correspondence, Box 311, Jim Bowmer (1966-1967), WODP. William O. Douglas, Speech before the Governor's Conference for California Beauty, January 11, 1966, Los Angeles, CA, YVM, 2; and William O. Douglas, Speech before the American Institute of Planners, October 25, 1971, San Francisco, CA, YVM, 4-5.

44. Douglas, *Wilderness Bill*, 100-10. Marsh emphasizes the importance of public hearings in democratizing wilderness management in *Drawing Lines*, 12-13.

45. Sigurd F. Olson, Ely, MN, to William O. Douglas, Washington, DC, September 21, 1965, in Correspondence, Box 362, Sigurd Olson (misc. correspondence), in WODP. Original emphasis.

46. Besides environmental causes, Douglas wrote about foreign affairs; see for example, *Democracy's Manifesto* (Garden City, NY: Doubleday, 1962); *Anatomy of Liberty: The Rights of Man without Force* (New York: Trident Press, 1963); and *International Dissent: Six Steps toward World Peace* (New York: Random House, 1971).

Chapter Four

1. William O. Douglas, "America's Vanishing Wilderness," *Ladies' Home Journal* (July 1964), 77.

2. Samuel P. Hays has most famously characterized the shift from conservation to environmentalism; see *Beauty, Health, and Permanence: Environmental Politics in the United States, 1955-1985* (New York: Cambridge University Press, 1987), 21-22. An alternative perspective is found in Robert Gottlieb, *Forcing the Spring: The Transformation of the American Environmental Movement*, revised and updated edition (Washington, DC: Island Press, 2005).

3. Some examples include the Buffalo River in Arkansas, Sunfish Pond in New Jersey, and Allagash River in Maine. See materials in Environment, Box 542, Buffalo River, AR (1961-62); Box 542, Buffalo River, AR (1962); Box 542, Buffalo River, AR (1964-1967); Box 562, Sunfish Pond, NJ (1967); Box 562, Sunfish Pond, NJ (1968 – May 1969); Box 562, Sunfish Pond, NJ (June 1969 - 1971); Box 541 Allagash River, ME (1963-1966), all in WODP; "Justice Douglas Aids Nature Lovers Who Oppose the Project," *New York Times*, May 20, 1962, 64; and "To Preserve Buffalo River," *New York Times*, May 28, 1962.

4. Douglas, "America's Vanishing Wilderness."

5. Isabelle Lynn and Kay Kershaw to William O. Douglas, January 14, 1958, folder 41, box 1, Double K Mountain Ranch Papers, Manuscripts, Special Collections, University Archives, University of Washington, Seattle, WA, [hereafter DKMRP]; Paul W. Hirt, *A Conspiracy of Optimism: Management of the National Forests since World War Two* (Lincoln: University of Nebraska Press, 1994), 226-29; and Michael McCloskey, "Wilderness Movement at the Crossroads, 1945-1970," *Pacific Historical Review* 41 (August 1972): 347-50.

6. William O. Douglas to Lawrence Barrett, June 12, 1954, Conservation 1951-1959 folder, box 548, Environment series, WODP. Please note that Douglas inconsistently spelled Barrett's first name; I have followed Douglas's usage.

7. All of the following 1960 correspondence is located in folder 42, box 1, DKMRP: William O. Douglas to David R. Brower, October 3; William O. Douglas to John Osseward, October 3; William O. Douglas to Pauline Dyer, October 3; and quotation from Douglas to Laurence O. Barrett, October 3. For jeeps in

Blankenship Meadows, see Kay Kershaw and Isabelle Lynn to Douglas, October 25; Douglas to L. O. Barrett, October 29; and Douglas to L. O. Barrett, November 2.

8. William O. Douglas to Barrett, October 3, 1960. Jackson's voice was a powerful one in the Senate on matters of land management, but it took time before he gave it much attention, despite his claim to Douglas: "You may be sure I am never too busy to look into a matter which you believe conflicts with the principles of good conservation." Jackson to William O. Douglas, October 18, 1960, folder 1, box 1, DKMRP. See also, William O. Douglas to Henry M. Jackson, November 15, 1960, folder 42, box 1, DKMRP.

9. William O. Douglas to L. O. Barrett, December 22, 1960, folder 42, box 1, DKMRP.

10. Douglas to Barrett, October 3, 1960.

11. William O. Douglas to Barrett, September 7, 1961, folder 1, box 1, DKMRP; and William O. Douglas to L. O. Barrett, October 12, 1961, Conservation (June-December 1961) folder, Environment series, box 548, WODP.

12. William O. Douglas to David R. Brower, September 7, 1961, Conservation (June-December 1961) folder, Environment series, box 548, WODP; William O. Douglas to Charles A. Reich, March 3, 1962, Conservation (January-April 1962) folder, box 549, Environment series, WODP; and Hirt, *Conspiracy of Optimism.*

13. Michael Frome, *Battle for the Wilderness*, rev. ed. (Salt Lake City, University of Utah Press, 1997), 145. The Wilderness Act, Public Law 88-577, is reproduced in Frome, 213-25. Mark Harvey, *Wilderness Forever: Howard Zahniser and the Path to the Wilderness Act* (Seattle: University of Washington Press, 2005); and Kevin R. Marsh, *Drawing Lines in the Forest: Creating Wilderness in the Pacific Northwest* (Seattle: University of Washington Press, 2007) furnish excellent context for this discussion.

14. William O. Douglas to Orville Freeman, December 8, 1965, Cougar Lakes Wilderness Area, WA (1962-1971) folder, Environment series, box 553, WODP. [Hereafter, materials from this folder will be cited by item name and CLWA, WODP.] Henry M. Jackson to William O. Douglas, February 23, 1971, in folder 1, box 1, DKMRP; and North Cascades Study Team, *The North Cascades Study Report* (Washington, DC, 1965), 14-15. One member of the study team, Owen S. Stratton, dissented from the proposal to declassify Cougar Lakes, see Study Team, *North Cascades Study Report*, 127-28. For context, see Marsh, *Drawing Lines*, 38-60; and Allan Ralph Sommarstrom, "Wild Land Preservation Crisis: The North Cascades Controversy," (Ph.D. diss., University of Washington, 1970).

15. William O. Douglas to Edward C. Crafts, November 4, 1964, in folder 1, box 1, DKMRP; and William O. Douglas to Patrick Goldsworthy, November 4, 1964 in CLWA, WODP.

16. William O. Douglas to Freeman, December 8, 1965; William O. Douglas to Orville L. Freeman, March 2, 1966; William O. Douglas to Orville L. Freeman, April 14, 1966; William O. Douglas to Harvey Broome, January 28, 1966; William O. Douglas to Goldsworthy, November 4, 1964; William O. Douglas to George A. Selke, November 14, 1964; William O. Douglas to Owen Stratton, March 4, 1966; and William O. Douglas to Henry M. Jackson, March 4, 1966; all in CLWA, WODP.

17. William O. Douglas to Freeman, January 25, 1966; William O. Douglas to Isabelle Lynn, January 14, 1966; and William O. Douglas to Robert F. Sutphen, January 21, 1966, all in folder 1, box 1, DKMRP; Douglas to Broome, January 28, 1966.

18. William O. Douglas to Cragg Gilbert, March 29, 1966; and William O. Douglas to Isabelle Lynn, February 26, 1966, both in CLWA, WODP. The statement was attached to Lynn's letter.

19. William O. Douglas to Freeman, March 2, 1966; and Freeman to William O. Douglas, April 8, 1966, both in CLWA, WODP.

20. Robert W. Lucas, "A Bumping Wilderness?" *Yakima (Washington) Herald Republic* April 26, 1971; and William O. Douglas to Editor, *Yakima Herald Republic*, April 30, 1971, in Cougar Lakes Wilderness Area, WA (1972-1976), Environment, Box 553, WODP.

21. Marsh, *Drawing Lines*; and Hays, *Beauty, Health, and Permanence*.

22. Eliot Porter, *The Place No One Knew: Glen Canyon on the Colorado* (San Francisco: Sierra Club Books, 1966).

23. 1 Kings 21: 1-29, quotations from 2-3 (Revised Standard Version); and William O. Douglas, *Farewell to Texas: A Vanishing Wilderness* (New York: McGraw-Hill, 1967), vii-ix.

24. Peter Gunter, *The Big Thicket: A Challenge for Conservation* (Austin and New York and Riverside, CN: Jenkins Publishing and The Chatham Press, 1971); and James J. Cozine, Jr., *Saving the Big Thicket: From Exploration to Preservation, 1685-2003* (Denton, TX: Big Thicket Association, University of North Texas Press, 2004).

25. The story of Douglas meeting Bowmer and Burleson is contained in James F. Simon, *Independent Journey: The Life of William O. Douglas* (New York: Harper & Row, 1980), 327.

26. Jim D. Bowmer, Temple, TX, to William O. Douglas, Washington, DC, October 13, 1965, Correspondence, Box 310, Jim Bowmer (1965), in WODP; and William O. Douglas, Washington, DC, to Jim D. Bowmer, Temple, TX, October 15, 1965, Correspondence, Box 310, Jim Bowmer (1965), in WODP.

27. Quoted in Congress, Senate, 89th Cong., 2nd sess., *Congressional Record* 112, pt. 7 (April 20, 1966), 8622.

28. Ibid.; and Cozine, *Saving the Big Thicket*, 107.

29. William O. Douglas, Washington, DC, to Jim D. Bowmer, Temple, TX, June 6, 1966, Correspondence, Box 311, Jim Bowmer (1966-1967), in WODP; and Stewart Udall, Washington, DC, to William O. Douglas, Washington, DC, June 17, 1966, Correspondence, Box 380, Stewart Udall (1957-1976), in WODP.

30. Douglas, *Farewell to Texas*, 2, 5, 7, and passim.

31. Ibid., 1, 18, 25, 26, 31, 33, 34.

32. Ibid., 20, 35.

33. Ibid., 14, 36; and Aldo Leopold, *A Sand County Almanac with Essays on Conservation from Round River* (New York: Ballantine Books, 1966).

34. Douglas, *Farewell to Texas*, 37. Nationalizing an environmental issue was not just a post-World War II strategy, as Hetch Hetchy demonstrates, but it became a particularly common and effective tactic during this period.

35. Ibid., 38-39, 56. Louis S. Warren explores similar dynamics of nationalizing resources focusing largely on wildlife in his excellent study, *The Hunter's Game: Poachers and Conservationists in Twentieth-Century America* (New Haven: Yale University Press, 1997). For the history of the park, see John Jameson, *The Story of Big Bend National Park* (Austin: University of Texas Press, 1996). Douglas was not the only high-level federal official traveling Texas in the mid-1960s. Lady Bird Johnson accompanied Secretary Udall on a raft trip in Big Bend National Park in an effort to promote its visibility.

36. Douglas, *Farewell to Texas*, 128, 134, 136; and Wendell Berry, *The Gift of Good Land: Further Essays Cultural and Agricultural* (San Francisco: North Point Press, 1981), 267-81.
37. Douglas, *Farewell to Texas*, 149; and Frome, *Battle for the Wilderness*, 93-102.
38. Douglas, *Farewell to Texas*, 155, 191; and William O. Douglas, Washington, DC, to Stewart L. Udall, Washington, DC, April 30, 1966, Correspondence, Box 380, Stewart Udall (1957-1976), in WODP.
39. Douglas, *Farewell to Texas*, 230, 231.
40. Ibid., 231.
41. Douglas to Bowmer, May 26, 1966. For Lady Bird Johnson's environmental activities, see Lewis L. Gould, *Lady Bird Johnson: Our Environmental First Lady* (Lawrence: University Press of Kansas, 1999).
42. Jim D. Bowmer, Temple, TX, to Editor, *Dallas Morning News*, Dallas, TX, February 22, 1968, Correspondence, Box 312, Jim Bowmer (1968-1969), in WODP.
43. Jim D. Bowmer, Temple, TX, to William O. Douglas, Washington, DC, March 10, 1967, Correspondence, Box 311, Jim Bowmer (1966-1967), in WODP.
44. Congress, Senate, 90th Cong., 2nd sess., *Congressional Record* 114, pt. 23 (October 8, 1968), 30012.
45. William O. Douglas, Washington, DC, to Jim D. Bowmer, Temple, TX, November 1, 1974, Correspondence, Box 312, Jim Bowmer (1972-1975), in WODP.
46. William O. Douglas, *Go East, Young Man: The Early Years: The Autobiography of William O. Douglas* (New York: Random House, 1974), 211.
47. William O. Douglas, "Sewage Treatment Plants—Not Dams," *National Parks Magazine* 36 (March 1962), 14; William O. Douglas, Washington, DC, to Abraham A. Ribicoff, Washington, DC, December 22, 1961, Environment, Box 561, Potomac Basin (1961-June 1965), in WODP; William O. Douglas, "The C&O Canal – 1959," speech at the Presidential Arms, Washington, DC, April 4, 1959, transcript in the Yakima Valley Museum [hereafter YVM]; William O. Douglas, "Pollution of the Potomac," speech before the League of Women Voters of DC, Washington, DC, January 19, 1960, transcript in YVM; and William O. Douglas, "The C&O Canal," speech before the Daughters of the American Revolution," Washington, DC, January 26, 1960, transcript in YVM. Context for the Potomac River development and opposition is found in Tim Palmer, *Endangered Rivers and the Conservation Movement* (Berkeley: University of California Press, 1986), esp. 62-63, 77-78.
48. Douglas, "C&O Canal – 1959" ; William O. Douglas, Washington, DC, to Governor Millard Tawes, Annapolis, MD, June 19, 1964, Environment, Box 561, Potomac Basin (1961-June 1965), in WODP; Douglas, "Sewage Treatment," 14-15; Douglas, "Pollution of the Potomac," 2; Douglas, "The C&O Canal" ; and William O. Douglas, *A Wilderness Bill of Rights* (Boston: Little, Brown and Company, 1965), 4-5.
49. William O. Douglas, Washington, DC, to Colonel Warren R. Johnson, Baltimore, MD, November 22, 1961, Environment, Box 561, Potomac Basin (1961-June 1965), in WODP.
50. Douglas to Tawes.

51. For some time, Douglas had condemned rural cooperatives, the primary lobbyists behind the dam, as greedy and selfish in their advocacy of basin development.
52. William O. Douglas, Washington, DC, to Russell E. Train, Washington, DC, November 11, 1965; Russell E. Train, Washington, DC, to William O. Douglas, Washington, DC, December 8, 1965; William O. Douglas, Washington, DC, to Russell E. Train, Washington, DC, December 13, 1965, Environment, Box 561, Potomac Basin (1965), all in WODP; and Douglas, "Sewage Treatment," 15. On Train, see J. Brooks Flippen, *Conservative Conservationist: Russell E. Train and the Emergence of American Environmentalism* (Baton Rouge: Louisiana State University Press, 2006).
53. Douglas, "C&O Canal," 4, 5; Douglas, "Sewage Treatment," 15; and Colin Ritter, " 'Walkin' … and Hollerin' …," *American Forests* 71 (June 1965), 60.
54. William O. Douglas, Washington, DC, to Stewart L. Udall, Washington, DC, December 8, 1960, Correspondence, Box 380, Stewart Udall (1957-1976), in WODP; Ritter, " 'Walkin'," 60-61; and Mackintosh, *C&O Canal*. At the Seventh Wilderness Conference in 1961, Douglas introduced Udall with glowing praise. William O. Douglas, "Introduction," in *Wilderness: America's Living Heritage*, ed. David Brower (San Francisco: Sierra Club Books, 1961), 86-90. For Udall's initial conservation work with the Kennedy Administration, see Thomas G. Smith, "John Kennedy, Stewart Udall, and New Frontier Conservation," *Pacific Historical Review* 64 (August 1995): 329-62.
55. Stewart L. Udall, Washington, DC, to William O. Douglas, Washington, DC, undated, Correspondence, Box 380, Stewart Udall (1957-1976), in WODP, original emphasis; William O. Douglas, Washington, DC, to Charles McC. Mathias, Jr., Washington, DC, June 2, 1966; and William O. Douglas, Washington, DC, to Stewart L. Udall, June 2, 1966, Environment, Box 544, C&O Canal Miscellaneous (1960-1967), in WODP.
56. Douglas to Udall, June 2, 1966; William O. Douglas, Washington, DC, to Stewart L. Udall, Washington, DC, December 29, 1966, Correspondence, Box 380, Stewart Udall (1957-1976), in WODP; William O. Douglas, "The C&O Canal as a National Historic Park," *Parks and Recreation* 3 (April 1968): 25-26, 52-53. William O. Douglas, Washington, DC, to Lyndon B. Johnson, Washington, DC, January 5, 1967, Environment, Box 544, C&O Canal Miscellaneous (1960-1967), in WODP; and Douglas, *Go East, Young Man*, 211.
57. William O. Douglas, Washington, DC, to Charles McC. Mathias, Washington, DC, September 1, 1967, Environment, Box 544, C&O Canal Miscellaneous (1960-1967), in WODP; William O. Douglas, untitled statement, March 1968, Environment, Box 544, C&O Canal Miscellaneous (1968-1969), in WODP; William O. Douglas, "The C&O Canal Becomes a Park," *National Parks and Conservation Magazine* 45 (May 1971), 8; William O. Douglas, *My Wilderness: East to Katahdin* (Garden City, NY: Doubleday & Company, 1961), 190; Ritter, " 'Walkin'," 60; and Mackintosh, *C&O Canal*, 182.
58. William O. Douglas, Washington, DC, to Henry M. Jackson, Washington, DC, December 30, 1970, Environment, Box 544, C&O Canal Miscellaneous (1970), in WODP.
59. Douglas, "Canal Becomes a Park," 5.
60. Ibid., 5, 8.

61. Mackintosh, *C&O Canal*, passim; Henry M. Jackson, to William O. Douglas, Washington, DC, December 22, 1970, Box 5, Folder 33: General Correspondence D-E (include Douglas, William O.), 1970, in Henry M. Jackson Papers, University of Washington Manuscripts and University Archives, Seattle, WA (hereafter HMJP); Department of Interior News Release, "C&O Canal National Historical Park Combines History and Natural Beauty," February 14, 1971, in Box 3:301, Folder: Correspondence: Michael Nadel: The C&O Canal, 1960s and 1970s, in Wilderness Society Records, CONS130, Conservation Collection, The Denver Public Library; Congress, House of Representatives, Representative Richard Ottinger of New York, H.R. 11226, 94th Cong., 1st sess., *Congressional Record* 121, pt. 32 (December 17, 1975): 41475; and Henry M. Jackson, Remarks, Box 245, Folder 43: Speeches and Writings: Justice Douglas Ceremony, C&O Canal, May 17, 1977, HMJP.

62. James Morton Turner, "The Politics of Modern Wilderness," in *American Wilderness: A New History*, ed. Michael Lewis (New York: Oxford University Press, 2007), 247 characterizes these trends of the wilderness movement from 1964 to the mid-1970s.

63. McCloskey, "Wilderness Movement."

Chapter Five

1. William O. Douglas, "Federal Policy and the Ecological Crisis," in *Ecocide ... and Thoughts toward Survival*, eds. Clifton Fadiman and Jean White (Santa Barbara, CA: Center for the Study of Democratic Institutions, 1971), 63.

2. Bob Woodward and Scott Armstrong, *The Brethren: Inside the Supreme Court* (New York: Avon, 1979), 46.

3. G. Edward White, "The Anti-Judge: William O. Douglas and the Ambiguities of Individuality," in *The American Judicial Tradition: Profiles of Leading American Judges*, expanded edition (New York: Oxford University Press, 1988): 369-420.

4. William M. Wiecek, "Sociological Jurisprudence," in *The Oxford Companion to the Supreme Court of the United States*, ed. Kermit L. Hall (New York: Oxford University Press, 1992), 803; Sheldon M. Novick, "Oliver Wendell Holmes," in *The Oxford Companion to the Supreme Court*, 406-7; Louis Menand, *The Metaphysical Club* (New York: Farrar, Straus and Giroux, 2001), 339-47; and G. Edward White, *The American Judicial Tradition: Profiles of Leading American Judges*, expanded edition (New York: Oxford University Press, 1988).

5. John W. Hopkirk, "The Influence of Legal Realism on William O. Douglas," in *Essays on the American Constitution: A Commemorative Volume in Honor of Alpheus T. Mason*, ed. Gottfried Dietze (Englewood Cliffs, NJ: Prentice-Hall, 1964): 59-76; Laura Kalman, *Legal Realism at Yale, 1927-1960* (Chapel Hill: The University of North Carolina Press, 1986), 3-44; Kermit L. Hall and Peter Karsten, *The Magic Mirror: Law in American History*, second edition (New York: Oxford University Press, 2009), 243-46, 292-94; and Edward A. Purcell, Jr., "American Jurisprudence between the Wars: Legal Realism and the Crisis of Democratic Theory," *American Historical Review* 75 (December 1969): 424-46.

6. Ibid.; William O. Douglas, *Go East, Young Man: The Early Years: The Autobiography of William O. Douglas* (New York: Random House, 1974), 156-73, quotation from 163; and Hall and Karsten, *Magic Mirror*, 294.

7. Howard Ball, "Loyalty, Treason, and the State: An Examination of Justice William O. Douglas's Style, Substance, and Anguish," in *"He Shall Not Pass This Way Again": The Legacy of William O. Douglas*, ed. Stephen L. Wasby (Pittsburgh: University of Pittsburgh Press for the William O. Douglas Institute, 1990), 7 (first quotation); Melvin I. Urofsky, "Getting the Job Done: William O. Douglas and Collegiality in the Supreme Court," in *"He Shall Not Pass This Way Again,"* 33 (second quotation), 34 (third quotation); Robert Jerome Glennon, "Commentary: Collegialism and Change over Time: William O. Douglas as Justice," in *"He Shall Not Pass This Way Again,"* 52; Melvin I. Urofsky, with the assistance of Philip E. Urofsky, eds., *The Douglas Letters: Letters: Selections from the Private Papers of Justice William O. Douglas* (Bethesda, MD: Adler and Adler, 1987), x; L. A. Powe, Jr., "Justice Douglas, the First Amendment, and the Protection of Rights," in *"He Shall Not Pass This Way Again,"* 76; and White, "Anti-Judge."

8. Douglas quoted in James C. Duram, *Justice William O. Douglas* (Boston: Twayne Publishers, 1981), 131 (first quotation); Donald W. Jackson, "Commentary: On the Correct Handling of Contradictions within the Court," in *"He Shall Not Pass This Way Again,"*, 60 (second quotation); and Douglas quoted in Michael Kammen, *A Machine That Would Go of Itself: The Constitution in American Culture* (New York: St. Martin's Press, 1994), 361 (third quotation). For process jurisprudence, see Hall and Karsten, *Magic Mirror*, 343; and White, "Anti-Judge," 415, 420.

9. *Edwards v. California*, 314 U.S. 160, 181 (quotation) (1941). Richard Neuberger, to William O. Douglas, December 4, 1941, in William O. Douglas Papers [WODP], Library of Congress, Washington, D.C., Correspondence, Box 359, Richard Neuberger (1940-1942); and Cathleen H. Douglas, "William O. Douglas: The Man," *Supreme Court Historical Society Yearbook* (1981), 8.

10. *Edwards v. California*, 173-75, 177-78 (first quotation), 178 (second quotation).

11. *Kent v. Dulles*, 357 U.S. 116 (1958); *Aptheker v. Secretary of State*, 378 U.S. 500 (1964); *Papachristou v. City of Jacksonville* 405 U.S. 156, 164 (quotation) (1972); Laura Krugman Ray, "Autobiography and Opinion: The Romantic Jurisprudence of Justice William O. Douglas," *University of Pittsburgh Law Review* 60 (1999), 736-39; and Bruce Allen Murphy, *Wild Bill: The Legend and Life of William O. Douglas* (New York: Random House, 2003), 383-84, 459-60. For his respect of Thoreau, see Douglas, *Go East, Young Man*, 204.

12. *Berman v. Parker*, 348 U.S. 26, 32-33 (first quotation), 33 (second quotation) (1954).

13. Mathew O. Tobriner and Michael A. Willemsen, "In Memoriam: William O. Douglas," *Ecology Law Quarterly* 8 (1980), 406 (first quotation); James M. Caragher, "The Wilderness Ethic of Justice William O. Douglas," *University of Illinois Law Review* (1986), 661-63; and *Village of Belle Terre v. Boraas*, 416 U.S. 1, 9 (second quotation) (1974). Douglas did not address the apparent class components that could make such exclusionary zoning laws discriminatory against the poor. One observer denied this bias and explained that *Belle Terre* simply "restated his belief, in a suburban rather wilderness area, that people can protect their environment if the fundamental rights of others are not violated." See Richard G. Huber, "William O. Douglas and the Environment," *Environmental Affairs* 5 (Spring 1976): 209-12, quotation from 211.

14. *Murphy v. Butler*, 362 U.S. 929, 930 (quotations) (1960); Mrs. David L. Cattanach, Houston, TX, to Justice Douglas, May 5, 1960, Supreme Court File, Box 1231, No. 662(d) *Murphy v. Butler*, October Term 1959, in WODP; "Dissent in Favor of Man," *Saturday Review* (May 7, 1960), photocopy in ibid.; Peter Manus, "Wild Bill Douglas's Last Stand: A Retrospective on the First Supreme Court Environmentalist," *Temple Law Review* 72 (Spring 1999), 160; Rachel Carson, *Silent Spring* (Boston: Houghton Mifflin, 1962; reprint, Boston: Houghton Mifflin, 2002), 158-59; and Linda Lear, *Rachel Carson: Witness for Nature* (New York: Henry Holt and Company, 1997), 306, 312-319.

15. Karl Boyd Brooks, *Public Power, Private Dams: The Hells Canyon High Dam Controversy* (Seattle: University of Washington Press, 2006).

16. Ibid., 220-21; *Udall v. Federal Power Commission*, 387 U.S. 428 (1967); and William Ashworth, *Hells Canyon: The Deepest Gorge on Earth* (New York: Hawthorn Books, 1977), 121-39.

17. Ashworth, *Hells Canyon*, 138-39; Brooks, *Public Power*, 221; Karl Boyd Brooks, " 'Powerless' No More: Postwar Judges and Pacific Northwest Hydroelectrification, 1946-1967," *Idaho Yesterdays* 45 (Winter 2001-02): 11-26; Charles F. Wilkinson, "Justice Douglas and the Public Lands," in *"He Shall Not Pass This Way Again,"* 239; and *Udall v. FPC*, 436 (first quotation, emphasis added), 437 (second quotation), 440 (third quotation). Douglas had held out the promise of alternative energy as a salvation to wilderness sanctuaries previously in *My Wilderness: The Pacific West* (Garden City, NY: Doubleday and Company, 1960), 64.

18. *Udall v. FPC*, 449-50 (emphasis added). Douglas, *Pacific West*, 64. James Morton Turner has shown how well how public-interest arguments were conservationists' most successful claims; see "'The Specter of Environmentalism': Wilderness, Environmental Politics, and the Evolution of the New Right," *Journal of American History*, forthcoming, copy in author's possession.

19. Brooks, *Private Power*, 221, 225; Wilkinson, "Douglas and Public Lands," 239; Ashworth, *Hells Canyon*, 143-49; Stew[art Udall], Washington, DC, to Bill [William O. Douglas], n.d., Correspondence, Box 380, Stewart Udall (1957-1976), in WODP; and Mr. and Mrs. Thomas J. Eley, Jr., Arcata, CA, to Justice Douglas, Washington, DC, October 2, 1967, Supreme Court File, Box 1392, Nos. 462, 463(c) *Washington Public Power v. FPC, Udall v. FPC*, O[ctober] T[erm] 1966, in WODP. Context for increased judicial review of administrative agencies is found in Hall and Karsten, *Magic Mirror*, 333-39.

20. Medicine Creek Treaty quoted in *Puyallup Tribe v. Department of Game of Washington*, 391 U.S. 392, 395 (1968); John R. Wunder, "Pacific Northwest Indians and the Bill of Rights," in *Terra Pacifica: People and Place in the Northwest States and Western Canada*, ed. Paul W. Hirt (Pullman: Washington State University Press, 1998), 162; and John R. Wunder, *"Retained by the People": A History of American Indians and the Bill of Rights* (New York: Oxford University Press, 1994), 181-82. Earlier, Douglas concurred with Justice Hugo Black that the state had the right to regulate Indian fishing for conservation. See *Tulee v. State of Washington*, 315 U.S. 681 (1942). He also ruled against Indians using fish traps in Alaska for conservation purposes in *Kake Village v. Egan*, 369 U.S. 60 (1962). The "reasonable and necessary" line comes from the Washington Supreme Court decision and is incorporated in *Puyallup v. Department of Game*, 401.

21. In cataloguing Douglas's participation in cases concerning American Indians, Ralph W. Johnson found that out of fifty-two Indian cases reaching the Court during his tenure, Douglas wrote fourteen majority, dissenting, or concurring opinions. Most often he voted with the Indian side. See, "'In Simple Justice to a Downtrodden People': Justice Douglas and the American Indian Cases," *He Shall Not Pass This Way Again,"* 191-213. *Puyallup Tribe v. Department of Game of Washington*, 391 U.S. 392, 398 (1968). At the time of *Puyallup I* Johnson strongly criticized the Court's decision to allow states the right to regulate Indian fishing; "The States versus Indian Off-Reservation Fishing: A United States Supreme Court Error," *Washington Law Review* 47 (1972): 207-36.

22. *Puyallup v. Department of Game*, 402; Johnson, "In Simple Justice," 200.

23. *Washington Game Dept. v. Puyallup Tribe*, 414 U.S. 44, 48 (first quotation), 49 (second and third quotations) (1973); Johnson, "In Simple Justice," 200-201; and Wunder, "Indians and the Bill of Rights," 163. In 1965, Douglas had argued that the federal government ought to acquire—that is, extinguish—Indian fishing rights through the power of eminent domain; see *A Wilderness Bill of Rights* (Boston: Little, Brown and Company, 1965), 152.

24. Excerpts of NEPA can be found in Louis S. Warren, ed., *American Environmental History* (Malden, MA: Blackwell, 2003), 290-93. J. Brooks Flippen, *Nixon and the Environment* (Albuquerque: University of New Mexico, 2000); Hal K. Rothman, *The Greening of a Nation?: Environmentalism in the United States since 1945* (Fort Worth: Harcourt Brace, 1998), 109-34; and James Morton Turner, "The Politics of Modern Wilderness," in *American Wilderness: A New History*, ed. Michael Lewis (New York: Oxford University Press, 2007), 243-49.

25. William H. Rodgers, Jr., "The Fox and the Chickens: Mr. Justice Douglas and Environmental Law," in *"He Shall Not Pass This Way Again,"* 217.

26. NEPA in Warren, ed., *American Environmental History*.

27. *San Antonio Conservation Soc. v. Texas Highway Department* 400 U.S. 968, 972, 978 fn. 3, 975 (first quotation) (1970). Justice Black also wrote a dissenting opinion that Douglas and Brennan joined.

28. Ibid., 977 (first quotation), 973-74, 980, 974 (second quotation), 978 (third quotation, emphasis added). The following spring, Douglas, with Black joining him, dissented from another denial of certiorari based in part on the lack of an EIS. *2,606.84 Acres of Land in Tarrant County, Texas v. United States* 402 U.S. 916. Manus characterized this dissent as "searing." "Douglas's Last Stand," 163.

29. *Committee for Nuclear Responsibility, Inc. v. Schlesinger*, 404 U.S. 917, 920 (first quotation), 923-30, 928 (second quotation), 929 (third quotation) (1971). The Council on Environmental Quality (CEQ), an advisory group to the president, resembled the Office of Conservation for which Douglas had called in *The Wilderness Bill of Rights*. James M. Caragher effectively analyzes Douglas's proposed Office of Conservation and the CEQ in "Wilderness Ethic of Justice Douglas," 655-61. Peter Coates, "Amchitka, Alaska: Toward the Bio-Biography of an Island," *Environmental History* 1 (October 1996): 20-45, is a valuable account of Project Cannikin, as well as being a creative environmental history of the island.

30. Roseanne Mlandenich to William O. Douglas, November 7, 1971, Supreme Court File, Box 1539, A. 483 App. For Stay (Amchitka) 1971, in WODP (Lt. Col. in USAF); Mrs. Richard Alexander to William O. Douglas, n.d., in ibid. (second

quotation); and R. W. Lamb to William O. Douglas, November 7, 1971, in ibid. (third and fourth quotations).

31. *Scenic Hudson Preservation Conference v. Federal Power Commission*, 407 U.S. 926, 933 (1972).

32. Ibid., 933.

33. *Life of the Land v. Brinegar*, 414 U.S. 1052, 1053-54 (first quotation), 1054 (second quotation), 1055 (third and fourth quotations) (1973).

34. Ibid., 1055-56. In a memoriam in *Ecology Law Quarterly*, California Supreme Court Associate Justice Mathew O. Tobriner and Senior Attorney on the Staff of the California Supreme Court Michael A. Willemsen singled out this dissent with only five others as important in making Douglas the chief legal spokesperson of conservationists, calling it "eloquent." "In Memoriam," 4.

35. Manus, "Douglas's Last Stand," 165 (first quotation), 153-56, 160-68, 166 (second quotation). For the changing nature of the administrative state, including an increased role for an active judiciary, see George Hoberg, *Pluralism by Design: Environmental Policy and the American Regulatory State* (New York: Praeger, 1992); and William M. Lunch, "Science, Civil Rights and Environmental Policy: A Political Mystery in Three Acts," a paper presented to the Western Political Science Association (March 2004), copy in author's possession.

36. William O. Douglas, *The Three Hundred Year War: A Chronicle of Ecological Disaster* (New York: Random House, 1972), 174 (first quotation), 175 (second and third quotations).

37. Background details in *Sierra Club v. Morton*, 405 U.S. 727, 727-34 (1972); John Warfield Simpson, *Visions of Paradise: Glimpses of Our Landscape's Legacy* (Berkeley: University of California Press, 1999), 220-22; and Michael McCloskey, *In the Thick of It: My Life in the Sierra Club* (Washington, DC: Island Press, 2005), 134-36.

38. *Sierra Club v. Morton*, 734-38; Christopher D. Stone, *Should Trees Have Standing? and Other Essays on Law, Morals and the Environment* (Dobbs Ferry, NY: Oceana Publications, 1996), 165-66.

39. *Sierra Club v. Morton*, 755-56 (first and second quotations), 756-58. Justice Brennan's dissent simply agreed with Blackmun's second alternative.

40. Ibid., 741 (first quotation), 743 (second quotation).

41. Ibid., 743 (first quotation), 744-45 (second quotation), 749 (third quotation), 750 (fourth quotation), 752 (fifth quotation).

42. Aldo Leopold, *A Sand County Almanac with Essays on Conservation from Round River* (New York: Ballantine Books, 1966). Stone's article has been reprinted numerous times. For instance, see Christopher D. Stone, *Should Trees Have Standing? Toward Legal Rights for Natural Objects*, New Preface for the 1988 edition, Foreword by Garret Hardin (Palo Alto, CA: Tioga Publishing, 1988), which includes all of the Supreme Court opinions in *Sierra Club v. Morton*. Stone's 1996 collection of essays, *Should Trees Have Standing? and Other Essays on Law, Morals and the Environment* explains that he wrote the article hurriedly to get it into a *Southern California Law Review* special issue on Law and Technology for which Douglas was coincidentally scheduled to write the preface. Although Stone's article did not really fit, it allowed Douglas to read the essay while *Sierra Club v. Morton* was still being decided, which was an important motivation for Stone in writing the article. See Stone, *Should Trees Have Standing* (1996), ix-x.

43. *Sierra Club v. Morton*, 743, footnote 5 criticizes mass recreation, while footnote 6 and 7 are scathing in their discussion of federal agencies' management of natural resources.

44. *Sierra Club v. Morton*, 758; KRR to Mr. Justice, 19 April 1972, Supreme Court File, Box 1545, No. 70-34, *Sierra Club v. Morton*, Law Clerks, in WODP; Woodward and Armstrong, *The Brethren*, 192-93; "Mr. Justice Douglas, Dissenting," *Living Wilderness* (Summer 1972), 19-29, quotation from 19; William O. Douglas with an Introduction by Joseph W. Meeker, "Nature's Constitutional Rights," *The North American Review* 258 (Spring 1973): 11-14, quotation from 11; John M. Naff, Jr., "Reflections on the Dissent of Douglas, J. in *Sierra Club v. Morton*," photocopy, Supreme Court File, Box 1545, No. 70-34 *Sierra Club v. Morton*, Misc. memos, Cert. memos, vote of Court (originally in *ABA Journal* August 1972), in WODP; Simpson, *Visions of Paradise*, 233, 234; Roderick Frazier Nash, *The Rights of Nature: A History of Environmental Ethics* (Madison: University of Wisconsin Press, 1989), 131; and Christopher D. Stone, "Commentary: William O. Douglas and the Environment," in *"He Shall Not Pass,"* 231. Incidentally, because of litigation delays and spiraling costs, Disney abandoned the development in Mineral King Valley and the valley was eventually included in Sequoia National Park.

Conclusion

1. William O. Douglas, *Go East, Young Man: The Early Years: The Autobiography of William O. Douglas* (New York: Random House, 1974), 465.

2. Robert Gottlieb and others have ably demonstrated that the movement never had been all that consensual. Nevertheless, the period after 1970 certainly experienced a much broader engagement with environmental questions resulting in a more fractured movement. *Forcing the Spring: The Transformation of the American Environmental Movement*, revised and updated edition (Washington, DC: Island Press, 2005).

3. William O. Douglas, *Points of Rebellion* (New York: Vintage Books, 1970), 50-51; and L. A. Powe, Jr., "Justice Douglas, the First Amendment, and the Protection of Rights," in *"He Shall Not Pass This Way Again": The Legacy of William O. Douglas*, ed. Stephen L. Wasby (Pittsburgh: University of Pittsburgh Press for the William O. Douglas Institute, 1990), 85.

4. Douglas, *Points*, 52, 71-72 (first quotation), 85, 87 (second quotation).

5. William O. Douglas, *The Three Hundred Year War: A Chronicle of Ecological Disaster* (New York: Random House, 1972), 171, 190 (quotation).

6. Ibid., 190-91.

7. Ibid., 147, 176.

8. This is a major point of both Michael Egan, *Barry Commoner and the Science of Survival: The Remaking of American Environmentalism* (Cambridge, MA: MIT Press, 2007); and Mark Hamilton Lytle, *The Gentle Subversive: Rachel Carson, Silent Spring, and the Rise of the Environmental Movement* (New York: Oxford University Press, 2007).

9. James Morton Turner has best made this argument. See "'The Specter of Environmentalism': Wilderness, Environmental Politics, and the Evolution of the New Right," *Journal of American History*, forthcoming, copy in author's possession.

10. Among others, Charles F. Wilkinson makes this point in "Justice Douglas and the Public Lands," in *"He Shall Not Pass This Way Again,"* 244-45.

11. Roderick Nash, *Wilderness and the American Mind*, third ed. (New Haven, CT: Yale University Press, 1982), 263 notes that Douglas's work was widely read and cited.

12. Stephen Fox, *The American Conservation Movement: John Muir and His Legacy* (Madison: University of Wisconsin Press, 1981), 239.

13. James F. Simon, *Independent Journey: The Life of William O. Douglas* (New York: Harper and Row, 1980), 446-54. Quotation from 447.

14. *Tributes to Honorable William O. Douglas, Associate Justice of the Supreme Court to Commemorate the Occasion of His Retirement from the Supreme Court, November 12, 1975,* 94th Congress, 2nd Session, House Document No. 94-622 (Washington, DC: US Government Printing Office, 1976), 58. As Douglas's representative, McCormack also noted: "I am sure the Douglases will not let me forget that they are my constituents. They inform me, not infrequently, of their interests, attitudes, and recommendations on pending legislation." (Ibid., 60.)

15. Ibid., 13.

16. Ibid., 150.

17. Ibid., 25.

18. Ibid., 46. Representative Gude continued in his testimony to explain Douglas's role in preserving the C&O Canal, an important one for a Maryland politician to note.

19. Ibid., 112.

20. Ibid., 75. For other general environmental praise, see ibid., 8, 55, 64, 78, 97, 102, 102-3, 114.

21. Ibid., 51.

22. Ibid., 153, 155.

23. Ibid., 1.

24. Ibid., 33.

25. Ibid., 104, 105. In 1955, Douglas took Robert F. Kennedy with him on a trip to the Soviet Union, and Kennedy's father was instrumental in Douglas's work with the SEC. William O. Douglas, *Russian Journey* (Garden City, NY: Doubleday, 1956). To tout his brother's efforts to promote physical fitness, RFK famously hiked fifty miles along the C&O Canal in seventeen hours in February 1963. See Barry Mackintosh, *C&O Canal: The Making of a Park* (Washington, DC: History Division, National Park Service, Department of the Interior, 1991), 180.

26. *Tributes*, 22-23.

27. Ibid., 45.

28. Ibid., 68. Preceding this remark, Representative Eckhardt included details of Douglas's efforts on behalf of Big Thicket preservation, a critical Texas conservation effort. See also, ibid., 120.

29. William O. Douglas, to Chief Justice and Associate Justices, November 14, 1975, in *The Douglas Papers: Selections from the Private Papers of Justice William O. Douglas*, edited with an introduction by Melvin I. Urofsky with the assistance of Philip E. Urofsky (Bethesda, MD: Adler and Adler, 1987), 417-18.

Bibliography

Manuscript Sources

Conservation Collection, Denver Public Library, Denver, CO
    —Wilderness Society Records
Library of Congress, Washington, DC
    William O. Douglas Papers
Manuscripts, Special Collections, University Archives, University of Washington,
    Seattle, WA
    —Double K Mountain Ranch Papers
    —Emily Haig Papers
    —Henry M. Jackson Papers
    —John Osseward Papers
Pacific Northwest Collection, Pacific Northwest Biographical Pamphlet files
    —Preston P. Macy Papers
Sierra Club Members Papers, Bancroft Library, University of California at Berkeley,
    Berkeley, CA
    —David R. Brower Papers
Sundquist Research Library, Yakima Valley Museum, Yakima, WA
    —William O. Douglas Speech Collection
Western History Collection, Denver Public Library, Denver, CO
    —E. Palmer Hoyt Papers

Newspapers

Coos Bay Times
Dallas Morning News
New York Times
Olympic Tribune
Oregon Labor Press
Port Angeles Evening News
Seattle Post-Intelligencer
Seattle Times
Washington Post
Washington Post and Times-Herald
Yakima Herald Republic

Court Cases

2,606.84 Acres of Land in Tarrant County, Texas v. U.S., 402 U.S. 916 (1971)
Aptheker v. Secretary of State, 378 U.S. 500 (1964)
Berman v. Parker, 348 U.S. 26 (1954)
Committee for Nuclear Responsibility, Inc. v. Schlesinger, 404 U.S. 917 (1971)
Edwards v. California, 314 U.S. 160 (1941)
Kake Village v. Egan, 369 U.S. 60 (1962)
Kent v. Dulles, 357 U.S. 116 (1958)
Life of the Land v. Brinegar, 414 U.S. 1052 (1973)
Murphy v. Butler, 362 U.S. 929 (1960)
Papachristou v. City of Jacksonville 405 U.S. 156 (1972)

Puyallup Tribe v. Department of Game of Washington, 391 U.S. 392 (1968)
San Antonio Conservation Soc. v. Texas Highway, 400 U.S. 968 (1970)
Scenic Hudson Preservation Conference v. Federal Power Commission, 407 U.S. 926
   (1972)
Sierra Club v. Morton, 405 U.S. 727 (1972)
Tulee v. State of Washington, 315 U.S. 681 (1942)
Udall v. Federal Power Commission, 387 U.S. 428 (1967)
Village of Belle Terre v. Boraas, 416 U.S. 1 (1974)
Washington Department of Game v. Puyallup Tribe, 414 U.S. 44 (1973)

Published Primary Sources

Ashworth, William. *Hells Canyon: The Deepest Gorge on Earth*. New York: Hawthorn
   Books, 1977.
Berry, Wendell. *The Gift of Good Land: Further Essays Cultural and Agricultural*. San
   Francisco: North Point Press, 1981.
Broome, Harvey. *Faces of the Wilderness*. Missoula, MT: Mountain Press Publishing
   Company, 1972.
Brower, David, ed. *Wilderness: America's Living Heritage*. San Francisco: Sierra Club,
   1961.
"The C and O Walkathon." *American Forests* 60 (May 1954): 18-19, 54.
Carson, Rachel. *Silent Spring*. Boston: Houghton Mifflin, 1962; reprint, Boston:
   Houghton Mifflin, 2002.
Congressional Record. 1939-1980.
Douglas, Cathleen H. "William O. Douglas: The Man." Supreme Court Historical
   Society Yearbook (1981): 7-9.
"Douglas, Jurist: Appointment to Supreme Court Puts Hard Hitter on the Bench."
   Newsweek 13 (March 27, 1939): 13.
Douglas, William O. *Of Men and Mountains*. New York: Harper and Brothers, 1950;
   reprint, San Francisco: Chronicle Books, 1990.
———. *Strange Lands and Friendly People*. New York: Harper and Brothers, 1951.
———. "The Black Silence of Fear." *New York Times Magazine* (January 13, 1952): 7,
   37-38.
———. *Beyond the High Himalayas*. New York: Doubleday, 1952.
———. "My Favorite Vacation Land." *The American Magazine* 154 (July 1952): 38-
   41, 94-99.
———. *North from Malaya: Adventure on Five Fronts*. Garden City, NY: Doubleday
   & Company, 1953.
———. "Foreword." In *Our National Forests*, Bernard Frank, vii-viii. Norman:
   University of Oklahoma Press, 1955.
———. *Russian Journey*. Garden City, NY: Doubleday & Company, 1956.
———. *West of the Indus*. Garden City, NY: Doubleday & Company, 1958.
———. *My Wilderness: The Pacific West*. Garden City, NY: Doubleday & Company,
   1960.
———. "Introduction." In *Wilderness: America's Living Heritage*, ed. David Brower,
   86-90. San Francisco: Sierra Club Books, 1961.
———. *A Living Bill of Rights*. Garden City, NY: Doubleday and Company, 1961.
———. *My Wilderness: East to Katahdin*. Garden City, NY: Doubleday & Company,
   1961.
———. *Democracy's Manifesto*. Garden City, NY: Doubleday, 1962.

———. "Sewage Treatment Plants—Not Dams." *National Parks Magazine* 36 (March 1962): 14-15.

———. *Anatomy of Liberty: The Rights of Man without Force.* New York: Trident Press, 1963.

———. "America's Vanishing Wilderness." *Ladies' Home Journal* 81 (July 1964): 37-41, 77.

———. *A Wilderness Bill of Rights.* Boston: Little, Brown and Company, 1965.

———. *Farewell to Texas: A Vanishing Wilderness.* New York: McGraw-Hill, 1967.

———. "The C & O Canal as a National Historic Park." *Parks and Recreation* 3 (April 1968): 25-26, 52-53.

———. *Points of Rebellion.* New York: Vintage Books, 1970.

———. "The C & O Canal Becomes a Park." *National Parks and Conservation Magazine: The Environmental Journal* 45 (May 1971): 4-8.

———. "Federal Policy and the Ecological Crisis." In *Ecocide ... and Thoughts toward Survival,* ed. Clifton Fadiman and Jean White, 63-74. Santa Barbara, CA: Center for the Study of Democratic Institutions, 1971.

———. *International Dissent: Six Steps toward World Peace.* New York: Random House, 1971.

———. *The Three Hundred Year War: A Chronicle of Ecological Disaster.* New York: Random House, 1972.

———. "Nature's Constitutional Rights," *The North American Review* 258 (Spring 1973): 11-14. With an Introduction by Joseph W. Meeker.

———. *Go East, Young Man: The Early Years: The Autobiography of William O. Douglas.* New York: Random House, 1974.

———. *The Court Years, 1939-1975: The Autobiography of William O. Douglas.* New York: Random House, 1980.

———. *The Douglas Letters: Selections from the Private Papers of Justice William O. Douglas.* Edited and introduced by Melvin I. Urofsky, with the assistance of Philip E. Urofsky. Bethesda, MD: Adler and Adler, 1987.

Fraser, Hugh Russell. Letter to "The Open Forum." *The American Mercury* 62 (February 1946): 251.

Frome, Michael. *Chronicling the West: Thirty Years of Environmental Writing.* Seattle: The Mountaineers, 1996.

Gunter, Peter. *The Big Thicket: A Challenge for Conservation.* Austin and New York and Riverside, CN: Jenkins Publishing and The Chatham Press, 1971.

"Justice Douglas, Journalists Debate C & O Canal Plans on 189-Mile Hike." *American Forests* 60 (April 1954): 42.

Lash, Joseph P., ed. *From the Diaries of Felix Frankfurter.* New York: W. W. Norton, 1975.

Leopold, Aldo. *A Sand County Almanac: With Essays on Conservation from Round River.* New York: Ballantine Books, 1966.

McCloskey, Michael. *In the Thick of It: My Life in the Sierra Club.* Washington, DC: Island Press, 2005.

"Mr. Justice Douglas, Dissenting." *Living Wilderness* (Summer 1972): 19-29.

Muir, John. *A Thousand-Mile Walk to the Gulf.* Boston: Houghton Mifflin, 1916; reprint, Boston: Houghton Mifflin, 1981.

Murie, Margaret E. *Two in the Far North.* New York: Knopf, 1962; reprint, Anchorage: Alaska Northwest Books, 1997.

Neuberger, Richard. *They Never Go Back to Pocatello: The Selected Essays of Richard Neuberger*. Edited and introduced by Steve Neal. Foreword by Maurine Neuberger. Portland: Oregon Historical Society Press, 1988.

Nixon, Edgar B., ed. *Franklin D. Roosevelt and Conservation, 1911-1945*. Volume One, 1911-1937. Hyde Park, NY: General Services Administration, National Archives and Records Service, Franklin D. Roosevelt Library, 1957.

O'Connor, Sandra Day, and H. Alan Day. *Lazy B: Growing Up on a Cattle Ranch in the American Southwest*. New York: Random House, 2002.

Politicus. "Justice Douglas—Headline Hunter." *The American Mercury* 83 (August 1956): 121-26.

Porter, Eliot. *The Place No One Knew: Glen Canyon on the Colorado*. San Francisco: Sierra Club Books, 1966.

"The Port Huron Statement." In *'Takin' it to the Streets': A Sixties Reader*. Second ed., eds. Alexander Bloom and Wini Breines, 50-61. New York: Oxford University Press, 2003.

Reich, Charles A. *The Greening of America*. New York: Random House, 1970.

Ritter, Colin. "'Walkin' ... and Hollerin' ...'" *American Forests* 71 (June 1965), 6-7, 60-61.

Rodell, Fred. "Bill Douglas, American." *American Mercury* 61 (December 1945): 656-65.

———. "I'd Prefer Bill Douglas." *Nation* 174 (April 26, 1952): 400-402.

Roosevelt, Theodore. *Winning of the West*. Four volumes. New York: G. P. Putnam's Sons, 1889-1896).

———. *Theodore Roosevelt: An Autobiography*. New York: Macmillan, 1913; reprint, New York: Charles Scribner's Sons, 1922.

———. "The Strenuous Life." In *The Works of Theodore Roosevelt: Volume XIII*. New York: Charles Scribner's Sons, 1926.

Schwartz, William, ed. *Voices for the Wilderness*. New York: Ballantine Books, 1969.

"Solitary Dissent." *Time* 63 (February 1, 1954): 15.

Tributes to Honorable William O. Douglas, Associate Justice of the Supreme Court to Commemorate the Occasion of His Retirement from the Supreme Court, November 12, 1975. 94th Congress, 2nd Session, House Document No. 94-622. Washington, DC: US Government Printing Office, 1976.

Turner, Frederick Jackson. "The Significance of the Frontier in American History." In *The Turner Thesis concerning the Role of the Frontier in American History*, revised ed., ed. George Rogers Taylor, 1-18. Boston: Heath, 1956.

"The Woods Walkers." *Time* 63 (March 29, 1954): 20.

Secondary Sources

Allin, Craig W. *The Politics of Wilderness Preservation*. Westport, CT: Greenwood Press, 1982.

Anderson, Terry H. *The Movement and the Sixties: Protest in America from Greensboro to Wounded Knee*. New York: Oxford University Press, 1995.

Backes, David. *A Wilderness Within: The Life of Sigurd F. Olson*. Minneapolis: University of Minnesota Press, 1997.

Ball, Howard. "Loyalty, Treason, and the State: An Examination of Justice William O. Douglas's Style, Substance, and Anguish." In *"He Shall Not Pass This Way Again": The Legacy of William O. Douglas*, ed. Stephen L. Wasby, 7-32. Pittsburgh: University of Pittsburgh Press for the William O. Douglas Institute, 1990.

Ball, Howard, and Phillip J. Cooper. *Of Power and Right: Hugo Black, William O. Douglas, and America's Constitutional Revolution*. New York: Oxford University Press, 1992.

Barbour, Michael G. "Ecological Fragmentation in the Fifties." In *Uncommon Ground: Toward Reinventing Nature*, ed. William Cronon, 223-55. New York: W. W. Norton, 1995.

Bederman, Gail. *Manliness and Civilization: A Cultural History of Gender and Race in the United States, 1880-1917*. Chicago: University of Chicago Press, 1995.

Bingham, Edwin R. "American Wests through Autobiography and Memoir." *Pacific Historical Review* 56 (February 1987): 1-24.

Boorstin, Daniel J. *The Image, or What Happened to the American Dream*. New York: Atheneum, 1962.

Bosmajian, Haig. "The Imprint of the Cascade Country on William O. Douglas." *Journal of the West* 32 (July 1993): 80-86.

Botkin, Daniel B. *Discordant Harmonies: A New Ecology for the Twenty-First Century*. New York: Oxford University Press, 1990.

Brinkley, Alan. *The End of Reform: New Deal Liberalism in Recession and War*. New York: Knopf, 1995.

Brockman, C. Frank *Recreational Use of Wild Lands*. New York: McGraw-Hill, 1959.

Brooks, Karl Boyd. "'Powerless' No More: Postwar Judges and Pacific Northwest Hydroelectrification, 1946-1967." *Idaho Yesterdays* 45 (Winter 2001-02): 11-26.

———. *Public Power, Private Dams: The Hells Canyon High Dam Controversy*. Seattle: University of Washington Press, 2006.

Budiansky, Stephen. *Nature's Keepers: The New Science of Nature Management*. New York: Free Press, 1995.

Callicott, J. Baird, and Michael P. Nelson, eds. *The Great New Wilderness Debate: An Expansive Collection of Writings Defining Wilderness from John Muir to Gary Snyder*. Athens: University of Georgia Press, 1998.

Caragher, James M. "The Wilderness Ethic of Justice William O. Douglas." *University of Illinois Law Review* (1986): 645-68.

Coates, Peter. "Amchitka, Alaska: Toward the Bio-Biography of an Island." *Environmental History* 1 (October 1996): 20-45.

Conte, Christopher. "Creating Wild Places from Domesticated Landscapes: The Internationalization of the American Wilderness Concept." In *American Wilderness: A New History*, ed. Michael Lewis, 223-41. New York: Oxford University Press, 2007.

Cooper, John Milton, Jr. *The Warrior and the Priest: Woodrow Wilson and Theodore Roosevelt*. Cambridge, MA: Belknap Press of Harvard University Press, 1983.

Cozine, Jr., James J. *Saving the Big Thicket: From Exploration to Preservation, 1685-2003*. Denton, TX: Big Thicket Association, University of North Texas Press, 2004.

Cronon, William, "The Trouble with Wilderness; or, Getting Back to the Wrong Nature." In *Uncommon Ground: Toward Reinventing Nature*, ed. William Cronon, 69-90. New York: Norton, 1995.

———, ed. *Uncommon Ground: Toward Reinventing Nature*. New York: W. W. Norton, 1995.

Decker, Jeffrey Louis. *Made in America: Self-Styled Success from Horatio Alger to Oprah Winfrey*. Minneapolis: University of Minnesota Press, 1997.

Dubbert, Joe L. "Progressivism and the Masculinity Crisis." In *The American Man*, eds. Elizabeth H. Pleck and Joseph H. Pleck, 303-20. Englewood Cliffs, NJ: Prentice-Hall, 1980.

Duram, James C. *Justice William O. Douglas*. Boston: Twayne Publishers, 1981.

Egan, Michael. *Barry Commoner and the Science of Survival: The Remaking of American Environmentalism*. Cambridge, MA: The MIT Press, 2007.

Flippen, J. Brooks. *Nixon and the Environment*. Albuquerque: University of New Mexico, 2000.

———. *Conservative Conservationist: Russell E. Train and the Emergence of American Environmentalism*. Baton Rouge: Louisiana State University Press, 2006.

Fox, Stephen. *The American Conservation Movement: John Muir and His Legacy*. Madison: University of Wisconsin Press, 1981.

Frome, Michael. *Battle for the Wilderness*. Revised edition. Salt Lake City: University of Utah Press, 1997.

Gayton, Don. *Landscapes of the Interior: Re-Explorations of Nature and the Human Spirit*. Gabriola Island, B.C., Canada: New Society Publishers, 1996.

Glancy, Dorothy J. "Douglas's Right of Privacy: A Response to His Critics." In *"He Shall Not Pass This Way Again": The Legacy of Justice William O. Douglas*, ed. Stephen L. Wasby, 155-77. Pittsburgh: University of Pittsburgh Press for the William O. Douglas Institute, 1990.

Glennon, Robert Jerome. "Commentary: Collegialism and Change over Time: William O. Douglas as Justice." In *"He Shall Not Pass This Way Again": The Legacy of William O. Douglas*, ed. Stephen L. Wasby, 51-56. Pittsburgh: University of Pittsburgh Press for the William O. Douglas Institute, 1990.

Gottlieb, Robert. *Forcing the Spring: The Transformation of the American Environmental Movement*, revised and updated. Washington, DC: Island Press, 2005.

Gould, Lewis L. *Lady Bird Johnson: Our Environmental First Lady*. Lawrence: University Press of Kansas, 1999.

Griswold, Robert L. "The 'Flabby American,' the Body, and the Cold War." In *A Shared Experience: Men, Women, and the History of Gender*, ed. Laura McCall and Donald Yacovone, 323-39. New York: New York University Press, 1998.

Hall, Kermit L., and Peter Karsten. *The Magic Mirror: Law in American History*, second edition. New York: Oxford University Press, 2009.

Hantover, Jeffrey P. "The Boy Scouts and the Validation of Masculinity." In *The American Man*, eds. Elizabeth H. Pleck and Joseph H. Pleck, 285-301. Englewood Cliffs, NJ: Prentice-Hall, 1980.

Harvey, Mark W. T. "Battle for Dinosaur: Echo Park Dam and the Birth of the Modern Wilderness Movement." *Montana: the Magazine of Western History* 45 (Winter 1995): 32-45.

———. *A Symbol of Wilderness: Echo Park and the American Conservation Movement*. Albuquerque: University of New Mexico Press, 1994; reprint, Seattle: University of Washington Press, 2000.

———. *Wilderness Forever: Howard Zahniser and the Path to the Wilderness Act*. Seattle: University of Washington Press, 2005.

———. "Loving the Wild in Postwar America." In *American Wilderness: A New History*, ed. Michael Lewis, 187-203. New York: Oxford University Press, 2007.

Hays, Samuel P. *Conservation and the Gospel of Efficiency: The Progressive Conservation Movement, 1890-1920*. Cambridge, MA: Harvard University Press, 1959; reprint, New York: Atheneum, 1975.

————, in collaboration with Barbara D. Hays. *Beauty, Health, and Permanence: Environmental Politics in the United States, 1955-1985*. Cambridge: Cambridge University Press, 1987.

Hazlett, Maril. "Voices from the *Spring: Silent Spring* and the Ecological Turn in American Health." In *Seeing Nature through Gender*, ed. Virginia J. Scharff, 103-28. Lawrence: University Press of Kansas, 2003.

Higham, John. "The Problem of Assimilation in the United States." In *Major Problems in American Immigration and Ethnic History*, ed. Jon Gjerde, 16-22. Boston: Houghton Mifflin, 1998.

Hirt, Paul W. *A Conspiracy of Optimism: Management of National Forests since World War Two*. Lincoln: University of Nebraska Press, 1994.

Hoberg, George. *Pluralism by Design: Environmental Policy and the American Regulatory State*. New York: Praeger, 1992.

Hoffert, Sylvia D. *A History of Gender in America: Essays, Documents, and Articles*. Upper Saddle River, NJ: Prentice Hall, 2003.

Hopkirk, John W. "The Influence of Legal Realism on William O. Douglas." In *Essays on the American Constitution: A Commemorative Volume in Honor of Alpheus T. Mason*, ed. Gottfried Dietze, 59-76. Englewood Cliffs, NJ: Prentice-Hall, 1964.

Huber, Richard G. "William O. Douglas and the Environment." *Environmental Affairs* 5 (Spring 1976): 209-12.

Hyman, Diana Rachel. "Defenses of Solitude: Justice Douglas, the Right to Privacy, and the Preservation of the American Wilderness." Ph.D. Dissertation, Harvard University, 2003.

Jackson, Donald W. "Commentary: On the Correct Handling of Contradictions within the Court." In *"He Shall Not Pass This Way Again": The Legacy of Justice William O. Douglas*, ed. Stephen L. Wasby, 57-62. Pittsburgh: University of Pittsburgh Press for the William O. Douglas Institute, 1990.

Jameson, John. *The Story of Big Bend National Park*. Austin: University of Texas Press, 1996.

Jarvis, Kimberly A. "Gender and Wilderness Conservation," in *American Wilderness: A New History*, ed. Michael Lewis, 149-65. New York: Oxford University Press, 2007.

Johnson, Benjamin. "Wilderness Parks and Their Discontents." In *American Wilderness: A New History*, ed. Michael Lewis, 113-30. New York: Oxford University Press, 2007.

Johnson, Michael L. *Hunger for the Wild: America's Obsession with the Untamed West*. Lawrence: University Press of Kansas, 2007.

Johnson, Ralph W. "The States versus Indian Off-Reservation Fishing: A United States Supreme Court Error." *Washington Law Review* 47 (1972): 207-36.

————. "'In Simple Justice to a Downtrodden People': Justice Douglas and the American Indian Cases." In *"He Shall Not Pass This Way Again": The Legacy of Justice William O. Douglas*, ed. Stephen L. Wasby, 191-213. Pittsburgh: University of Pittsburgh Press for the William O. Douglas Institute, 1990.

Kalman, Laura. *Legal Realism at Yale, 1927-1960*. Chapel Hill: The University of North Carolina Press, 1986.

Kammen, Michael. *A Machine That Would Go of Itself: The Constitution in American Culture*. New York: St. Martin's Press, 1994.

Kasson, John F. *Houdini, Tarzan, and the Perfect Man: The White Male Body and the Challenge of Modernity in America.* New York: Hill and Wang, 2001.

Kaye, Roger. *Last Great Wilderness: The Campaign to Establish the Arctic National Wildlife Refuge.* Fairbanks: University of Alaska Press, 2006.

Lear, Linda. *Rachel Carson: Witness for Nature.* New York: Henry Holt and Company, 1997.

Lears, T. J. Jackson. *No Place of Grace: Antimodernism and the Transformation of American Culture, 1880-1920.* New York: Pantheon Books, 1981.

Lewis, Michael. "Wilderness and Conservation Science." In *American Wilderness: A New History,* ed. Michael Lewis, 205-21. New York: Oxford University Press, 2007.

Lien, Carsten. *Olympic Battleground: The Power Politics of Timber Preservation.* San Francisco: Sierra Club Books, 1991.

Louter, David. *Windshield Wilderness: Cars, Roads, and Nature in Washington's National Parks.* Seattle: University of Washington Press, 2006.

Lunch, William M. *The Nationalization of American Politics.* Berkeley: University of California Press, 1987.

———. "Science, Civil Rights and Environmental Policy: A Political Mystery in Three Acts." A paper presented to the Western Political Science Association. March 2004. Copy in author's possession.

Lytle, Mark Hamilton. *America's Uncivil Wars: The Sixties Era from Elvis to the Fall of Richard Nixon.* New York: Oxford University Press, 2006.

———. *The Gentle Subversive: Rachel Carson,* Silent Spring, *and the Rise of the Environmental Movement.* New York: Oxford University Press, 2007.

Mackintosh, Barry. *C & O Canal: The Making of a Park.* Washington, D.C.: History Division, National Park Service, Department of the Interior, 1991.

———. "Shootout on the Old C.&O. Canal: The Great Parkway Controversy, 1950-1960." *Maryland Historical Magazine* 90 (Summer 1995): 141-63.

Maher, Neil M. *Nature's New Deal: The Civilian Conservation Corps and the Roots of the American Environmental Movement.* New York: Oxford University Press, 2008.

Manus, Peter. "Wild Bill Douglas's Last Stand: A Retrospective on the First Supreme Court Environmentalist." *Temple Law Review* 72 (Spring 1999): 111-96.

Marsh, Kevin. *Drawing Lines in the Forest: Creating Wilderness in the Pacific Northwest.* Seattle: University of Washington Press, 2007.

McCloskey, Michael. "Wilderness Movement at the Crossroads, 1945-1970." *Pacific Historical Review* 41 (August 1972): 347-50.

Menand, Louis. *The Metaphysical Club.* New York: Farrar, Straus and Giroux, 2001.

Merchant, Carolyn. "Women of the Progressive Era Conservation Movement, 1900-1916." *Environmental Review* 8 (Spring 1984): 57-85.

Miller, Char. *Gifford Pinchot and the Making of Modern Environmentalism.* Washington, DC: Island Books, 2001.

Muncy, Robyn. "Trustbusting and White Manhood in America, 1898-1914." *American Studies* 38 (Fall 1997): 21-37.

Murphy, Bruce Allen. *Wild Bill: The Legend and Life of William O. Douglas.* New York: Random House, 2003.

Nash, Gerald D. *Creating the West: Historical Interpretation, 1890-1990.* Albuquerque: University of New Mexico Press, 1991.

Nash, Roderick. *Wilderness and the American Mind.* Third ed. New Haven: Yale University Press, 1982.

————. *The Rights of Nature: A History of Environmental Ethics.* Madison: University of Wisconsin Press, 1989.

Nelson, Michael P. "An Amalgamation of Wilderness Preservation Arguments." In *The Great New Wilderness Debate: An Expansive Collection of Writings Defining Wilderness from John Muir to Gary Snyder,* eds. J. Baird Callicott and Michael P. Nelson, 154-98. Athens: University of Georgia Press.

Nicholson, Marjorie Hope. *Mountain Gloom and Mountain Glory: The Development of the Aesthetics of the Infinite.* Ithaca: Cornell University Press, 1963, reprint; Seattle: University of Washington Press, 1997.

Novick, Sheldon M. "Oliver Wendell Holmes." In *The Oxford Companion to the Supreme Court of the United States,* ed. Kermit L. Hall, 406-7. New York: Oxford University Press, 1992.

Nugent, Walter. *Into the West: The Story of Its Peoples.* New York: Alfred A. Knopf, 1999.

Oelschlaeger, Max. *Caring for Creation: An Ecumenical Approach to the Environmental Crisis.* New Haven, CT: Yale University Press, 1994.

Palmer, Tim. *Endangered Rivers and the Conservation Movement.* Berkeley: University of California Press, 1986.

Parrish, Michael E. "Cold War Justice: The Supreme Court and the Rosenbergs." *American Historical Review* 82 (October 1977): 805-42.

Patterson, James T. *Grand Expectations: The United States, 1945-1974.* New York: Oxford University Press, 1996.

Posner, Richard A. *Public Intellectuals: A Study of Decline.* Cambridge, MA: Harvard University Press, 2001.

Powe, L. A., Jr. "Justice Douglas, the First Amendment, and the Protection of Rights." In *"He Shall Not Pass This Way Again": The Legacy of Justice William O. Douglas,* ed. Stephen L. Wasby, 69-90. Pittsburgh: University of Pittsburgh Press for the William O. Douglas Institute, 1990.

Purcell, Jr., Edward A. "American Jurisprudence between the Wars: Legal Realism and the Crisis of Democratic Theory." *American Historical Review* 75 (December 1969): 424-46.

Ray, Laura Krugman. "Autobiography and Opinion: The Romantic Jurisprudence of Justice William O. Douglas." *University of Pittsburgh Law Review* 60 (1999): 707-44.

Reich, Charles A. "Foreword: 'He Shall Not Pass This Way Again.'" In *"He Shall Not Pass This Way Again": The Legacy of Justice William O. Douglas,* ed. Stephen L. Wasby, xi-xiii. Pittsburgh: University of Pittsburgh Press for the William O. Douglas Institute, 1990.

Righter, Robert W. *The Battle over Hetch Hetchy: America's Most Controversial Dam and the Birth of Modern Environmentalism.* New York: Oxford University Press, 2005.

Rodgers, William H., Jr. "The Fox and the Chickens: Mr. Justice Douglas and Environmental Law." In *"He Shall Not Pass This Way Again": The Legacy of Justice William O. Douglas,* ed. Stephen L. Wasby, 215-26. Pittsburgh: University of Pittsburgh Press for the William O. Douglas Institute, 1990.

Rome, Adam. *The Bulldozer in the Countryside: Suburban Sprawl and the Rise of American Environmentalism.* New York: Cambridge University Press, 2001.

————. "'Give Earth a Chance': The Environmental Movement and the Sixties." *Journal of American History* 90 (September 2003): 525-54.

Rothman, Hal K. *The Greening of a Nation?: Environmentalism in the United States since 1945*. Fort Worth, TX: Harcourt Brace College Publishers, 1998.

————. *Devil's Bargains: Tourism in the Twentieth-Century American West*. Lawrence: University Press of Kansas, 1998.

Runte, Alfred. *National Parks: The American Experience*. 3rd ed. Lincoln: University of Nebraska Press, 1997.

Sachs, Aaron. *The Humboldt Current: Nineteenth-Century Exploration and the Roots of American Environmentalism*. New York: Viking, 2006.

Said, Edward W. *Representations of the Intellectual: The 1993 Reith Lectures*. New York: Vintage Books, 1994.

Schmitt, Peter J. *Back to Nature: The Arcadian Myth in Urban America*. New York: Oxford University Press, 1969; reprint, Baltimore: Johns Hopkins University Press, 1990.

Schrepfer, Susan R. *Nature's Altars: Mountains, Gender, and American Environmentalism*. Lawrence: University Press of Kansas, 2005.

Sellars, Richard West. *Preserving Nature in the National Parks: A History*. New Haven, CT: Yale University Press, 1997.

Shils, Edward. *The Intellectuals and the Powers and Other Essays*. Chicago: University of Chicago Press.

Simon, Bryant. "'New Men in Body and Soul': The Civilian Conservation Corps and the Transformation of Male Bodies and the Body Politic." In *Seeing Nature through Gender*, ed. Virginia J. Scharff, 80-102. Lawrence: University Press of Kansas, 2003.

Simon, James F. *Independent Journey: The Life of William O. Douglas*. New York: Harper & Row, 1980.

Simpson, John Warfield. *Visions of Paradise: Glimpses of Our Landscape's Legacy*. Berkeley: University of California Press, 1999.

Sitkoff, Harvard. *The Struggle for Black Equality, 1954-1992*. Revised ed. New York: Hill and Wang, 1993.

Slotkin, Richard. *Gunfighter Nation: The Myth of the Frontier in Twentieth-Century America*. New York: Atheneum, 1992; reprint, Norman: University of Oklahoma Press, 1998.

Smith, Thomas G. "John Kennedy, Stewart Udall, and New Frontier Conservation." *Pacific Historical Review* 64 (August 1995): 329-62.

Soest, Sally Warren, ed., *Voice of the Wild Olympics*. Seattle: Olympic Park Associates, 1998.

Sommarstrom, Ralph. "Wild Land Preservation Crisis: The North Cascades Controversy." Ph.D. diss., University of Washington, 1970.

Sowards, Adam M. "Spiritual Egalitarianism: John Muir's Religious Environmentalism." In *John Muir in Historical Context*, ed. Sally M. Miller, 123-36. New York: Peter Lang Publishing, 1999.

————. "William O. Douglas: The Environmental Justice and the American West." In *The Human Tradition in the American West*, ed. Benson Tong and Regan Lutz. Wilmington, DE: Scholarly Resources, forthcoming.

Steen, Harold K. *The U.S. Forest Service: A History*. Centennial Edition. Durham, NC, and Seattle: Forest History Society in association with University of Washington Press, 2004.

Steinberg, Ted. *Down to Earth: Nature's Role in American History*. New York: Oxford University Press, 2002.

Stoll, Mark. "Religion 'Irradiates' the Wilderness." In *American Wilderness: A New History*, ed. Michael Lewis, 35-53. New York: Oxford University Press, 2007.

Stone, Christopher D. *Should Trees Have Standing? Toward Legal Rights for Natural Objects*. New Preface for the 1988 edition. Palo Alto, CA: Tioga Publishing, 1988.

———. "Commentary: William O. Douglas and the Environment." In *"He Shall Not Pass This Way Again": The Legacy of Justice William O. Douglas*, ed. Stephen L. Wasby, 227-32. Pittsburgh: University of Pittsburgh Press for the William O. Douglas Institute, 1990.

———. *Should Trees Have Standing?: and Other Essays on Law, Morals and the Environment*. Dobbs Ferry, NY: Oceana Publications, 1996.

Sutter, Paul S. *Driven Wild: How the Fight Against Automobiles Launched the Modern Wilderness Movement*. Seattle: University of Washington Press, 2002.

Testi, Arnaldo. "The Gender of Reform Politics: Theodore Roosevelt and the Culture of Masculinity." *Journal of American History* 81 (March 1995): 1509-33.

Tobriner, Mathew O., and Michael A. Willemsen. "In Memoriam: William O. Douglas." *Ecology Law Quarterly* 8 (1980): 405-8.

Turner, James Morton. "The Politics of Modern Wilderness." In *American Wilderness: A New History*, ed. Michael Lewis, 243-61. New York: Oxford University Press, 2007.

———. "'The Specter of Environmentalism': Wilderness, Environmental Politics, and the Evolution of the New Right." *Journal of American History*, forthcoming. Copy in author's possession.

Urofsky, Melvin I. "Getting the Job Done: William O. Douglas and Collegiality in the Supreme Court." In *"He Shall Not Pass This Way Again": The Legacy of William O. Douglas*, ed. Stephen L. Wasby, 33-49. Pittsburgh: University of Pittsburgh Press for the William O. Douglas Institute, 1990.

———. "William O. Douglas and Felix Frankfurter: Ideology and Personality on the Supreme Court." *The History Teacher* 24 (November 1990): 7-18.

———. "Review of Bruce Allen Murphy, *Wild Bill: The Legend and Life of William O. Douglas*." H-Law, H-Net Reviews [June, 2003]. URL: http://www.h-net.org/reviews/showrev.cgi?path=284821059374840. Accessed July 9, 2007

Walker, Richard A. *The Conquest of Bread: 150 Years of Agribusiness in California*. New York: The New Press, 2004.

Warren, Louis. *The Hunter's Game: Poachers and Conservationists in Twentieth-Century America*. New Haven: Yale University Press, 1997.

———. *Buffalo Bill's America: William Cody and the Wild West Show*. New York: Vintage, 2005.

———, ed., *American Environmental History*. Malden, MA: Blackwell, 2003.

Wasby, Stephen L., ed. *"He Shall Not Pass This Way Again": The Legacy of Justice William O. Douglas*. Pittsburgh: University of Pittsburgh Press for the William O. Douglas Institute, 1990.

———. "Introduction." In *"He Shall Not Pass This Way Again": The Legacy of Justice William O. Douglas*, ed. Stephen L. Wasby, 69-90. Pittsburgh: University of Pittsburgh Press for the William O. Douglas Institute, 1990.

Watkins, T. H. "Commentary: Justice Douglas Takes a Hike." In *"He Shall Not Pass This Way Again": The Legacy of Justice William O. Douglas*, ed. Stephen L. Wasby, 249-53. Pittsburgh: University of Pittsburgh Press for the William O. Douglas Institute, 1990).

Weart, Spencer. *The Discovery of Global Warming*. Cambridge, MA: Harvard University Press, 2003.

West, Elliott. *Growing Up with the Country: Childhood on the Far Western Frontier*. Albuquerque: University of New Mexico Press, 1989.

White, G. Edward. *The American Judicial Tradition: Profiles of Leading American Judges*. Expanded edition. New York: Oxford University Press, 1988.

White, Richard. "Frederick Jackson Turner and Buffalo Bill." In *The Frontier in American Culture: An Exhibition at the Newberry Library, August 26, 1994-January 7, 1995*, ed. James R. Grossman, 7-65. Berkeley: University of California Press, 1994.

————. "'Are You an Environmentalist or Do You Work for a Living?': Work and Nature." In *Uncommon Ground: Toward Reinventing Nature*, ed. William Cronon, 171-85. New York: W. W. Norton, 1995.

Wiecek, William M. "Sociological Jurisprudence." In *The Oxford Companion to the Supreme Court of the United States*, ed. Kermit L. Hall, 803. New York: Oxford University Press, 1992.

Wilkinson, Charles F. "Justice Douglas and the Public Lands." In *"He Shall Not Pass This Way Again": The Legacy of Justice William O. Douglas*, ed. Stephen L. Wasby, 233-48. Pittsburgh: University of Pittsburgh Press for the William O. Douglas Institute, 1990.

————. *Crossing the Next Meridian: Land, Water, and the Future of the West*. Washington D.C.: Island Press, 1992.

Woodward, Bob, and Scott Armstrong. *The Brethren: Inside the Supreme Court*. New York: Avon, 1979.

Worster, Donald. *Rivers of Empire: Water, Aridity, and the Growth of the American West*. New York: Oxford University Press, 1985.

————. "The Ecology of Order and Chaos." In *The Wealth of Nature: Environmental History and the Ecological Imagination*, 156-70. New York: Oxford University Press, 1993.

————. "John Muir and the Roots of American Environmentalism." In *The Wealth of Nature: Environmental History and the Ecological Imagination*, 184-202. New York: Oxford University Press, 1993.

————. *Nature's Economy: A History of Ecological Ideas*. Second edition. New York: Cambridge University Press, 1994.

Wunder, John R. *"Retained by the People": A History of American Indians and the Bill of Rights*. New York: Oxford University Press, 1994.

————. "Pacific Northwest Indians and the Bill of Rights." In *Terra Pacifica: People and Place in the Northwest States and Western Canada*, ed. Paul W. Hirt, 159-88. Pullman: Washington State University Press, 1998.

Index

Abbey, Edward, 29
Adams, Ansel, 73
Adams, John Quincy, 35
Adirondacks, 78
Administrative Procedures Act (1946), 79
Ahab (biblical parable), 92, 95
Allagash River, 65
Alpine Lakes Wilderness Area, 88, 145
Amchitka, 127-28
American Forests, 40, 45, 46
American Magazine, The, 48
American Mercury, 23
"America's Vanishing Wilderness," (Douglas, 1964), 1, 8, 81
Anadromous Fish Act (1965), 121
Aptheker v. Secretary of State (1964), 117
Army Corps of Engineers, 82, 103-5, 106, 107
Atomic Energy Commission, 127-28
Audubon Society, 36, 37, 39, 41
automobiles. *See* roads

Badillo, Herman, 144
balance of nature idea, 66-68
Barnes, Irston, R., 36
Barrett, Larry, 85, 86, 89, 90
Beall, J. Glenn, 41
Beaumont, Texas, 93
Berman v. Parker (1954), 118
Berry, Wendell, 98
Big Bend, 94, 97; Big Bend National Park, 98
Big Thicket, 93-97, 99, 100, 101, 110, 146
Big Thicket Association, 97
Bill of Rights, 74, 76, 77, 110, 143
Bird Creek Meadows, 61-62, 65
Black, Hugo, 127
Blackmun, Harry, 133, 135, 136
Blankenship Meadow, 85, 90
Blue Ridge Parkway, 35

Boone, Daniel, 1, 17, 90
Bowmer, Jim, 93-94, 100, 101
Brackenridge Basin-Olmos Basin, 127
Brandeis, Louis, 21
Braun, Frederic W., 89
Brennan, William, 127, 133
Brethren, The (Woodward and Armstrong, 1979), 112
Brooks Range, 61, 66
Broome, Harvey, 40, 41, 42, 43, 46, 49, 52
Brower, David, 56, 85, 86
Bureau of Outdoor Recreation, 100
Bureau of Roads, 36
Burleson, Bob, 94

Cahn, Edmond Nathaniel, 76
Capote Falls, 99, 100-01
Carhart, Arthur, 68
Carson, Rachel, 59, 73, 119, 141
Cascade Mountains, 11-12, 25, 27, 81, 83, 85, 87, 89, 91, 142, 143, 145
Cascadians, 88
case method, legal, 114
Chesapeake and Ohio Canal, 5, 31, 34-48, 57, 82, 102, 106-10, 139, 142, 145; C&O Canal Association, 88, 105, 109; C&O Canal Committee, 44, 46, 107; "C&O Canal Song, The," 43-44; 1954 hike, 39-45, 59, 86, 89; reunion hikes, 46, 109, 143
civic action. *See* grassroots activism
Civilian Conservation Corps, 34, 74
civil rights movement, 59, 72, 138, 165n31
Clean Water Act, 112
Clements, Frederic L., 67
Cleveland, Washington, 10-11
Cliff, Ed, 85, 90
Cody, Buffalo Bill, 17, 18
Columbia Law School, 19-20, 113, 114